THE ENGLISH LAKES

BY THE SAME AUTHOR

The Sun King's Garden

THE
ENGLISH LAKES

A History

Ian Thompson

BLOOMSBURY
LONDON · BERLIN · NEW YORK

First published in 2010

The author and publishers are grateful to the sources below for permission to reproduce images on the following pages: 3, 231 – from the author's copy of *Lake Scenery* by Thomas Allom; 4 – PA Wire; 11, 130–31, 193 – Reproduced by courtesy of Abbot Hall Art Gallery, Kendal, Cumbria; 18, 114 – © The National Gallery, London; 25 – © The National Museums Liverpool (Walker); 30, 42, 46, 80, 88, 94, 98, 107, 116, 120, 127, 136, 166, 188, 198, 206, 209, 228 – The Wordsworth Trust; 53, 119, 152 – © Abbot Hall Art Gallery, Kendal, Cumbria / The Bridgeman Art Library; 62, 70, 165 – scanned from Alan Hankinson's *The Regatta Men*; 65 – With permission from the Provost and Scholars of King's College Cambridge; 109 – Scottish National Portrait Gallery; 122 – © Tate, London 2009; 125, 156, 163 – Reproduced by courtesy of Abbot Hall Art Gallery, Kendal, Cumbria; 129, 134 – V&A Images / Victoria and Albert Museum; 141, 146 – Carlisle Library; 170, 184, 232, 237, 244, 247, 252 – © The Francis Frith Collection; 175 – © All Rights Reserved. The British Library Board; 180 – St Louis Art Museum; 214 – © abrahamphotographic; 219, 222 – © abrahamphotographic. Reproduced by permission of the FRCC; 258 – © Frederick Warne & Co., 1907, 2002. Reproduced by permission of Frederick Warne & Co.; 262 – © Frederick Warne & Co., 1903, 2002. Reproduced by permission of Frederick Warne & Co.; 288 – © The Estate of A. Wainwright 1966. First published by Frances Lincoln 2003; 291 – © The Estate of A. Wainwright 1955. First published by Frances Lincoln 2003; 265 – Popperfoto / Getty Images; 278 – Courtesy of Kendal Museum; 283 – Courtesy of Willow Publishing; 270 – copyright details unknown; 274 – Reprinted by permission of The Random House Group Ltd; 306 – Hardman Collection; 308 – © Anthony John West / CORBIS. All images not credited belong to the author

Bloomsbury Publishing Plc, 36 Soho Square, London W1D 3QY
Bloomsbury USA, 175 Fifth Avenue, New York, NY 10010

www.bloomsbury.com
www.bloomsburyusa.com

Bloomsbury Publishing, London, New York and Berlin

A CIP catalogue record for this book is available from the British Library.
Cataloging-in-Publication Data is available from the Library of Congress

ISBN 978 0 7475 9838 1 (UK edition)
ISBN 978 1 60819 226 7 (US edition)

10 9 8 7 6 5 4 3 2

Typeset by Hewer Text UK Ltd, Edinburgh
Printed in Singapore by Tien Wah Press

Half-title page: Tarn Hows
Previous page: Grasmere from the southern shore

In memory of my father,
John (Jack) Healey Thompson,
who loved the fells.

CONTENTS

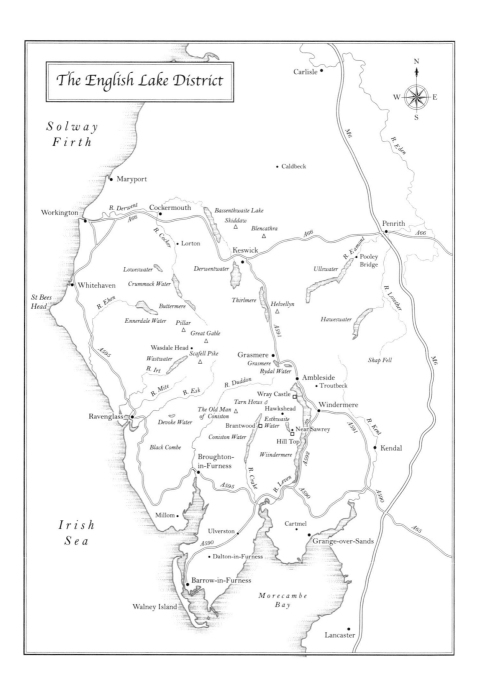

The English Lake District

Solway Firth

Irish Sea

Morecambe Bay

Carlisle

Caldbeck

Maryport

Workington
Cockermouth
R. Derwent
A66
R. Cocker
Lorton
Keswick

Bassenthwaite Lake
Skiddaw
Blencathra
A66
Penrith
R. Eamont
Pooley Bridge

Whitehaven

St Bees Head

Loweswater
Crummock Water
Derwentwater
Ullswater

R. Ehen

Thirlmere
Helvellyn
Haweswater
R. Lowther

Buttermere
Ennerdale Water
Pillar
Great Gable

Wasdale Head
Scafell Pike
Wastwater
R. Irt
R. Mite
R. Esk

Grasmere
Grasmere
Rydal Water
Shap Fell

A591

Ambleside
Troutbeck

R. Duddon
Tarn Hows
Wray Castle
Hawkshead
Windermere
R. Kent

Ravenglass
Devoke Water
The Old Man of Coniston
Brantwood
Esthwaite Water
Near Sawrey
Hill Top

Black Combe
Coniston Water
Kendal

Broughton-in-Furness
Wiindermere

A595
R. Crake
R. Leven
A590

Millom

Ulverston
A590
Cartmel
Grange-over-Sands
A65

Dalton-in-Furness

Barrow-in-Furness

Walney Island

Lancaster

M6
R. Eden

Introduction

IN 1773 A PLEASURE barge buffeted its way through the choppy waters of Ullswater. Members of the crew carried French horns and the boat was armed with six swivelling brass cannon, not for piracy or protection, but to shatter without conscience the tranquillity of a Lake District valley. On board were William Hutchinson, a solicitor from Barnard Castle, who wrote the account of the expedition, and his brother, who would have provided the illustrations had not the strong southerly breeze whipped up the waves into a fair resemblance of the sea. The boat had been put at their disposal by the Duke of Portland, who also provided the four strong oarsmen who laboured against the swell.

After lunch in the bay of Water Mellock, they rowed out to a spot which held the reputation for the finest echoes, then discharged one of the cannon. 'The report was echoed from the opposite rocks, where by reverberation it seemed to roll from cliff to cliff, and return through every cave and valley; till the decreasing tumult gradually died away upon the ear,' wrote Hutchinson.[1] As the noise faded, the sound of every distant waterfall could be heard, but only for an instant. The stillness was swiftly interrupted by the crash of the returning echo, like a peal of thunder above the tourists' heads. This too faded away, but the energy of the blast continued to bounce around the mountains, making its way up every winding creek and dell before returning to its point of origin. In this way the distant music of the waterfalls was interrupted seven times for every detonation.

Who could resist letting all the cannon off at once? Hutchinson reported the results of a general discharge which roused the company to new astonishment: 'although we had heard with great surprise the former echoes, this exceeded them so much that it seemed incredible'.[2]

Though the party returned to this rowdy entertainment throughout the afternoon, at intervals they lightened their programme with tunes upon the French horn, but once again they were mostly interested in the echoes, which took on different qualities depending upon the surrounding land-scape. 'Here,' wrote Hutchinson, 'the breathings of the organ were imitated, there the bassoon with clarinets; in this place from the harsher sounding cliffs, the cornet; in that from the wooded creek, among the caverns and the water-falls, we heard the soft-toned lute accompanied with the languish-ing strains of enamoured nymphs; whilst in the copse and grove was still retained the music of the horns.'[3]

On their way to the firing place, this aesthetically inclined party passed Gowbarrow Park, the place where the world's most celebrated drift of daffodils can still be found, but, at the time of their pyrotechnic escapade, William Wordsworth, the poet of naturalness and rural seclusion, was still a three-year-old infant, playing undisturbed in a Cockermouth garden. Wordsworth and the Lake District are so inextricably linked that it is easy to imagine that it was the poet and his circle who created the fashion for lakes and mountains, but this enthusiasm began more than thirty years before the poet was born, and had its roots in the experiences of the Grand Tourists who crossed the Swiss Alps on their way to the cultural honeypots of Italy.

In the context of Lake District tourism, Hutchinson and his brother were among the first on the scene, visiting only one year later than William Gilpin, who would do so much to swell the craze for the Picturesque, but Gilpin's *Observations on Cumberland and Westmoreland* would not be published for another thirteen years, so it is not so surprising that the North Country solicitor and his companions should have been so engrossed in the sensory diversions of the Ullswater soundscape, particularly when augmented by artillery, rather than preoccupied with the picture spotting that entertained later tourists. Gilpin and others had yet to lay down the rules of that particular game.

What is evident from Hutchinson's account is that even in 1773 there was an emerging itinerary for Lake District tourists, or 'Lakers' as they came to be known. The Duke of Portland's barge was already fitted with cannon, and his boatmen knew exactly which spot – or 'station' – they needed to reach to provide the anticipated seven echoes.

Soon tourists would be comparing the echoes like connoisseurs and the innkeepers who catered for this trade made boats and guns available.

The Second Reach of Ullswater (mid-nineteenth century) by Thomas Allom,
engraved by J. Sands, from *Lake Scenery*

One of the best regarded was the cannon provided by the Lodore Inn, a
hostel which was already well placed for the celebrated waterfall. Pointed
towards Blea Crag it could rouse nine distinct echoes. So popular did this
pastime become that prices inevitably rose. In 1799 the Lodore cannon
could be discharged for one shilling and sixpence, but by the following
decade two strengths of gunpowder were on offer, the most powerful
costing four shillings. Robert Southey, writing in the guise of a fictional
Spanish tourist, remarked that 'English echoes appear to be the most
expensive luxuries in which a traveller can indulge'.[4]

The Lake District has become one of our most cherished landscapes and
tourism has grown into an enormous industry, measured both in terms of
the money it brings into the local economy and in 'tourist days'. Recent
figures from Cumbria Tourism claim that more than eight million visitors
came to the National Park in a single year (the resident population, for sake
of comparison, is around 43,000).[5] The visitors stayed long enough to clock
up 14,600,000 tourist days and they spent over £600 million.[6] The keen hillwalkers who drive up in the morning from Manchester, find a grass verge
wide enough to park on, eat their sandwiches on Silver How or Sergeant

Man and head for home before dusk probably escape the count entirely. The official figures are modest estimates and the true numbers can never be known, although an assessment carried out by the National Park Authority in 1994, which involved roadside surveys on the main roads into the District and also at various popular destinations, suggested that the annual number of visitor days was in excess of twenty-two million. Five per cent of the visitors come from overseas. The appeal of the English Lakes is truly inter-national, yet the District is little more than thirty miles wide and its highest fell, Scafell Pike, reaches only 3,210 feet (978 metres), considerably less than Scotland's highest mountain, Ben Nevis, at 4,409 feet (1,344 metres) and a pygmy when set against the Matterhorn, which attains 14,6934 feet (4,478 metres). Whatever accounts for the reputation and cultural significance of this closely packed region, it cannot be sheer size.

But popularity brings problems. In March 2005 the National Park Authority imposed a 10 mph speed limit on motorboats on Windermere, effectively putting an end to water-skiing and other high-speed activities on the lake. It was a contentious decision and there are still some who would defy the ban, but when the issue was tested at a public inquiry the government inspector concluded that there was a fundamental incompatibility between

Donald Campbell's jet hydroplane *Bluebird* at speed on Coniston Water, 1 December 1966

high-speed power-boating and gentler forms of water-based recreation, such as sailing and canoeing. Power-boating thus came to an end despite the Lake District's long association with speed. On Friday, 13 June 1930, Sir Henry Segrave set a new world waterspeed record on Windermere of 98.76 mph in the elegant *Miss England II*, which broke up on its third run, killing both Sir Henry and his chief engineer. Donald Campbell established a new world record of 202.15 mph on Ullswater in 1955, but met the same fate as Segrave while attempting to reach 300 mph in *Bluebird K7* on Coniston Water in 1967. On his second run the boat lifted out of the water and cart-wheeled across the lake. Campbell's teddy-bear mascot, Mr Whoppit, was found floating among the debris, but his body was not recovered from the lake until 2001.

Though it was safety rather than noise that proved the decisive issue, the speedboat controversy illuminates two very different visions of the Lake District. On one hand it has been the unlicensed playground, the place where one could roam freely on the fells, dangle from ropes, tear up mountain passes in sports cars, leap off crags with no support other than a flimsy sail, or indeed let off a cannon in the middle of a lake. On the other hand it has been the secluded retreat of poets, painters and philosophers, a place to escape from the pressures of city life, the grime of industry and the corrupt values of the metropolis. It has been other things, too: a vision of Arcadia, a miniature Alps and a budding Blackpool among the mountains. To the early Forestry Commissioners it was an empty space, blank on the map, that they hoped they could fill up with trees, while to the burghers of Manchester it was a giant cistern full of healthy, fresh water. These competing visions or identities have jostled one another for three centuries. Today, and for the foreseeable future, it is the conservation values which dominate policy, but it might have been otherwise. What we take to be a natural state of affairs is really nothing of the kind.

Depending upon your beliefs, it was either God or the massive, impersonal forces of geology and meteorology that created the Lake District, with some help from Herdwick sheep and the descendants of those distant Norse settlers who made these narrow valleys home. In another sense the Lake District which tourists flock to see is a human construction, elaborated by the countless artists, poets and topographical writers who discovered qualities here to stir their pens and brushes. The story of the Lake District is both social history and the story of an imaginative idea.

Ninety years before the Wright brothers' earliest gliders drifted over the sand dunes of North Carolina, William Wordsworth gave wings to the readers of his first Lake District guidebook. He asked them to place themselves on a cloud floating midway between the peaks of Great Gable and Scafell and from this lofty platform he offered them an aerial portrait of the landscape he loved so well. 'We shall see stretched at our feet a number of valleys,' he wrote, 'not fewer than eight, diverging from the point, on which we are supposed to stand, like spokes from the nave of a wheel.'[7] In two hundred years no one has bettered this topographical summary, and, since this interlude would not even count as a tick of the geological clock, the poet's image is as powerful today as it was when he framed it.

With our feet planted firmly on this cloud we can rotate slowly clockwise and count off the major valleys, as Wordsworth did for his readers. First, to the south-east, is Langdale, which connects with the long lake known to the poet as Winandermere; then comes the Vale of Coniston running up likewise from the sea, followed by the valley of the Duddon, where there is no lake but the most picturesque of rivers, winding its way down through rocks and fields toward the sands of an estuary. The fourth is the valley of the Esk, which issues into the Irish Sea below the Roman town of Ravenglass; the fifth, almost directly to the west, is steep-sided Wasdale, where forbidding screes run straight into the deepest and most sombre of the lakes; next is Ennerdale, wild, remote and less visited than its fellows, then comes the Vale of Buttermere, where the lake of that name lines up with Crummock Water, separated only by a tongue of green pasture. Finally, we come to Borrowdale, of which the Vale of Keswick, much favoured by the early tourists, is a continuation, but the wheel analogy breaks down at this point. With a geographer's exactness, Wordsworth would not count the eastern valleys of Ullswater and Haweswater as spokes, because they did not connect with the central hub but were associated with a secondary massif dominated by Helvellyn.

These valleys do, however, share in the general radial arrangement which generates so much of the Lake District's scenic interest and has made it such a paradise for walkers. A great part of its appeal lies in the way that a little exertion can provide rapidly changing views: whether one is clambering over rocks to reach a ridge or gripping the steering wheel of a car while negotiating the tortuous twists of a mountain pass, there is always the promise of rewarding views on the other side. And the fells of the Lake District feel larger than they really are. Most walks begin from not much above sea level so to reach a summit or follow a ridge gives the day walker a satisfying sense of achievement and lets everyman feel like a mountaineer.

Wordsworth was in no doubt that the Lake District enjoyed a decided superiority over the mountainous areas of Scotland and Wales and that this rested in the variety of aesthetic experience that was available within such a narrow compass. 'Yet, though clustered together,' he observed, 'every valley has its distinct and separate character; in some instances, as if they had been formed in studied contrast to each other, and in others with the united pleasing differences and resemblances of a sisterly relationship.'[8]

The Lake District may resemble a wheel when seen from above, but at its centre is a dome composed of rocks spewed out during the Ordovician era, 450 million years ago, by volcanoes as powerful as Etna or Vesuvius, then humped and crumpled into shape by massive tectonic movements, some 400 million years ago, before being carved by glaciers which flowed as recently as 13,000 years ago, just yesterday in geological terms. The ice shaped the mountains into pyramidal peaks, leaving sharp arêtes like the celebrated Striding Edge, which offers plucky walkers a thrilling way on to Helvellyn, and scoured the valleys into their characteristic U-shaped profiles, making many of them hospitable to lakes. It is no accident that the Lake District is a miniature version of the Alps for in both places the same vast forces were at work.

The face of the Lake District is determined, at least in part, by the under-lying bone structure of its geology, and this is complex, accounting for much of the variation one can observe between different valleys or different groups of fells. Showing how very different areas acquired their dominant characteristics goes some way to explaining why the northern fells were those favoured by the early tourists, why the first rock-climbers were so enamoured of Wasdale, and why wealthy businessmen were so attracted to the shores of Windermere.

First Skiddaw, that massive, hump-like presence which forms the back-drop to Keswick: here are some of the oldest rocks, formed 510–460 million years ago and known to geologists as the Skiddaw Slates, though they are much too soft and friable to put on the roof of your house. Indeed, there was once a layer of this material, some 4,000 metres thick, laid down on an ocean floor, but it was soft and easily worn away. Since there was no harder material to offer resistance, the erosion was even, which is why Skiddaw and such near neighbours as Skiddaw Little Man, Ullock Pike and Great Calva are symmetrical in form with smooth, regular slopes clothed with grass, heather or bracken, rather than broken up by jagged crags. Their shapes are soothing to the eye and the walking is easy, if rather dull. The first tourists might have been keen to scale a mountain, but most of them were not natural mountaineers and the gradients on Skiddaw made ascent on horseback an easier option.

Where the central dome of the Lake District now sits, the sedimentary rocks were not allowed to erode gently over aeons. Somewhere between 510 and 460 million years ago they were blown apart by shattering volcanic eruptions. The area became a gargantuan pressure cooker in which the rocks were transmuted into more resistant forms, but the products of this alchemy varied in their qualities and this shaped the way the mountains appear today. The cooling lavas produced very durable rocks such as basalts, rhyolites and andesites, while the rocks formed from the pyroclastic ash flows were softer. Where there are peaks and perpendicular crags they are made of the solid, hard-wearing substance, but they are interspersed with gentler slopes of the less resistant material.

The collective name for this group of rocks is the Borrowdale Volcanics, but most of the rugged core of the Lake District is made of them, including all of the most memorable mountains: Coniston Old Man, Wetherlam, the Scafells, Great Gable, the Langdale Pikes and Helvellyn. The area's Vulcan furies are long spent and none of these summits any longer resembles a volcano – the sites of the prehistoric volcanoes are unknown – but the harsher, more challenging face of the Lake District was born of fire before it was scoured by ice. These are the rocks which have made the Lake District a magnet for adventurous walkers and climbers.

The District's third great geological division runs diagonally from the mouth of the Duddon estuary across the heads of both Coniston Water and Windermere to Ambleside. To the south and west of this line, and mostly lying in the old counties of Lancashire and Westmorland, sedimentary rocks laid down in the Silurian period are found. Known as the Windermere Group, they are softer than their neighbours to the north and were thus more easily eroded to produce a gentler landform with lower hills and harmless slopes, often draped now with woodland. It is a more hospitable, less demanding terrain, not a place for testing oneself against nature, but for settling down and building a rural retreat, preferably one with a view over water to distant hills.

These, then, are the three main divisions, but they do not complete the picture. Other features ought to be mentioned, such as the strip of coastal sandstone, deposited in a prehistoric red desert, which runs from St Bees Head down to the tip of the Furness peninsula, where it was quarried to build Furness Abbey, the granite intrusions around Wastwater, Ennerdale and Eskdale, the Carboniferous coal measures around Workington and Whitehaven, and the limestone pavements, cliffs and scars around Morecambe Bay.

At a finer level of detail, the joints and cracks between the shifting bodies of rock became mineral veins, as copper, lead, zinc and silver crystallised out of the cooling groundwater. It is one of the Lake District's ironies that it became, in the eyes of many, a place to escape the ravages of industry, when in truth it had already been an industrial site for centuries.

In 1564 Elizabeth I invited a company of German miners to extract copper from the Newlands valley. At first they came in small numbers, but later in their hundreds. Despite an initially frosty reception from the locals, they stayed, many of them marrying Cumberland girls, sometimes biga-mously. This now tranquil vale once echoed with the shouts of workers, the clang of hammers and the thumping of the crushing mills. The miners made a base for themselves on Derwent Island in Derwentwater, and built the largest smelting works in England just outside Keswick, which was thus an industrial town long before it became a tourist capital. There were copper mines near Coniston and in the Caldbeck fells, iron bloomeries in the lower hills of the south-west, a celebrated wad mine deep within Borrowdale where graphite, otherwise known as blacke-cawke, black-lead or plumbago, was extracted. This versatile material was prized by the military-industrial complex of the day for its tolerance to high temperatures, which made it an ideal lining for the moulds in which cannonballs were cast. As 'a lover of the pencil', the artist William Gilpin cherished Borrowdale graphite for its more peaceable virtues as an artistic medium and it later became the basis of a profitable pencil manufacturing business founded in Keswick in 1832.[9]

What is also evident from an aerial perspective, or indeed from just study-ing a map, is how isolated the Lake District is from the rest of Britain. It is wrapped on three sides by the sea, the Solway Firth to the north, the treach-erous but glisteningly beautiful sands of Morecambe Bay to the south, with the chilly beaches of the Cumberland coast in between. To the east the Lake District is kept apart from the Pennines by the broad, fertile Eden valley in the north and by the lesser valley of the River Kent to the south. All the main communication routes, whether drove roads, railways or motorways, have taken this line of least resistance, slogging their way over the elevated moorland wastes of Shap Summit and skirting the Lakes altogether. The natural seclusion of the Lake District is underlined by the fact that the main route to the monastery of Furness, for centuries the dominant institution in the area, lay across Morecambe Bay's shifting sands, where a knowledgeable local guide was needed to prevent calamity.

Wordsworth's aerial picture must have done much to fix the idea of a 'district' in people's minds. The early guidebooks had cumbersome titles, like Thomas West's *A Guide to the Lakes of Cumberland, Westmoreland and Lancashire*, which respected historical administrative boundaries, but did nothing to kindle the imagination. It was not until writers started to use phrases like the 'Lake District', the 'English Lakes' and 'Lakeland' that the region began to appear as a distinct entity, separate from those bits of its constituent counties that did not fit the Picturesque ideal. Since the Lake District is an imaginative construction it has no real boundaries, physical or historical, and there can always be argument about what is in or out. Early tourist itineraries often included a trip to the Cistercian ruins at Furness Abbey, and a boat trip to Piel Island in Morecambe Bay, but this was before haematite ore was found and Barrow boomed as a centre for steel-making and shipbuilding.

When the National Park boundary was drawn, the principal criterion was that it should include areas of 'high-landscape quality'. There were other considerations, such as a preference for distinguishable physical boundaries and a wish to stretch the limits to include anything of scientific, historical or architectural value on the margins, but the 'high-quality' factor was the main one. Its corollary was that only features that represented the rural economy and community life should be included, while anything that smacked of urban or industrial development should be left out, and this included quarrying and mining.[10] It is not so easy to define 'high-landscape quality' but at least there was a rationale for leaving out places like Barrow with its dockside cranes, Carlisle with its biscuit factory and the west coast with its legacy of coal mining. But the main market towns of Cockermouth, Penrith, Kendal and Ulverston were also excluded and, even more strangely, so was the tip of the Cartmel peninsula, including Cartmel itself, a charming village clustered around the Priory and an old square.

Several writers have bridled against the artificiality of throwing a cordon around the central hills and valleys and declaring them special, while shutting out the remainder of the county. One such was Norman Nicholson, lifelong

Loading Slate at Coniston (1771) by John 'Warwick' Smith

resident of Millom and an almost Poet Laureate, whose books about the Lake District easily outsold his verses. In *Greater Lakeland* he argued that what the rest of the country called 'Lakeland' would die from the edges inwards 'to become in the end little more than a beautiful, embalmed corpse in a rotting coffin'[11] if efforts were not made to maintain the economic vibrancy of the surrounding area. But he was a Millom lad, born and bred, and he wrote the first page of his book on the very day on which the ironworks that had sustained life in his home town for a century were shut down.

Nicholson was no sentimentalist and he observed that the mountain mass at the heart of the Lake District had often served to keep people apart rather than to bring them together, so that the people of High Furness mixed little with those Back o' Skiddaw or the folk across in the Eden valley. The valleys lead outwards, so it is natural for dalesfolk to look to their nearest market towns and these are found around the rim of the mountains. Ullswater looks to Penrith, Coniston to Ulverston and Buttermere to Cockermouth. Local government reform in 1974 created the workable new county of Cumbria, but one does not have to dig too deeply to find continuing allegiance to the old counties.

Cumbria has probably endured as an administrative entity because, as

Nicholson believed, it makes good geographical, social and economic sense to link the valleys of the central dome with the towns of the surrounding collar, but it also helps that it is an attractive and evocative name, redolent with historical associations. Topographical accounts always draw attention to the Norse place names that lie over the Cumbrian fells as densely as leaf litter. They point out that 'force', the Cumbrian term for a waterfall, is very close to Norse *fors*, that 'beck' is derived from *bekkr*, 'tarn' from *tjorn*, 'dale' from *dalr* and 'fell' from *fjall*, while the common ending '-thwaite' (as in Satterthwaite) came from the Norse term for a clearing made among woods. Most of the land to the west of the Pennines was previously in the hands of the Cymry, the Britons who held sway from the River Clyde right down the west coast to Wales and Cornwall. We owe place names like Derwent, which means thick with oak trees, and Blencathra, which is said to derive from 'Blain' and 'Cadeir' meaning 'hill of the chair', to the Cymry. Cumbria was Celtic before it became Nordic.

In time Anglian settlers would push across from the east, isolating Wales and Cornwall, while Cumbria became part of the kingdom of Strathclyde. The Anglians occupied much of the lower, flatter land in Cumbria too, spreading through the Eden valley and along the coastal margins, but the mountains and narrow valleys were not to their taste. The Norsemen, when they arrived, were not really the Vikings of our imagination. Archaeologists tell us that they came from Ireland, via the Isle of Man, rather than from Scandinavia, and that they did not come as hostile invaders. They left the Anglian hamlets alone and pushed on into the dales, which they found familiar and congenial. Although this is the *English* Lake District containing the *English* Lakes, there is a sense in which this region has always been alien and other, a fragment of Celtic or Nordic wildness that has worked its way into the English heart.

By the beginning of the seventeenth century the so-called 'statesmen' or 'estatesmen', descendants of the original Norse-Irish settlers, had emerged as the most powerful social group in the Lake District valleys. They were independently minded yeomen farmers, either small freeholders or customary tenants. In the second half of that century, with the troubles on the Scottish border finally settled, the statesmen began to rebuild their farmsteads in the local stone. They also built the characteristic dry-stone walls which helped them to gather in their flocks from the fellsides. Though the Lake District summits can appear rugged and untamed, the sheltered valleys have a domestic, almost garden-like quality.

During the eighteenth and nineteenth centuries this isolated and intro-
verted area was opened up by forces which belonged to a much wider world.
The village of Grasmere lies close to the heart of the Lake District, and
during the years of Wordsworth's residence it also became the centre of
a literary and artistic circle which prized seclusion, yet it is only thirty
miles, as the crow flies, to Lancaster and only seventy-five to the middle
of Manchester, the first city of the Industrial Revolution. The growth in
the popularity of the Lake District is shadowed by the utter transformation of Manchester from a modest market town to an industrial behemoth.
During the 1770s, while Gilpin was touring Britain in search of picturesque scenes for his sketchbook and William Wordsworth was growing up
in Cockermouth, Manchester was establishing itself as the centre of the
cotton industry in Lancashire. A year before the death of Wordsworth,
Angus Reach, a writer for the *Morning Chronicle*, visited Manchester and
wrote the following description of his arrival:

> You shoot by town after town – the outlying satellites of the great cotton
> metropolis. They have all similar features – they are all little Manchesters.
> Huge, shapeless, unsightly mills, with their countless rows of windows,
> their towering shafts, their jets of waste steam continually puffing in
> panting gushes from the brown grimy wall. Some dozen or so of miles so
> characterised, you enter the Queen of the cotton cities – and then amid
> smoke and noise, and the hum of never ceasing toil, you are borne over the
> roofs to the terminus platform. You stand in Manchester.[12]

Manchester is emblematic of all the great industrial cities and it stands
in polar contrast to the naturalness found less than a hundred miles to the
north. As numerous parliamentary committees would report, conditions in
the new urban areas were wretched, and as the radical newspaper proprietor Archibald Prentice observed: 'The volumes of smoke which, in spite of
legislation to the contrary, continually issue from factory chimneys, and
form a complete cloud over Manchester, certainly make it less desirable as a
place of residence than it is as a place of business.'[13] The lives of the inhabitants would be greatly improved, thought Prentice, if they could breathe
a purer atmosphere and see a little sun. It is not surprising that those
who made their money in Manchester or in similar towns soon wanted
to live outside them, a choice not available to the workers, whose cramped
and often unsanitary houses were crushed together in the manufacturing

districts. No wonder, then, that the aesthetically minded gentlefolk who had become attached to the peaceful seclusion of the Cumbrian valleys soon found that they had the company of those who had made money in business or the professions and who were not content just to visit the Lake District, but wanted to own a portion of it.

In the chapters to follow, the story of the Lake District's opening up will be told. It is difficult to avoid the word 'discovery' in this context, although, like the discovery of America or Africa, this implies a kind of colonisation. The Lake District was not, of course, unknown to its indigenous inhabitants before it was explored by visitors from polite society.

Many visitors describe their first encounter with the area in terms that might come from a romantic novel. People fall in love with this landscape, sometimes so deeply that they feel they must transplant their entire lives. Others return year after year and feel a sense of ownership which does not depend upon holding the deeds to a cottage in Hawkshead or Coniston.

It is also striking that so many of the people who have heaped praise upon the Lake District were not born within its valleys. The Cumbrian term for those who move into the area is 'off-comers' and it is often said that it takes many generations to lose that status. This may be true in farming circles, but it does not seem to hold in cultural ones. It is remarkable how many of the figures most closely associated with the Lake District seem to be off-comers, and even those who were born, raised or resided within the present boundaries of Cumbria often belonged more to the rim than to the hub. Thomas West, the author of the most influential early guidebook, lived at Tytup Hall near Dalton-in-Furness; the artist William Green moved to Ambleside from Manchester; John Ruskin was born in London and was already over fifty when he bought Brantwood on the shores of Coniston Water; Beatrix Potter was proud of an old family connection with Monk Coniston, but she grew up in Kensington, in London, and was only able to reinvent herself as a Lake District farmer in middle age; Arthur Ransome, author of *Swallows and Amazons*, was the son of a history professor in Leeds; Alfred Wainwright, creator of the famous fellwalking guidebooks, moved to Kendal from Blackburn when he was almost thirty-five. Even William Wordsworth did not settle permanently in Grasmere until he was twenty-nine.

The story of the Lake District as a cultural phenomenon is therefore as much a story about off-comers and outsiders as it is about the place itself, its farming communities or its local traditions. At times the visitors and the locals have seen things very differently. What is truly remarkable about the Lake District is the way that such an enormous range of people from such a wide variety of backgrounds have come to feel an affinity with the place, a sense of belonging, even a sense of possession.

Overleaf: The Duddon Estuary and Black Combe from Roanhead

Landscape with Hagar and the Angel (1646) by Claude Lorrain

1

The English Alps

From Defoe's 'horrid mountains' to a Revolution in Taste

IN 1722, THREE YEARS after the publication of *Robinson Crusoe*, the novelist, journalist, pamphleteer and political spy Daniel Defoe began work on *A Tour Through the Whole Island of Great Britain*. Published in three volumes, each describing a number of circuits or tours which the author purported to have made, it is the best account we have of the state of the nation on the eve of the Industrial Revolution. London-based Defoe did not get to the Lake District until Volume III, which appeared in August 1726, although the title page read 1727, a ploy to boost sales by keeping the book looking fresh. This stratagem over the publication date is not the only dubious thing about the book; indeed, it has been suggested that Defoe neither made the journeys he described, nor even visited many of the places he mentioned.[1] The elderly but industrious hack was a consummate gatherer of information and a masterful weaver of fictions.

Whether or not his opinions were based on first-hand acquaintance, Defoe had no time for mountains; they were 'high and formidable' and they had 'a kind of unhospitable terror in them'. For him the hills of Cumberland and Westmorland had no redeeming features; they had no rich pleasant valleys like the Alps, no lead mines like the Peak District, no coal pits like the hills around Halifax and no gold like the Andes. They were 'all barren and wild, of no use or advantage either to man or beast'. For Defoe there was nothing spiritually uplifting or aesthetically pleasing about mountain scenery. He noticed the snow on the 'unpassable hills' of Westmorland and concluded that 'all the pleasant part of England was at an end'.[2]

The Britain through which Defoe toured, whether physically or just in his imagination, was still largely rural. The industrial metropolis of Manchester existed only in embryo. England had some fashionable spas, but there were no seaside resorts and Whitehaven was the third busiest

port after London and Bristol. Most of the population still derived a living
from the land. The countryside was a site of labour, not a place to which
an urbanised population would flee for escape. Defoe's *Tour* was a form of
economic journalism which charted the productive life of the nation, taking
pleasure in every weekly market, fertile plain, well-made road, navigable
river, comfortable inn or fruitful manufactory. As an experienced journalist,
he knew what his readers wanted to see, so his opinions about mountains
were by no means out of step with the conventional pre-Romantic view.

The seventeenth-century English traveller James Howell put this anti-
pathy to mountains in the most forthright terms. In his *Instructions for Forraine
Travell* of 1642, he described the Pyrenees as 'not so high and hideous as
the Alps' and as 'uncouth, huge, monstrous Excrescences of Nature, bearing
nothing but craggy stones'.[3] Mountains could not be cultivated, they were
difficult to traverse and they were associated with bad weather and other
hazards like rock falls and avalanches. Their very inaccessibility made them
a suitable home for imaginary demons and dragons; these, perhaps, were the
mischievous agents that brought down such calamities upon humankind.

Though Defoe reproduced the conventional Western view, earlier travellers had been more even-handed about the Lake Counties. In 1586 the
antiquary William Camden had written of Cumberland:

> The Country although it be somewhat with the coldest, as lying farre
> North, and seemeth as rough by reason of hilles, yet for the variety
> thereof it smileth upon the beholders, and give contentment to as many
> as travaile it. For after the rockes bunching out, the mountaines standing
> thicke togither, rich of mettal mines, and betweene them great meeres
> stored with all kindes of wild-foule, you come to pretty hills good for
> pasturage and well replenished with flockes of sheepe, beneath which
> againe you meet with goodly plaines spreading out a great way, yeelding
> corne sufficiently. Besides all this, the Ocean, driving and dashing upon
> the shore, affourdeth plenty of excellent good fish, and upbraideth, as it
> were, the Inhabitants there abouts with their negligence, for that they
> practise fishing no more than they doe.[4]

The barb at the end might be a gratuitous poke at foolish northerners,
intended to please an Oxford readership, but the description of the landscape is not calculated to cause a shudder. Camden's *Britannia*, from which
this extract is taken, described the North Country as an uncouth place,

remote from the experience of most Englishmen, but not entirely lacking in comforts and interesting enough to be worth visiting.

Another celebrated traveller, Celia Fiennes, a distant forebear of the polar explorer Ranulph Fiennes, set out on horseback to visit every county in England. Her journeys took place between 1684 and 1703, predating Defoe's, but the memoir she wrote was intended for family reading only and so was not published in its entirety until 1888, when it appeared under the title *Through England on a Side Saddle*. Fiennes travelled to get 'a change of aire and exercise'. For most of the time she rode with only one or two servants for company. In contrast to the professional polish of Defoe's prose, Fiennes' writing is garrulous and often ungrammatical, jumping around among the subjects which interested her, but while reading her one is in no doubt that she was describing things that she actually saw.

Around Kendal she was struck by the lanes which were too narrow for carriages of the usual size. Instead the locals used 'very narrow ones like little wheele-barrows'. They also used horses with panniers, loading them with hay, turf, lime or dung, as required. 'The reason,' wrote Fiennes, 'is plaine, from the narrowness of the lanes where is good lands they will loose as little as they can, and where its hilly and stoney no other carriages can pass . . .'[5]

Like Defoe, Fiennes was writing before the characteristic vocabulary of the Picturesque movement had been developed. She did not talk of foregrounds, middle distances, side-screens, roughness, sudden variation or the play of light and shade. She was matter-of-fact and not prone to exaggeration, but she thought no better of mountains than Defoe. At the northern end of Ullswater she admired a fine round hill, full of wood and fruitful with grass and corn, but then she took leave of 'the desart and barren rocky hills', noting that they were not limited to Westmorland, for she wrote that if she had ventured father into the left-hand corner, into Cumberland, she would have found more hills 'farr worse for height and stony-ness about White haven side and Cockermouth'.[6] Neither did she find anything charming about the vernacular architecture, nor indeed the local society:

> Here I came to villages of sad little hutts made up of drye walls, only stones piled together and the roofs of same slatt; there seemed to be little or noe tunnells for their chimneys and have no morter or plaister within or without. For the most part I tooke them at first sight for a sort of houses or barns to fodder cattle in, not thinking them to be dwelling houses, they being scattering houses, here one, there another, in some

places they may be 20 or 30 together; and the churches the same. It must needs be very cold dwellings, but it shews some thing of the lazyness of the people; indeed here and there was a house plaister'd, but there is sad entertainment – that sort of clap bread and butter and cheese and a cup of beer all one can have, they are 8 mile from a market town and their miles are tedious to go both for illness of way and length of the miles.[7]

All of this sounds very different from the Lake District eulogised by William Wordsworth. Some sixty years later, the young poet, returning home on vacation from his Cambridge college, would be so profoundly moved by these same hills and valleys that, recalling the experience in middle age, he could liken them to the highest and purest regions of heaven:

> The Sea was laughing at a distance; all
> The solid Mountains were as bright as clouds,
> Grain-tinctured, drenched in the empyrean light,
> And, in the meadows and the lower grounds,
> Was all the sweetness of a common dawn,
> Dews, vapours, and the melody of birds,
> And Labourers going forth into the fields.
> – Ah! Need I say, dear Friend, that to the brim,
> My heart was full?[8]

Laughing? Sweetness? Melody? Can this really be the same district which so underwhelmed Fiennes and was dismissed in such disparaging terms by Defoe? What might account for these conflicting perceptions? Defoe was born in London, the son of a butcher, Fiennes was a colonel's daughter from Wiltshire, whereas Wordsworth was born in Cockermouth, within sight of the hills he would grow to love so deeply. Many of us feel a particular affection for the landscapes in which we grew up. The flatlander from Cambridgeshire finds a move to Inverness unpalatable, while the highlander cannot cope with the big skies of Lincolnshire. But in this matter the evidence is insufficient to state a general rule, and many facts point in the opposite direction, as any survey of second-home ownership in upland areas would show. The startling difference between Defoe's pejorative prose and Wordsworth's joyful verse cannot be explained away so easily. Something happened in the course of the eighteenth century that amounted to an outright revolution in taste. The 'horrid mountains' which featured in accounts of travel up to the eighteenth century came to be considered as places which could provide aesthetic pleasure and spiritual elevation. They ceased to be landscapes which travellers would avoid and became places of recreation and resort.

The craze for mountain scenery which took hold towards the end of the eighteenth century had its origins in the Grand Tour, an almost obligatory period of continental travel, which could last anything from a few months to several years, and served as a form of education for the sons (and later the daughters) of the English upper classes. Italy was the destination for most, although some went on to explore Greece and the wilder shores of the Mediterranean. For a culture obsessed with classicism this trip was a feasible way of making first-hand contact with antiquity, and the tourists ostensibly went to study architecture and the arts, although it is some indication of the manners of these young aesthetes that the tutors who accompanied them were known as 'bearleaders'.

The Alps presented a difficult obstacle for the Tourists. They either tried to circumvent them by taking a boat from France to Italy, though this carried the risks of shipwreck or an attack by Barbary pirates, or they chanced the mountain passes. Some of the travellers seem to have enjoyed the experience. Thomas Brand, who made the crossing in October 1783, reported that:

> The porters whisk you with incredible strength and celerity down a steep stony road with sharp angles at each turn. Perhaps for the first five or six minutes I was under some fright but the firmness of their steps soon set me at ease and the beautiful cascades that present themselves on every side and the majesty of the hoary mountains that surrounded me furnished me with sufficient matter of admiration and surprise.[9]

It is thought that Joseph Addison was the first Englishman to admire the Alps. In his *Remarks on Several Parts of Italy* of 1705 he commented upon the 'agreeable kind of horror' presented by 'one of the most irregular mis-shapen scenes in the world'.[10] The poet Thomas Gray, travelling with his friend Horace Walpole in 1739, visited the monastery of the Grande Chartreuse in the mountains of Savoy and enthused about 'a monstrous precipice, almost perpendicular, at the bottom of which rolls a torrent'.[11] In a stunning revision of customary aesthetic standards, qualities that would have repelled a writer like Defoe were now to be exalted. The scene was 'the most solemn, the most romantic' that Gray had ever seen. 'I do not remember to have gone ten paces without an exclamation, that there was no restraining,' he

gushed, 'not a precipice, not a torrent, not a cliff, but is pregnant with religion and poetry.'[12]

From being an obstacle to the Grand Tour, the Alps became an essential part
of the itinerary. By the time the Napoleonic Wars put an end to the Grand Tour
and to Alpine tourism, the English taste for mountain scenery was securely
established. Those with a taste for travel now paid attention to the hills of their
Celtic cousins and to the miniature Alps on their doorstep, the Lake District.

The Grand Tourists who set out for Italy had been schooled in Greek and
Latin. Their imaginations were half-filled with visions of Classical antiquity before they even crossed the English Channel. They knew as much
about Roman history as they did of their own, and on the Alpine passes
they dreamt of Hannibal and his elephants. Their taste in painting was
shaped by the works of two Frenchmen who had based their studios in the
Eternal City: Nicolas Poussin (1594–1665) and Claude Lorrain (1600–82).
Both had painted visions of an Arcadian landscape based upon the countryside around Rome, where they would sometimes go together to sketch, but
intended to evoke the sparsely populated mountains of southern Greece.
Modern Arcady is a province of the Peloponnese, but in mythology it is the
domain of Pan and his spirits of nature. Arcadia has become synonymous
with any form of utopian rural paradise. Here shepherds were thought to
live blissfully in an eternal summer of dancing, drinking and generally
taking it easy. It represented a land of lost innocence and there are paral-
lels with Rousseau's notion of the 'noble savage' which was to have such an
influence upon the Romantics. A parallel literary tradition, with its origins
in the bucolic poetry of Theocritus and Virgil, came into English at the
Renaissance when Edmund Spenser wrote a series of pastorals entitled *The
Shepheard's Calendar*. The tradition continued into the eighteenth century
with Alexander Pope, who consciously echoed Spenser in his rustic poems.
Throughout these works the life of the Mediterranean shepherd is often
presented as sunny and appealing, but is not without its hazards and heart-
breaks. Wolves attack the sheep, lovers are rejected, friends sometimes die
and the weather can turn hostile, but all these adversities are natural, which
is to say that they are not caused by corruption or tyranny in human society.
The utopia presented in visions of Arcadia was not one devised by ingenu-
ity and it had no politics or constitution; it was the spontaneous result of a
life lived close to nature, away from the iniquitous influences of civilisation.
This was the way that some people came to regard the Lake District.

Landscape with Hermit (*c.* 1662) by Salvator Rosa

Poussin and Claude are often bracketed together as landscape painters, but Poussin's subjects were usually historical or mythological figures arranged against a landscape backcloth, whereas Claude promoted the background landscape to the status of subject, although he could not quite let go of the idea that a serious painting had to have some gods or peasants in the foreground, so he made them small and inconspicuous. A third painter, the Italian Salvator Rosa (1615–73), belonged to a later generation and was able to shake off more of the conventions. He shunned the calm, pastoral views of Arcadia to create broodingly rough and melancholic landscapes, full of rocks and ruins and peopled with brigands, shepherds, sailors and others from the margins of

society. As part of his personal myth, he cultivated the idea that he too had
run with bandits in the mountains of the Abruzzo. He was destined to become
a darling of the Romantics and to play an important role in the elaboration
of the Lake District as a cultural edifice. In early prints of Cumberland kilted
Scottish raiders took the place of Rosa's *banditti.*

It can be seen that the origins of the change in taste which would transform the fortunes of the Lake District lay well outside the area, but, if the
tributaries of change rose in such faraway places as Arcady and the Roman
campagna, the first local signals were hoisted by two local men who were
ahead of the general surge by a decade or more. 'Local', in this case, again
means 'of the rim', since the first of these heralds, Dr John D. Dalton,
was born at Dean, which lies about halfway between Cockermouth and
Workington, while the second, Dr John Brown, was born in Wigton. The
two Johns had much in common. John Dalton was an Oxford don, while
John Brown enjoyed similar standing at Cambridge. Both were clergymen
and both were literary men in a minor way.

Dr Dalton wrote a poem, published in 1755, which enumerated the beauties of the Vale of Keswick. These are the opening lines:

> Horrors like these at first alarm,
> But soon with savage grandeur charm,
> And raise to noblest thoughts the mind.[13]

This is a succinct statement of the psychological processes which Dalton
thought were involved in viewing mountainous scenery, but it can also be
read as a summary of the way in which opinions were swinging around the
fulcrum of taste in the mid-eighteenth century, with thoughts of nobility
and grandeur replacing alarm and revulsion. Later in the verse the poet
adopts the aerial perspective of a soaring kite, surveying 'channels by rocky
torrents torn' and 'rocks to the lake in thunders borne', before bringing
his readers back to the more comforting curves of the bay and the verdant
islands of Derwentwater. Revealingly, the poem is addressed to 'Two Young
Ladies at their Return from Viewing the Mines at Whitehaven', which indicates that the taste for viewing landscapes had not yet found its grip, while
the kind of economic tourism represented by a trip to the coalfield was
well established. Industry, by the middle of the eighteenth century, had not
acquired the negative associations that would cling to it like ingrained soot
from the nineteenth century onwards.

Though Dr John Brown portrayed similar scenes in prose rather than in verse, his *Description of the Lake and Vale of Keswick* proved even more influential. It was written around 1753 as a private letter to Lord Lyttelton. In it Brown compared the Vale of Keswick with Dovedale in Derbyshire, which had already attracted the attention of scene-hunting tourists. Derwentwater came out well from the comparison. Whereas Dovedale was a 'narrow slip of a valley', Keswick enjoyed 'a vast amphitheatre, in circumference above twenty miles'. While Dovedale had some fine rocks 'pointed and irregular', the Derbyshire hills were 'both little and unanimated', but the slopes above Derwentwater had 'rocks and cliffs of stupendous height, hanging broken over the lake in horrible grandeur, some of them a thousand feet in height, the woods climbing up their steep and shaggy sides, where mortal foot never yet approached'. Brown set a fashion for exaggerating the dramatic horrors of the Lake District which later writers would find hard to relinquish.

'The full perfection of Keswick,' added the doctor, 'consists of three circumstances, beauty, horror and immensity united; the second of which alone is found at Dovedale.'[14] Charles Avison, composer and organist at Newcastle Cathedral, made a similar remark some years later when he said of Derwentwater, seen from Friar's Crag, that here was 'beauty lying in the lap of horrour'.[15]

Having made a reasonable fist of describing the valley, Brown confessed that he was not really up to the task. 'To give a complete idea of these three perfections as they are joined at Keswick,' he wrote, 'would require the united powers of Claude, Salvator, and Poussin.' Claude would 'throw his delicate sunshine over the cultivated vales, the scattered cots, the groves, the lake, and wooded islands'; Salvator would 'dash out the horror of the rugged cliffs, the steeps, the hanging woods, and foaming water-falls' while it would be left to Poussin (it has been suggested that Brown did not mean Nicolas but his brother-in-law Gaspard, who took his name and was his pupil[16]) to fill in the 'impending mountains'.[17]

This letter, commending the Lake District in terms of Italian painting, re-emerged fifteen years later when it was published as a pamphlet in Newcastle which circulated among the cognoscenti of England. It was this which persuaded Thomas Gray to visit the English Lakes and Gray was an influential arbiter of taste. The Lake District had begun its ascent to cultural significance.

Overleaf: Brothers Water from Kirkstone Pass

Four ovals of perfect scenery (*c.* 1796) by William Gilpin

2

Pathfinders

From Thomas Gray to William Gilpin

'I AM A TRAVELLER, YOU are a tourist, he is a tripper.' The origin of this aphorism is uncertain, but the general idea is that the traveller is not far short of an explorer, an intrepid individual who seeks out unusual experiences in places seldom visited. Tourists, on the other hand, follow an established itinerary, while the tripper is often disparaged for a complete lack of taste or discernment. There is nothing new about the snobbery all this reveals. The Lake District has had more than its portion.

We could safely say that the antiquaries Camden and Leland were travellers, and so too were Fiennes and Defoe (even if the latter made some of his journeys solely within his head). Their visits to the Lake District followed no established itineraries, and were short stops taken in the course of much longer expeditions. They were not principally interested in scenery. The case is different when we come to Thomas Gray. His curiosity had been spiked by passages in Dr Brown's descriptive letter and he came specifically to look for himself. It is often said that he was the Lake District's first tourist.

If so, he was a very eminent one. At Eton he had counted Horace Walpole, the son of prime minister Sir Robert Walpole, among his closest friends, along with Richard West, whose father was a future Lord Chancellor of Ireland. Although he had sheltered away for much of his life in Cambridge colleges, by the time he visited the Lakes in 1769 Gray's reputation as one of the century's leading poets was already established, mostly on the strength of his *Elegy Written in a Country Churchyard.*

Gray was not new to tourism. On his trip to the Alps with Walpole he had seen sights 'that would awe an atheist into belief, without the help of other argument'.[1] At times he had felt as though death was perpetually before his eyes 'only so far removed, as to compose the mind, without frightening it'.

Gray had the sensitivity and imagination to be scared easily. He was shy and reclusive by nature and not one for vigorous outdoor pursuits. Gray quarrelled with Walpole in Italy, a breach that took several years to heal; it seems that the gregarious Walpole and the studious Gray had different ideas of fun. Yet the Alps had clearly given the poet a frisson of excitement and he was looking to recapture these thrills when he came to the Lake District.

Pernickety and obsessional, Gray drew great comfort from a well-planned itinerary. His first attempted tour in 1767 was cut short before it began when his companion, Dr Wharton, was taken ill at Keswick. Wharton was again ill in 1769 but this time Gray resolved to carry on alone, posting an epistolary journal to his friend so that he might share the experience. He spent ten days in the Lake District, arriving in Penrith on 30 September, from where he made an excursion to Ullswater. For the next six days his base was in Keswick 'lap'd in Elysium'. His sightseeing took in Bassenthwaite, Castlerigg Stone Circle and Borrowdale, including the celebrated Wad Mine. On 8 October his intention was to relocate to Ambleside via Dunmail Raise and Grasmere, but he found that the best room at the Salutation Inn was as 'dark and damp as a cellar' so he pressed on to Kendal, where he spent his last two nights in the District.

Gray was an appreciative visitor with a lucid style of prose. He rose at seven on 3 October, 'a heavenly day', and set out across the hoarfrost towards Borrowdale, noticing the diversity of the views and the way that the prospects changed every ten paces. On the margins of Derwentwater he found 'the most delicious view' his eyes had ever beheld:

> Opposite, are the thick woods of Lord Egremont, and Newland valley, with green and smiling fields embosomed in the dark cliffs; to the left, the jaws of Borrowdale, with the turbulent chaos of mountain behind mountain, rolled in confusion; beneath you and stretching far away to the right, the shining purity of the lake reflecting rocks, woods, fields, and inverted tops of hills, just ruffled by the breeze, enough to shew it is alive, with the white buildings of Keswick, Crosthwaite church and Skiddaw for a background at a distance.[2]

But as Gray penetrated more deeply into Borrowdale, he found the prospects increasingly alarming:

... soon after we came under Gowdar-crag, a hill more formidable to the eye, and to the apprehension, than that of Lowdore; the rocks at the top deep-cloven perpendicularly by the rains, hanging loose and nodding forwards, seen just starting from their base in shivers. The whole way down, and the road on both sides is strewed with piles of the fragments strangely thrown across each other and of a dreadful bulk; the place reminds me of those passes in the Alps, where the guides tell you to move on with speed, and say nothing, lest the agitation of the air should loosen the snows above, and bring down a mass that would overwhelm a caravan. I took their counsel here, and hastened on in silence.[3]

Passages such as this have attracted much derision, and they only make sense if we think of Gray as a neurotic with a low threshold for excitement. He was, after all, looking for thrills and it seems that his imagination could supply all that he needed. He was also making use of voguish aesthetic theory.[4] None of this quite rescues the timorous Gray from ridicule. When Robert Southey wrote about the same valley forty years later, he mocked the guidebooks which talked of terrific precipices and stone avalanches, and he clearly had Gray in mind when he laughed at 'the fear of some travellers who had shrunk back from the dreadful entrance to Borrowdale'.[5] Southey, writing under the nom de plume of a visiting Spanish tourist, found no difficulty in walking along a good road 'which coaches of the light English make travel every summer's day'. A century later and the laughter had not abated. The historian C. G. Collingwood took another poke at the poet in *The Lake Counties*. As a keen walker and a resident of Coniston he would have liked to drag Gray up to the bold alpine scenery at the back of the Old Man: 'he found the Jaws of Borrowdale so terrible,' he wrote, 'that it would have been pleasant to watch him accumulating adjectives half way up Dow Crags'.[6]

Though Gray was eloquent and observant and wrote with a directness which had the power to attract others to the area, he was – in twentieth-century slang – a bit of a wally, both gullible and inept. His trip up Borrowdale got no further than Grange. Ignoring an ancient and well-used packhorse route over the pass at Sty Head, he concluded that there was nothing more than a little winding path beyond Seathwaite, known only to dalesmen and passable only for a few weeks of the year. He convinced himself that 'all farther access is here barred to prying mortals'. He had had quite enough excitement for one day, so he turned back to his lodgings. Nevertheless, Gray's place in the history of the Lake District is secure. No one doubts that it was he who cranked the tourist engine into life, and if you believe that tourists are a blessing to the area (opinions differ) then Gray should be given suitable credit.

In the same year as Gray's second visit, the Flintshire natural historian and antiquary Thomas Pennant also passed through the Lake District on his way back from Scotland, and he stopped off again in the course of a return trip across the border in 1772. A Fellow of the Royal Society from 1761, he shared the eighteenth-century predilection for cataloguing and classifying. Dr Johnson, championing Pennant, replied to one of his detractors: 'He's Whig, sir; a sad dog. But he's the best traveller I have ever read; he observes more things than anyone else does.'[7] Johnson was probably right, but Pennant did not have an original mind, nor was there much poetry in his soul. He categorised the southern end of Borrowdale as a composition of 'all that is horrible', contrasting it with the northern view where Skiddaw 'rises over the country like a gentle generous lord, while the fells of Borrowdale frown on it like a hardened tyrant',[8] but if this seems hackneyed today it was fresh enough in its time for later writers to copy.

Pennant's descriptions of the mines at Whitehaven convey a greater sense of wonder and excitement than anything he wrote about lakes or mountains. In this passage concerning the dangers of explosive gases underground, his imagination is unshackled:

> Formerly the damp or fiery vapour was conveyed through pipes to the open air, and formed a terrible illumination during the night like the eruptions of a volcano; and by its heat water could be boiled; the men who worked in it inhaled inflammable air, and, if they breathed against a candle, puffed out a fiery stream.[9]

Here he was evidently relishing stories he had been told, not describing things he had seen, but the whole passage from which this is taken can be regarded, like early paintings of Coalbrookdale, as a token of the industrial sublime. Industry on a large scale, especially if illuminated by sheets of flame, could be every bit as awe-inspiring as any natural phenomenon. The mind-boggling fact which brought tourists to Whitehaven was that most of the mines stretched under the Irish Sea. Just as any real danger had to be absent from crags and precipices for them to appear sublime, so too the hardships and perils of industry had to be bracketed out for polite consumption.

Another writer who toured the North Country was Arthur Young. He was an astute social observer, a political economist and an advocate for agricultural improvement, with an eye for landscape and an interest in paintings and landscape gardens, although he confined his comments on these latter subjects to lengthy footnotes. He drew an extraordinary contrast between the valleys of Cumberland and the gardens of Versailles: 'What are the effects of Louis's magnificence to the sportive play of nature in the vale of Keswick! How trifling the labours of art to the mere pranks of nature!'[10] Yet he felt that 'a vast many edges of precipices, bold projections of rock, pendent cliffs, and wild romantic spots, which command the most delicious scenes' were dangerously inaccessible and that it would be a good idea if someone cut winding paths in the rock and made resting places for the weary traveller. From the beginning it was clear that the tourists were going to alter what they came to see.

Pennant and Young may have written 'tours' but they were really travellers and topographers in the school of Defoe and Fiennes. The relative merits of views had already emerged as a lively topic for discussion, but neither Pennant nor Young attempted to write a Picturesque guidebook. The first to do that was another resident of the 'rim', Father Thomas West, a Jesuit priest who lodged with the Matsons of Tytup Hall. West was born and educated in Scotland and took holy orders in 1751. He studied at Liège and was then assigned to the English Mission, which in his case meant being sent to Furness, where the Royal Abbey of Saint Mary – to give the local ruins their Sunday-best title – lay secluded in the Vale of Nightshade. He became absorbed by the history of the area and wrote *The Antiquities of Furness*, published in 1774. It was a guidebook of sorts, and successful enough to make West think of writing another.

This was the more ambitious and more commercial *A Guide to the Lakes of Cumberland, Westmoreland and Lancashire*, first published in Kendal and London in 1778. In his introduction West commented on the improved condition of the region's roads even since Mr Pennant's trip (only six years earlier) and upon the increasing numbers of 'persons of genius, taste, and observation' – it never hurts to flatter readers – who were now making tours of their own country. Unfortunately West died the year after publication, so he can have known little of the book's success. A second edition was published in 1780 which included an appendix of extracts from Gray's *Journal*, Brown's *Description* and Dalton's *Descriptive Poem*. These days there would be a paperback with the title *The Essential Lake District*. West's *Guide* was a hit and remained in print for over fifty years.

West's bright idea was to condense the essence of the Lake District into easily swallowed gobbets of scenic pleasure. Other writers had remarked about particular views from particular places. He would pick through their writings, catalogue all the 'stations' from which these favoured views had been described, then verify them with 'his own repeated observations'. Finally, he would add a few remarks of his own and provide such other incidental information as might 'relieve the traveller from the burthem of those tedious enquiries on the road, or at the inns, which generally embarrass, and often mislead'.[11]

That West chose to refer to his chosen viewpoints as 'stations' is revealing: they were places to station oneself or to be stationary. The implication is that West has already done all the work of selection, so all that the visitor needs to do is follow his pedantic instructions to find the best spots available. His guidebook turned a tour of the Lakes into a sort of scenic orienteering, where finding the authorised station was more important than experiencing the journey (although it would be several years before the stations were accurately mapped by Peter Crosthwaite). The best way to show West's method is to give an example. Here is his description of his first station on Coniston Water, which is found at Water Park:

> STATION I. – A little above the village of Nibthwaite, the lake opens in full view. From the rock, on the left of the road, you have a general prospect of the lake, upwards.
>
> This station is found by observing where you have a hanging rock over the road on the east, and an ash tree on the west side of the road. On the opposite shore, to the left, and close by the water's edge, are some stripes of meadow and green ground, cut into small inclosures, with some dark-coloured houses under aged yew trees. Two promontories project a great way into the lake; the broadest is finely terminated by steep rocks, and crowned with wood; and both are insulated when the lake is high.[12]

The Jesuit believed that visitors would leave 'with a sense of the Creator's power, in heaping mountains upon mountains, and enthroning rocks upon rocks'. Such a collection of sublime and beautiful objects was supposed to 'excite both rapture and reverence'. By giving all the credit to God, West was overlooking any contribution made by generations of farmers to the look of the land, but in retrospect we can see that West himself, by the very act of selection, was constructing something too. He had done more than establish an itinerary; he had created an official canon of those views which just had to be seen.

West's guidebook, together with improvements in roads, helped to create a fashion for the Lake District. Though it must have been of genuinely practical assistance, it was also the launch pad and reference system for countless high-flown conversations. West himself had taken issue with Gray by suggesting that Grasmere was best approached from the south rather than over Dunmail Raise: now others could chatter about the pros and cons of West's various stations.

William Wilberforce must have had a copy of West's *Guide* to hand when he visited the Lakes in 1779 for he remarked in his journal that he 'join'd the Borrowdale Road & found or thought I found West's 3rd station (somewhere below Walla Crag) which I should like better if one did not look across the water'.[13] Neither was he much impressed by Station I at Cockshut Hill, of which he wrote, 'I cannot say that this View of the Lake pleases me so well as many others', nor with Station II, where his verdict was 'Crow Park is not at all a favourite Station with me'.

Although no one talks about viewing stations in this way any more – the railway usage probably ended all that – we still recommend viewpoints, mark them on maps and delineate them on the ground with parking bays, paths and picnic tables, while coach parties still make their way around a pre-arranged itinerary of stops. There is not too much wrong with this – not everyone is interested in walking for its own sake, or fit enough to do it – but those who turn up their noses at the more sedentary ways of appreciating the Lake District would point to the inauthenticity of experiencing the place in salami-style slices. Norman Nicholson became heated when he wrote about the Picturesque approach to landscape. He thought that it reduced the world 'to a mere scribbling pad for man'.[14] It ignored the biological, geological, organic and physical complexity of the place and that ultimately it was 'not even a half-truth, or a quarter truth, but a lie'. Fierce words, and he went too far. It is not immoral to look at a view as if it were a picture in a gallery, but for many people – most, perhaps – the aesthetic appreciation of landscape is, in any case, far more engaged. West and his ilk were certainly wrong to think that there were privileged viewpoints from which the Lake District had to be seen. We stroll around lakes, slog up steep paths, clamber over stiles, pick our way through fields of boulders, heave our heavy bodies over rocky outcrops. The whole body is involved, not just the eyes.

Everyone who produces a guidebook or writes about the Lake District sees the area through the lens of their own interests and preconceptions. West was an antiquary at heart and was probably more comfortable writing about church history than describing views, though he knew enough about Poussin and Rosa to invoke them in his description of the view from Belle Isle on Windermere. He also added his fourpennorth on the differences between the lakes. The 'delicate touches of Claude' were verified on Coniston Water, the 'noble scenes of Poussin' exhibited on Windermere and the 'stupendous, romantic ideas of Salvator Rosa, realized on Derwentlake'. Weighing the virtues of the various waterbodies would become part of the aesthetic game. West's own preference was for Windermere, but that is what one might expect from someone who lived to the south of the District.

West sanctioned the use of a small device which Gray had also carried on his Lake District exploration. This was a portable convex mirror, usually known as a Claude glass, because it was tinted in such a way that it could be used to frame reflected scenery so that it resembled a painting by Claude Lorrain. West thought it would 'furnish much amusement in this tour', which suggests that he thought of it as a plaything rather than a serious tool for artists. Without a shutter or a roll of film, it is difficult to see what the tourist was supposed to do with his Claudian view, once he had found it. Perhaps he called the rest of the party over and they all tried to peer over his shoulder, while gushing about his skill at composition. But the view in the mirror had to be given up, like an angler throwing a fish back into a lake. Glasses of various radiuses were available, with different backings. West recommended a dark glass for sunny days and one with silver foil for days when it was gloomy.

West was certainly no great walker or mountain man. His stations are all relatively low-lying with just enough elevation to provide good views across water. At this time it was still the lakes themselves, together with certain fairly accessible waterfalls, that were the main focal points of tourist attention. West did, however, defend the fells against adverse comparisons with the Alps or Apennines:

> our northern mountains are not inferior in beauty of line, or variety of summit, number of lakes, and transparency of water; not in colouring of rock, or softness of turf; but in height and extent only. The mountains here are all accessible to the summit, and furnish prospects no less surprising, and with more variety than the Alps themselves. The tops of

the highest Alps are inaccessible, being covered with everlasting snow, which commencing at regular heights above the cultivated tracts, of wooded and verdant sides, form, indeed, the highest contrast in nature; for there may be seen all the variety of climate in one view. To this, however, we oppose the sight of the ocean, from the summit of all the higher mountains, as it appears intersected with promontories, decorated with islands, and animated with navigation; which adds greatly to the perfection and variety of all grand views.[15]

If West was the person who guided people towards what they ought to see, it was another cleric, William Gilpin, who told them how to look: indeed, he wrote the rulebook for Picturesque tourism. Like so many of the crucial figures in this history, Gilpin's origins were 'of the rim' since he was born at Scaleby Castle, near Carlisle, and schooled at St Bees on the Cumberland coast, though his ancestors had lost manorial lands in the Kentmere valley in the time of Cromwell. William's father, Captain John Bernard Gilpin, was a soldier, but also an enthusiastic amateur painter, while his younger brother, Sawrey, became a professional artist specialising in horses and other animals for the sporting set. The Gilpin family history was also peppered with notable churchmen, and this was the occupation which William initially chose in life, graduating from Oxford and becoming first a curate at Irthington in Cumberland, then later the headmaster of Cheam School in Surrey. He stayed at Cheam until 1777, when he retired to become the vicar of Boldre in the New Forest. He had a good reputation as an enlightened and progressive teacher, but we are not so much interested in his professional accomplishments as in what he did on his holidays.

The first indication Gilpin gave of his interest in landscape aesthetics was in an anonymously published dialogue concerning Viscount Cobham's garden at Stowe (1748). It was by no means an outlandish enthusiasm for someone of Gilpin's class, for this was the heyday of the English landscape garden and being able to articulate views on architecture and garden making was one of the marks of a gentleman. Stowe was a landscape studded with temples and embellished by Arcadian scenes, many crafted by William Kent, the gardener who, in Horace Walpole's famous phrase, had 'leap'd the fence and seen that all nature is a garden'.[16] The discussion of landscape aesthetics was about to follow Kent over the garden fence. The appearance of the countryside in general would soon be a favoured topic for conversation and connoisseurship, and Gilpin's views would be at the centre of the discussion.

Perhaps it is not surprising that someone raised within view of the
Cumbrian fells should have developed a taste for rugged scenery. Then, as
now, schoolmasters were blessed with long vacations and Gilpin used his
to visit the hillier parts of Britain. Using his knowledge of landscape painting he conducted a quasi-scientific investigation of the qualities which he
thought made landscapes suitable subjects for artistic depiction. In his *Essay
on Prints* of 1768 he defined the Picturesque as 'that kind of beauty which
is agreeable in a picture'.[17] Without further elucidation this would have
been a ludicrously circular definition – what is agreeable in a picture is the
Picturesque which is what is agreeable in a picture – but Gilpin also set out
his 'little rules', which, though often fuzzy, offered guidance to tourists in
search of Picturesque views and to artists who hoped to create Picturesque
paintings.

Gilpin visited the Wye valley in 1770 and toured his native Lake District
in 1772 – the same year as Pennant's second visit and Hutchinson's frolics
on Ullswater, and six years before West's *Guide to the Lakes* first appeared in
print. As was the fashion, he committed his thoughts to notebooks, illustrat-
ing them with spontaneous sketches. He showed these first to friends, such
as the poet William Mason, then circulated them in manuscript form to a
wider circle, including Gray and Walpole. Finally, his confidants persuaded
him that they should be published. The first to appear, in 1782, was his tour
of the Wye valley, but his *Observations relatively chiefly to Picturesque Beauty
made in 1772, on several parts of England; particularly the Mountains and Lakes
of Cumberland and Westmoreland* appeared in 1786. Further titles (equally
long and informative) appeared over the next twenty-three years, relating
to tours of Scotland, the West Country, the Isle of Wight and East Anglia.
Gilpin attracted a following and the Picturesque became a cult. It is even
said that King George III was a fan.

Gilpin's 'little rules' provided everyone with a checklist for Picturesque
Correctness. Rebecca Solnit has likened them to those etiquette guides
which told socially aspiring members of the middle classes what knives and
forks to use.[18] Texture was important; scenes should be rough, intricate,
varied or broken. Compositionally, there should be a dark 'foreground',
a brighter 'middle distance' and beyond that a 'distance' indistinctly
perceived. Such terms have become so much part of our linguistic toolkit
that we use them now without much thought, but Gilpin used other terms
like 'frontscreen' and 'sidescreen' which have not lasted in the same way.
Like West, Gilpin favoured low viewpoints because they accentuated the

sublime characteristics of a landscape. Unlike earlier guidebook writers, he had very little to say about old churches, stone circles and so on, unless they helped to compose a scene. He thought that nature was good at producing colours and textures, but not so reliable when it came to composition, so he gave licence to his intended readership of artists to move things around a little. Infamously, he suggested that the ruins of Tintern Abbey could be improved by the judicious application of a mallet, though he did not mean this to be taken literally.

By the time Jane Austen drafted the story that would become *Northanger Abbey*, appreciation of the Picturesque was such a well-established social game that the novelist could not resist a poke at it. When her hero- ine Catherine Morland, out walking with Henry Tilney, confesses that she would give anything in the world to be able to draw, her companion launches into a disquisition about 'foregrounds, distances, and second distances – side-screens and perspectives – lights and shades'. Catherine is such a promising scholar that by the time they reach their destination 'she voluntarily rejected the whole city of Bath as unworthy to make part of a landscape'.[19] Austen did not visit the Lake District, but it is intriguing to imagine what she might have made of it. In *Pride and Prejudice*, first drafted in 1796–7, another heroine, Elizabeth Bennet, looks forward to a tour of the Lakes in the company of her aunt and uncle:

> 'My dear, dear Aunt,' she rapturously cried, 'what delight! What felicity! You give me fresh life and vigour. Adieu to disappointment and spleen. What are men to rocks and mountains? Oh! What hours of transport we shall spend! And when we *do* return, it shall not be like other travellers, without being able to give one accurate idea of any thing. We *will* know where we have gone – we *will* recollect what we have seen. Lakes, mountains, and rivers shall not be jumbled together in our imaginations; nor, when we attempt to describe any particular scene, will we begin quarrelling about its relative situation. Let *our* first effusions be less insupportable than those of the generality of travellers.'[20]

As the story develops the projected trip to the North is curtailed and Elizabeth must make do with Derbyshire, but satire at the expense of the Picturesque in these novels shows that it was much more than a fringe enthusiasm. Gilpin and his theories were satirised in a crueller, more knock- about way by the poet William Combe in his *Tour of Doctor Syntax in Search*

of the Picturesque (1809–11), which was wickedly illustrated by Thomas
Rowlandson. At the start of this long comic poem, first published in serial
form in monthly editions of the *Poetical Magazine*, a hen-pecked and impe-
cunious curate and schoolmaster called Syntax (the name is a satire upon
Gilpin's 'little rules') suddenly realises how he can make some money. As he
explains to his wife:

> I'll make a TOUR – and then I'll WRITE IT.
> You well know what my pen can do,
> And I'll employ my pencil too: –
> I'll ride and *write*, and *sketch* and *print*,
> And thus create a real mint;
> I'll *prose* it here, I'll *verse* it there,
> And *picturesque* it ev'ry where[21]

Syntax is a cartoon character in whom aspects of the real-life Gilpin are
merged with the tall, bony figure of Don Quixote, but, in place of Rocinante,
Syntax has his trusty grey mare, Grizzle, and rather than the deluded
pursuit of chivalric honour, his quest is to track down some profitably
Picturesque views. At one point in the story, Syntax declines an invitation
to join a hunt, saying:

Dr Syntax Sketching a Lake (1817) by Thomas Rowlandson

Your sport, my Lord, I cannot take,
For I must go and hunt a lake;
And while you chase the flying deer,
I must fly off to Windermere.
Instead of hallooing to a fox,
I must catch echoes from the rocks[22]

Syntax's travels take him to Oxford and to York, but eventually he reaches Keswick. On the way he is set upon by robbers, swindled in inns and chased by a bull. On the shores of Derwentwater he takes out his sketchbook as the wind whips up a storm, but old Grizzle stumbles and dumps him into the lake. Combe was ultimately merciful to his accident-prone hero, rewarding him with a publishing success and a comfortable stipend in Cumberland, both of which helped to improve the temper of his wife. He was less generous to the Picturesque, heaping ridicule throughout upon the idea that artists could exaggerate proportions or move things around in their paintings just for effect.

The adjective 'picturesque' is a washed-out word nowadays. Many people use it as if it were synonymous with 'beautiful' or 'sublime', rolling together three aesthetic categories that eighteenth-century theorists were keen to keep apart. It often degenerates into the kitsch or the twee. William Gilpin is certainly not a household name, and yet, for all this, when tourists take out their compact cameras and point them at the landscape – whether in the Lake District or on the opposite side of the planet – there is a very good chance that they are following the fuzzy rules set down by the Cumbrian schoolmaster.

Overleaf: Furness Abbey

William Wordsworth (1818) by Benjamin Robert Haydon

3

'Settled contentment'

The Lake District of Wordsworth's Youth

Wordsworth's autobiographical poem *The Prelude* gives us glimpses of the apparent idyll of his infant years in Cockermouth. His playmate was the 'beauteous stream' of the River Derwent, which flowed beside the terraced walk that terminated the back garden of the family home. Here, as a five-year-old boy, he would make 'one long bathing of a summer's day'; or he would course through the sandy fields, leaping through groves of groundsel as free as a naked savage. Even though Cockermouth lies outside the boundaries of the present National Park and belongs more to the coastal plain than to the mountains, Wordsworth rightly judged himself 'much favoured' in his birthplace.

William was born on 7 April 1770 in one of the back bedrooms of a four-square Georgian town house on the main street. His siblings were also born there: his elder brother Richard, his beloved sister Dorothy (born on Christmas Day the following year) and the two younger boys, John and Christopher. Their father, John Wordsworth, was a steward for Sir James Lowther, the local landowner, who would later become the first Earl of Lonsdale. This connection is unlikely to have made the Wordsworths popular, since Wicked Jimmy Lowther (also known as the Bad Earl, the Gloomy Earl and Jimmy Grasp-all) was deeply disliked. His huge land-holdings and the coal that went with them made him the most powerful man in Cumberland. Lowther was ruthless in business, fought duels, kept mistresses and had a number of parliamentary seats in his pocket. A contemporary, Alexander Carlyle, wrote that Sir James was 'more detested than any man alive' and concluded that he was 'truly a madman, but too rich to be confined'.[1]

The first calamity to shake William's world was the death of his mother before he was eight years old. She had fallen ill after visiting a friend in

London, where she is said to have slept in a damp bed, and was dead within two months. His father, kept busy by Lowther business, could not cope with his children alone, so Dorothy was dispatched to Halifax to live with cousins, while William and Richard were packed off to the grammar school in Hawkshead.

This was not the misfortune it might have been, because the school was good and William was happy there. It had been founded in 1585 by Edwyn Sandys, Archbishop of York, who was born at Esthwaite Hall, about one mile south of the village, and in William's day its reputation was so high that it drew pupils from across the north of England. It taught Latin and Greek and 'other sciences' which included arithmetic and geometry, but William had teachers who encouraged him in his liking for literature, notably the headmaster William Taylor, who set him poetry exercises.

William was fortunate, too, in his lodgings because he was looked after by Hugh Tyson, the local joiner, and his wife Ann, who ran a grocery shop. The couple were elderly but good-natured and William enjoyed both the security of a loving home and the liberty to wander the woods, fields and fellsides. *The Prelude* is packed with his childhood roamings and transgressions. By night he would rove the hillsides looking for snares set by others, occasionally helping himself to a trapped bird. In springtime he hung by his fingertips to slippery rocks while plundering birds' nests among the crags. Once he stole a shepherd's skiff from the shores of Ullswater and rowed it stealthily to the middle of the silent lake, only to become alarmed by a rearing cliff which seemed to stride after him like a living thing, compelling him to row back, hands trembling, to the mooring place. Wordsworth was no conscienceless tearaway; he was sensitive to the moral lessons which the 'presences of nature' and 'souls of lonely places' could teach him. Nevertheless his was a remarkably untrammelled boyhood, in which there was time for ice-skating on frozen lakes, following hounds through darkened woods, racing around the islands of Windermere in rowing boats and galloping on hired horses past Furness Abbey in the Vale of Nightshade.

Though William had not been unhappy in Cockermouth, his abrupt transplantation to the centre of the Lake District seems to have done him nothing but good. His affection for his 'grey-haired Dame' and for the village of Hawkshead itself, its lowly cottages so beautiful among the fields, is evident in *The Prelude*. His surrogate parents, the Tysons, were intimately involved in village life in a way that his own parents, by virtue of their social position, could never have been in Cockermouth and the experience infused

William with an egalitarian spirit which burned brightly in his youth and never entirely left him, despite his drift towards the Tory party in later life. Farming life in the valleys furnished him with a template for a robust and self-sufficient existence, where individuals cooperated with their neighbours and prospered in harmony with nature. When he came to write his *Guide to the Lakes* he described 'a perfect Republic of Shepherds and Agriculturists' to be found at the heads of the dales. It was, he wrote:

> a pure Commonwealth; the members of which existed in the midst of a powerful empire, like an ideal society or an organized community, whose constitution had been imposed by the mountains which protected it. Neither high-born nobleman, knight, nor esquire, was here; but many of these humble sons of the hills had a consciousness that the land, which they had walked over and tilled, had for more than five hundred years been possessed by men of their name and blood.[2]

These statesmen farmers held their land in various forms of customary tenure which lay somewhere between freehold and the sort of copyhold frequently found in southern England. These traditions provided security and a rough sort of equality.[3] Those who held their land by custom could pass on any improvements to their descendants or even sell it, so the statesmen became a modestly affluent yeomanry, not quite gentry but a long way from being peasants.

The farmhouses which Wordsworth came so greatly to admire were mostly built in the later decades of the seventeenth century or the early part of the eighteenth. By the time he knew them, they would have weathered for several generations, colonised by mosses, lichens and ivy, making them seem as though rooted in the landscape since time immemorial. These stone-built dwellings, made from locally quarried materials, replaced the cruck-framed, wattle-and-daub or turf-walled huts of previous centuries, none of which have survived. The stone houses, like that of the sensible piggy in the nursery rhyme, have endured, and at Townend, near Troutbeck, the National Trust has preserved a fine example of a statesman's home, which belonged to the Browne family from 1623 up until 1944. This is no stately pile or country seat, but it is nevertheless substantial and imposing in its way, with oak-mullioned windows and tall cylindrical chimneys capped with slanting slates. Inside it is dark but cosy with much oak-panelling. Statesmen farmers were people of the middling sort and, like aspirational types throughout the ages, they could get ideas above their station: without ever having been given the right to display arms, the Brownes went ahead and carved a coat of arms into the door of a downstairs cupboard.

In Wordsworth's day there would have been fewer of the dry-stone walls that are now such a characteristic and much-loved landscape feature. Although the irregular field patterns in valley-bottom places such as Wasdale Head and Great Langdale suggest an origin earlier than the eighteenth century, the movement to enclose large areas of the fells did not get going in earnest until the early 1760s, a decade before the poet was born. The patterns of the walls reveal much social history. From the earliest times a wall, known as the 'ring-garth', marked the boundary between the valley floor and the fellside commons. Some farmers became wealthy enough to enclose large fields on the slopes outside this wall and these were known as 'intakes'. This privatising tendency was offset by a cooperative idea: so that every farmer could get his sheep to the open fells, passages called 'rakes' or 'outgangs' were left through the encircling intake land.[4]

As with the enclosure movement elsewhere, larger landowners had the political and economic muscle to seize what had once been common to all. It was the beginning of an upheaval that would change the social structure of the area, as smaller farmers lost their rights to gather wood or graze their animals on common land. Many were forced to work as hired labourers or to make their way to the burgeoning industrial cities. Much as we might admire dry-stone walls today, and marvel at the skill and audacity of the wallers who built them up such steep hillsides and seemingly impossible crags, they must have had an altogether more depressing significance for those who witnessed their livelihoods being walled away.

There has been a continuous tradition of sheep-farming in the Lake District for over a thousand years. On his six-month tour of the north of England in 1771, Arthur Young noted flock sizes of between 100 and 1,000 head, and his description of Kendal manufactories gives us an idea of the significance of the woollen industry at the time:

> Kendal: It is famous for several manufactories; the chief of which is that of knit stockings employing near 5000 hands by computation. They reckon 120 wool-combers, each employing five spinners and each spinner four or five knitters: if four, the amount is 2400.[5]

The Herdwick, with its white face and feet and its disreputable overcoat of bluish wool, has been the characteristic sheep of the Lake District for centuries, as much part of the scenery as the crags and the dry-stone walls, though in numbers they have now lost ground to other mountain breeds such as Swaledales, Rough Fells and Teeswaters. Constitutionally suited to the rigours of life on windswept uplands, Herdwicks are renowned for their stay-at-home inclinations. They are 'hefted', which means that they have an instinct to return to the fellsides on which they were weaned. This has several advantages for the farmer, who always knows where to look for his sheep and can leave them on the unenclosed fell without worrying about them wandering off. A few sheep will stray, of course, but the shepherds have devised ingenious ways of displaying ownership by clipping 'lug' marks into their ears and by dying their fleeces with distinctive marks, traditionally using red iron oxide or Borrowdale wad. As a child in Cockermouth, Wordsworth would have known little about the customs of shepherds, but at school in Hawkshead and later in Grasmere he came to know this way of life and to admire it for its organic connection to the land, the weather and the seasons.

The fleece of the Herdwick has enabled the breed to withstand the fiercest winters and there are stories of sheep surviving in snowdrifts, but the wool has never been prized for its quality. In 1390 it was described as 'the worst wool in the realm'.[6] It found its market, however, for rough, hard-wearing cloths such as 'Hodden Grey' and the famous 'Kendal Green', which was coloured with locally growing dyer's broom (*Genista tinctoria*). Though Kendal was the centre of the woollen industry, Hawkshead also had its 'tenter grounds' where cloth could be stretched and bleached.

There is no longer any market for Herdwick wool; indeed, it costs more to shear the sheep than can be recouped from sale of the fleeces. The heyday of the Lakeland woollen industry was in the sixteenth century and by Wordsworth's time it was already in decline. It had been largely a cottage industry, with much of the carding, spinning and weaving dispersed among the farms, some of which had outside spinning galleries to take maximum advantage of the light. Small water-driven fulling mills, where cloth was scoured and thickened, were scattered through the dales. Wordsworth admired the self-reliance of Lake District families and appreciated all their small-scale industries, not only those linked to wool, but also coppicing, charcoal burning and basket weaving. But the apparently settled state of the valleys was an illusion. Vast social changes were afoot, and the Lake District had no indemnity.

Living among the dalesfolk, Wordsworth became aware of the precariousness of their existence. Several of his most affecting poems are concerned with their reactions to undeserved adversity. *Michael* is the sad tale of an ancient shepherd of Green-head Gill and his hard-working son, to whom the old man hopes to pass on his land and his flock. The narrator, who sounds much like Wordsworth himself, talks of his love for these hardy men, 'not for their own sakes but for the fields and hills where was their occupation and abode'. The poem opens with a settled scene: Old Michael's wife spinning at one of her two wheels (one for flax, the other for wool) as the shepherd and his son Luke card wool for the spindle, while warming themselves at the fireside. The close working bond between father and son is broken when Michael's nephew falls into some unspecified misfortune and the shepherd, who had agreed to stand surety for his relative, is faced with the prospect of selling land to raise funds to help him. It is an early example of property being used as security for a business risk. As hefted to the land as any of his sheep, Michael is dismayed by this prospect and proposes that Luke should go to work in the city for a relative who is prosperous in trade. But in the dissolute city Luke quickly falls 'to evil course: ignominy and shame' and ultimately flees the country. Old Michael's heart is broken; so too is the ancestral link with the land. Confident of Luke's successful return, he had started to build a new sheepfold. Now he can hardly lift a stone. Upon his death, and that of his widow soon afterwards, the farm is sold to a stranger who demolishes the cottage which once harboured such settled contentment.

The storyline of *The Last of the Flock* has a similar melancholy. Here a prosperous hill farmer is forced to sell his sheep, one by one, to feed his six children. The poem shows him in tears, cradling the last of his lambs, having given up all hope of keeping his family out of poverty. In both poems there is the sense that powerful social and economic pressures, only dimly understood by the narrators or the characters themselves, could tear apart the established envelope of their lives. The hard truth was that the statesmen farmers often had insufficient capital to enclose and improve their lands, so many of them were forced to sell up.

Rapid change was facilitated by improved communications. When the first travellers came to the Lake District, they found it an adventure. Most made a suitably dramatic entrance through the amphibian world of Morecambe Bay, across the treacherous sands. It has always been a dangerous place. In

1326 the Abbot of Furness petitioned the King to let him have a coroner
because so many people had drowned while crossing the sands to attend
the coroner's court on the other side, while the monks of Conishead Priory
would say a mass for travellers on Chapel Island, a limestone outcrop on the
Ulverston Sands.

But, for all its perils, the route across the sands remained the principal
southern approach to the Lake District until the construction of the Levens
turnpike in 1818. Quick though the sands can be to suck down an incautious
cockle-picker, a cart or a tractor, and fickle though the tides and the mists
have always proved, there was, for decades, a regular coach service across
the bay. It began in 1781 and continued until 1857, and it was only the opening of the Ulverston and Lancaster Railway that finally killed it. Stay on the
right line and the sands could be as hard as stucco, as one traveller, the Hon.
Mrs Murray, observed (it is a good comparison, too, since stucco was traditionally made from sand, lime and water), but wander off course and one
could be lost in a deadly deliquescence. Passengers had a better chance of
an uneventful crossing if they travelled in a diligence carrying three or four
persons including the driver; larger coaches carrying twelve or more also
hazarded the crossing, but there was a much greater risk of getting stuck in

The High Sheriff of Lancashire crossing Morecambe Sands (*c.* 1795–8)
by Thomas Sunderland

the liquefying sands. Paintings from the time show that the route was busy, for the coach might be followed by pack ponies and travellers on foot.

There are places – as I can testify – where the stucco path leads to a slippery-sided channel where walkers must wade. When I made the crossing, in the company of the official guide, our party straggled ashore with mud up to our knees, an alarming apparition for people taking afternoon tea in Grange-over-Sands.

Advertisements for the coach service across the bay reassured customers that they would be in the hands of 'a sober and careful driver, who is well acquainted with the sands'.[7] The crossing did not just offer a route to Furness and the southern Lakes, but was part of a longer route which linked Lancaster and Whitehaven, which had also to negotiate the Duddon Sands and the estuaries of the rivers Esk, Mite and Irt.

In the central Lake District, before the construction of the turnpikes, wheeled vehicles were rare. Most produce was transported by pack ponies and the numerous little stone bridges that can still be found over becks and rivers were built with low parapets to allow the lurching packs to cross. Huge wooden sledges were used to get slate from elevated quarries down to the valley floors. Period dramas always make travel in eighteenth-century England look grim, with rutted roads, sweating horses, swaying coaches, highwaymen and overcrowded inns, but this image obscures the very real improvements that were being made throughout the century. Local Turnpike Trusts were empowered to levy tolls on the users of particular stretches of road, employing funds secured against this income to improve and maintain the fabric of the highway. A turnpike in this context, rather than the military one from which the term first came, was simply a toll gate across the road. In this way, the costs of improving roads were met by the users rather than by the local population in general, many of whom might be quite stay-at-home. The first Turnpike Trust in Cumbria was set up in Whitehaven in 1739 with more to follow in the 1750s and 1760s. There were fifteen by the close of the century. By the time Wordsworth was born, the journey from London to the Lake District took three days; forty years earlier it had taken nine.

Most of the eighteenth-century tourists in the Lakes, however, were prosperous enough to own their own coaches or could afford to hire them. Because horses became exhausted, travel was arranged in stages of about fifteen miles. The owner of a coach would set out with his own horses, but hire others along the way from posting stations (Penrith, Cockermouth, Ulverston and Kendal were all significant coaching towns). There were sportier versions of the standard coach, such as the more manoeuvrable chariot or diligence, which also bestowed an assured social cachet, and the phaeton, a vehicle for upper-crust boy racers. At the top of the range was the open-topped landau, the sort of carriage which nowadays carries the Queen on various state occasions. Even in the eighteenth century, one of these would have been a very rare sight in the Lake District, so it is not surprising that when Dorothy Wordsworth saw one in 1800 she thought it worth noting in her diary: 'A coroneted Landau went by when we were sitting on the sodded wall. The ladies (evidently Tourists) turned an eye of interest upon our little garden & cottage.'[8]

Arthur Young made detailed notes about the turnpikes he used on his travels and he thought those in the Lake District were generally sound:

> To *Penrith*. Turnpike. Very good.
> To *Keswick*. Ditto. Ditto; except a mile over a rotton common, which is as bad.
> To *Hull's Water*. Cross. Middling; a coach may pass it very tolerably.
> To *Shapp*. Turnpike. Very good.
> To *Kendal*. Turnpike. Exceedingly hilly and some very steep, but the road itself is excellent.[9]

It might have been that these roads were good because they did not carry heavy traffic; Young had much worse to say about the roads in industrial Lancashire. His advice on roads prefigured the modern form of guidebook, as did his reviews of the various inns he had occasion to use. Christopher Fenton at the King's Arms in Kendal, for example, kept a 'good clean house' and offered 'a brace of woodcocks, veal cutlets, and cheese' for one shilling or 'a boiled fowl and sauce, a roast partridge, potted charr, cold ham, tarts and three or four sorts of foreign sweetmeats' for eight shillings.

With his keen interest in agricultural improvement, Young found Cumbrian farming practices behind the times. 'They have no beans, very few pease, and as little rye,' he wrote of the farmers around Keswick. 'They know but little of clover: one or two of the farmers have tried it with barley, but found it good for nothing: It must have been strange land.'

Young's paradoxical-sounding remedy for backward agriculture was to urge landlords to increase rents, as this would act as a spur to those who practised good husbandry. This was the hard medicine of the times. The choice lay between progress and paternalism, but progress, in the countryside just as much as in the towns, could be a painful business with many losers.

Improving roads did not bring prosperity for all. Farmers found that they were competing with cheap grains from abroad. Outsiders came into the area and bought up failing farms. Pedlars who had made a living hawking their wares around remote farms and hamlets found that their customers were now going to shops in the nearest towns. Those who could find no way to make a good living in the countryside went off to the industrial towns. We hear a great deal about how bad conditions were in cities like Manchester, but how much worse they must have appeared to some in rural areas if the satanic mills were considered a desirable alternative.

Scholarly monks, such as those who kept the library at Furness Abbey, have provided modern-day academics with one of their favourite metaphors for landscape. Because vellum scrolls were expensive, the frugal scribes used to erase them and write on them again, but traces of the previous text would always show through. Such a document was called a palimpsest and landscapes are layered and reinscribed in a similar way, with traces from earlier times remaining. Every generation adds something new to these repositories of collective memory, and change is inevitable, although we might sometimes try to slow it down by preservation or conservation.

One of the changes most lamented in Wordsworth's time was the felling of the oaks on the estates that had once belonged to James Radcliffe, the third Earl of Derwentwater, including those that previously formed a glade at Crow Park on the shores of the lake. The earl had been one of the leaders of the failed Jacobite rising of 1715 and was beheaded for treason at Tower Hill in London in February of the following year. His estates were confiscated and conferred upon the Greenwich Hospital, whose commissioners were more concerned with their own funding problems than with the aesthetics of a northern lake, so they sold the oaks and they were cut down in 1751, despite much local opposition. Landscapes which are appreciated locally can often fall victim to decisions taken at a remote distance. This was an early instance in the Lake District which showed that beauty was vulnerable and might need to be defended.

Felling woodlands is the quickest, and therefore one of the most noticeable, ways of changing the character of a landscape, but planting trees can, within a few years, have just as much impact. Many of the aesthetic disputes that beset the Lake District were concerned with changes to the tree cover of one sort or another. On the positive side, there were landowners who set out to beautify their holdings by planting trees and succeeded beyond their dreams, leaving gifts of loveliness for generations to follow. One such man was John Christian – or John Christian Curwen as he became when he changed his name legally after marrying his second wife. This was his younger cousin Isabella Curwen, the heiress to a fortune derived from coal mining in the Workington area. From all accounts the marriage was a happy one and the wealth it brought Curwen provided him with the platform for his political career. A leading advocate for agricultural improvement, he was one of the founders of the Royal Agricultural Society. Though Curwen, like other landowners of the period, planted larches for profit, he also planted oak trees for posterity. In a single year – 1798 – he planted fourteen acres of them. He is reckoned to have planted a million trees on the slopes of Windermere.[10] Curwen was dedicated to the creation of a prosperous northern Arcadia, believing it was not only the right of an owner to develop his land, but his duty. His aesthetics went happily hand in hand with his economics.

A true wilderness could never be considered Arcadian. In paintings by Claude and Poussin, the pastoral idyll required not only peaceful fields and contented livestock, but an architectural presence that signified civilisation. In the eighteenth century, landowners the length of Britain took these images to heart and built Classical temples and Palladian mansions on their estates. Inevitably this enthusiasm reached the Lake District, where the first Arcadian villa to be conceived was John Plaw's circular mansion for Thomas English, on the Windermere island then known by its Norse name of Long Holme.

To place this event in context, it is worth noting that Wordsworth had not left Cockermouth when construction began in 1774 and that he was still under Ann Tyson's charge in Hawkshead when English's money ran out and the island was bought for Isabella Curwen and renamed Belle Isle in her honour. This was 1781, the year before Isabella's marriage to John Christian, who completed the house, but removed the formal gardens and fashionable chinoiserie trappings put in by English. Curwen appointed a landscape gardener called Thomas White to replace them with something smooth, simple and grassy in the style of 'Capability' Brown. Plaw used the house to illustrate the frontispiece of his *Rural Architecture* of 1794. In this view the house stands proud as the focal point of the lake, but nowadays it is softened and screened by mature woodland and the best view requires a trip on the Windermere ferry.

Though the house had curiosity value from the outset, it took heavy blows from the critics. One such was William Gell, who made a tour in 1797 and would one day become a respected archaeologist. 'As to the house itself,' wrote Gell, 'when the observer stands in such a position as not to perceive the portico, it wants only a little green paint and a label of Souchong or fine Hyson to make it exactly like a large tea shop canister.'[11] Dorothy Wordsworth later compared Plaw's mansion to a pepperpot. William Cockin, on the other hand, who took it upon himself to update West's *Guide to the Lakes*, thought the development on Belle Isle a precedent to be pursued. What the island needed was a bridge from the shore, and what the lake needed was more houses, so that it might 'become a rival to the celebrated lake of Geneva, which owes its principal superiority over all other lakes to its having a city at one end and being surrounded with palaces'.[12]

Curwen's other celebrated addition to the Windermere landscape was a piece of Picturesque whimsy, the architectural equivalent of a Claude glass. This was Claife Station, so called because it stood on the site of West's first recommended viewpoint on Windermere, on the western shore, up a steep slope from the ferry landing. In 1799 the reclusive rector of Hawkshead, the Reverend William Braithwaite, built an octagonal pleasure house here, and when the Curwens acquired the land in 1802 they grafted castellations and a massive rectangular bay on to the previous structure. The ruins of this curious hybrid can still be found amid woodland now managed by the National Trust, but originally planted by Curwen. The Station was a folly, but its foolishness had a function. There was a dining room on the ground floor, but it was the sitting room on the upper floor which gave the building its purpose. The glass in its various windows was tinted to provide a variety of experiences: green to convey the verdancy of spring, yellow to suggest a warm sunny day, orange for autumn tints, blue to cast a cold, wintry spell and purple to conjure the sense of an impending storm.

Though Lake Windermere never did become Lake Geneva, the Round House on Belle Isle was the first of many grand villas to be built on its shores during Wordsworth's lifetime. The eleventh edition of West's *Guide* (1821) mentioned the following: 'by Mr. Law, at Brathay; Miss Pritchard, Croft-Lodge, Clappersgate; Mr. Harrison, above Ambleside; Mrs. Taylor, Cottage, Ambleside; the late Bishop of Llandaff, Calgarth; Mr. North, Ambleside; Mrs.

Taylor, Bellfield, near Bowness; Mr. Crump, Ferney-Green; Mr. Bellasis, Holly-Hill; Mr. Greaves, Old England; John Bolton, Esq., Storrs; Mr. Taylor, Townhead; Mr. Dixon, Fell-foot; Mr. Machel, Newby-bridge; &c.'

The *Guide* then gave them all its blessing: 'these objects, as works of art, most of which are done in styles suitable to their situation, give an air of consequence to the country, and, with the surrounding natural beauties, have lately made this neighbourhood, and particularly about Ambleside, a place of the greatest celebrity.'

One of the ideas caught in the popular imagination is that Wordsworth discovered the Lake District, or was the person who did most to popularise it. Reading one or two accounts by early tourists is enough to dispel these ideas. Clearly the Lake District would have been celebrated without him. Nevertheless, Wordsworth was destined to become one of the key attractions of the area, while his particular vision of his native landscape would have an enduring influence upon its future. The associated myth is that the Lake District of Wordsworth's time was a prelapsarian Eden where self-sufficient farmers lived in the contented and stable rhythms of their forefathers. As we have seen, this was not the case, even in the poet's boyhood. On the contrary, the Lake District was a place where farming was being squeezed, established ways of life were being threatened and new people and new influences were pouring in.

Overleaf: Derwentwater from Great Wood

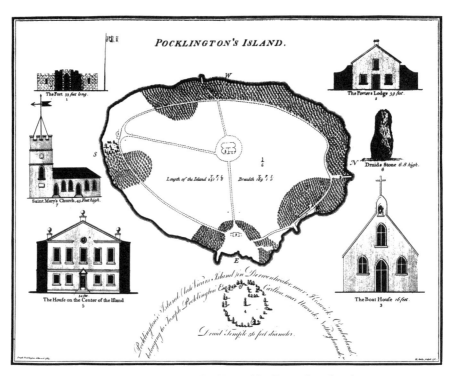

Map of Pocklington's Island (1783) by Peter Crosthwaite

4

Showmen

'King Pocky' and 'Admiral' Crosthwaite

IN 1778, A YEAR before Wordsworth was sent to school at Hawkshead, a middle-aged bachelor named Joseph Pocklington paid £300 for an island close to the northern shore of Derwentwater and began to transform it. Pocklington was the son of Nottinghamshire banker, and he was wealthy, having come into a legacy at the age of twenty-six, but during a succession of visits to the Lake District in the 1770s he fell in love with the region, in his own eccentric way, and decided that he must make his home beside a lake.

The island he bought was the one that had once provided a home to the migrant workers of the Company of Mines Royal, but over the centuries it has borne many names. The Norsemen called it Hestholm, or 'Stallion Island'; later it became Vicar's Island and now it is Derwent Island; but for seventeen years it was Pocklington's Island, and its ruler, soon dubbed 'King Pocky' by the locals, was determined to stamp his mark upon it. Pocklington was happy to scatter whimsical features liberally around his new realm; in addition to a brand-new mansion, there was a church, with a mocked-up timber nave, designed to be seen from across the water, a boathouse built in the style of a Nonconformist chapel, and a white-painted porter's lodge. To the south of the island were the ramparts of Fort Joseph, another sham construction, which housed a battery of brass guns, but the 'improvement' that caused most consternation was the so-called Druid's Circle. This was modelled on the prehistoric stone circle at Castlerigg, just above Keswick, but Pocklington had the nerve to proclaim it as a new archaeological discovery, 'the most compleat and last-built Temple in Europe' – which, of course, it was.

Pocklington's fanciful schemes provided local employment and he was charitable to the poor, but his lack of taste condemned him in the eyes of

more cultured types. Gell was disgusted with 'the folly and childishness of
what is now called Pocklington's island, where is an house that appears to
have dropped from the clouds, one or two batteries with pasteboard battlements and a spruceness in the whole, which cannot accord in any degree
with the surrounding scenery'.[1] He found the 'awkward jumble of fantastic
gew gaws' utterly risible, but, as one might expect from an antiquary-in-
the-making, he was particularly scathing about the Druid's Circle, which
turned out to be as impermanent as the rest:

> A druid temple was the next thing to employ his [Pocklington's] genius
> and accordingly he collected a number of large stones, placed them in a
> circle, and had them fixed upright on the southern shore. Unfortunately
> for all lovers of British antiquity a storm arose in the lake, and the waves
> washed down the labours of some days.[2]

King Pocky's local popularity had much to do with the regattas he organised with his friend Peter Crosthwaite, the owner of a museum in Keswick.
The son of a farmer at Dale Head, near Thirlmere, Crosthwaite had enjoyed
a short but colourful career with the East India Company and a spell in
the Customs Service at Blyth in Northumberland. When he returned to
Keswick at the age of forty-four he was one of the first to recognise the
commercial possibilities presented by the visiting tourists. The collection
of unusual artefacts was a popular hobby at the time and many fine country houses boasted a cabinet of curiosities. Crosthwaite assembled his own
display and charged for entry.

Pocklington and Crosthwaite were natural allies. Pocklington was affluent and upper-class with a university education, and, as a bachelor cared
for by a retinue of servants, he had all the time in the world to indulge his
whims and pastimes. He had money and connections but lacked local knowledge. Crosthwaite's life, conversely, had been much tougher. The local man
had fought his own way up from humble beginnings and had a wife and
two children to support. He was pugnacious, self-taught and relentlessly
self-promoting but with a playful streak that must have struck a chord with
King Pocky, because soon after Crosthwaite's return the two men were
planning the first of the Derwentwater regattas.

The regattas on Derwentwater were not the first the Lake District had seen.
John Spedding of Armathwaite Hall set the precedent in 1779 when he organised an event at the northern end of Bassenthwaite Lake. Three more were

Pocklington's Island (1794) by John 'Warwick' Smith

held there in subsequent years and Pocklington and Crosthwaite borrowed some ideas for their events, such as the equine swimming race where a raft of horses would be towed to the middle of the lake and sunk, so that spectators could place bets on the animal most likely to be first ashore. With two such showmen at the helm, it was certain that the Derwentwater festivities would be more spectacular. An announcement which appeared on the front page of the *Cumberland Pacquet* on 21 August 1781 promised generous cash prizes for the races, but also held out the prospect of some pyrotechnic fun:

> Pocklington's Island (late Vicar's Island) will be attacked by a formidable Fleet, when a stout resistance is to be made, especially from the Half Moon Battery; and it is to be thought the circling Mountains will bear a Part in this Tremendous Uproar . . .[3]

Stalls and sideshows were erected on the meadows between the town and shore of the lake, with refreshment tents and marquees. As neither Pocklington nor Crosthwaite had ever imbibed the faintest drop of

Puritanism, there were plenty of opportunities to drink and to gamble. It is no wonder that people came in droves, not just locals, but gentry from further afield who arrived in their carriages.

Crosthwaite styled himself the 'Admiral of the Keswick Regatta' and supplied enough naval knowledge to make the mock battles on the lake seem convincing. The day always culminated in the invasion of Pocklington's Island. A fleet of boats, laden with musketeers and cannon, would appear in formation from behind Friar's Crag. The Admiral, who, by his own account, had once captained the gunboat *Otter* to protect East India Company ships from Malay pirates, was in charge of the attacking forces, while King Pocky organised the defence. The whole event was choreographed by signalling flags from the island.

The fickle Cumbrian weather dampened spirits at the first Derwentwater Regatta. Incessant rain meant that the naval crews, mindful of the need to keep their powder dry, had to postpone their assault until the evening, by which time many of the sodden spectators had drifted away. But the *Cumberland Pacquet* was able to give a more upbeat account of the following year's amusements:

> About 4 o'clock preparations were made for the attack on Pocklington's Island: the fleet retired behind Friar Crag to prepare for action, previous to which a flag of truce was sent to the governor, with a summons to surrender upon honourable terms; a defiance was sent, upon which the fleet appeared advancing with great spirit before the batteries, when after forming in a curved line, a terrible cannonade began on both sides, accompanied with a dreadful discharge of musquetry, which continued a considerable time, occasioning the most tremendous roar that can be conceived, which was frequently echoed back from hill to hill in a variety of sounds. After a severe conflict, the enemies were driven from the attack etc.[4]

Compared with the six cannon on Hutchinson's boat, the cumulative noise made by a whole fleet of little gunships, together with their armed marines and the island's cannons, must have been deafening, particularly as the latter were packed with moss and damp rags to make them even louder. French horns were also part of the occasion, just as they had been for Hutchinson's party. In between the attacks there would be musical interludes creating 'an almost supernatural tide of harmony'. The local press claimed that the battle could be heard as far away as Appleby, and the reporters were probably not exaggerating.

When it came to business, Crosthwaite was a very prickly character who resented competition. He clearly saw the regattas as his own enterprise and disliked others trying to muscle in. In his memorandum books, which are now in the Keswick Museum and Art Gallery, he referred to his rivals collectively as the 'Junto' and was convinced that he was the victim of a conspiracy. It seems that at one of the regattas a number of men who were nominally under the self-styled Admiral's command 'fled their colours' and went to the island, where, by 'uttering many great swelling lies', they persuaded the gentry that Crosthwaite would not fight and 'by this means they filled their boats with the very flower of the Cumberland Gentry at a shilling a head . . .'[5]

Even though this was intended to be a faux battle, Crosthwaite appears to have been wounded as much by the slight on his manly courage as he was by the loss of custom, because the episode is mentioned several times in his notebooks.

Planting follies around an island, like so many decorations on an iced cake, could not quench Pocklington's appetite for building. He built an odd house in Portinscale, which drew more critical remarks from William Gell, who drew comfort (wrongly, as it turned out) from the fact that 'his houses are so slightly built that the people think they cannot stand long to be the eye sores of the lake'.[6] This particular building, much extended and altered, is now known as Derwent Bank and is a popular Holiday Fellowship guest-house, while Pocklington's third mansion, Barrow House, on the eastern side of the lake, today serves as a youth hostel. Pocklington called the latter Cascade House, and had men with picks and shovels divert the course of a stream to create a waterfall that could be seen from its windows. It was intended to be a rival to neighbouring Lodore Force, which was already well established on the tourist circuit. Coleridge thought it 'commonplace'[7] but for once Gell had something positive to say. 'The fall was really grand,' he wrote, 'and the walks not ill suited to the place, a most unusual circumstance where Mr. Pocklington is concerned.'[8]

But Pocky being Pocky could not resist a few more embellishments. According to Gell, there was a 'white embattled hermitage' situated on a nearby eminence, and Pocklington had offered half a crown a day to anyone who would take up residence. That no one presented themselves for this well-remunerated position might have had something to do with the conditions of employment: the small print stated that the hermit was never to leave the place, nor to hold any conversations with anyone for seven years, never to wash and to allow both his hair and nails to grow as long as nature would permit them.

Even in the early years of the century, Pocklington's taste would have been questionable, but he began to embellish his properties around Derwentwater at just the moment in garden history when picturesque naturalness was on the rise. The art of the landscape designer was to make it seem as if no art had been applied, but this was never the eccentric Pocklington's way. At Cascade House another curiosity was his 'ghost tree', which was supposed to shimmer in the moonlight. Coleridge, who was living in Keswick at this time, was dismissive: 'Pocklington shaved off the branches of an Oak, Whitewashed and shaped it into an Obelisk – Art beats Nature.'[9]

But nature produces oddities, too, and, with his eye for the unusual, Pocklington could scarcely overlook them. In 1789 he bought the land where the celebrated Bowder Stone, a massive fragment of volcanic rock, had perched since time immemorial. At over eight metres high and about eighteen metres long the stone is the largest free-standing boulder in the Lake District, but it is also famous for its crazily teetering angle, for it is like the building block of a giant child who has thrown it down carelessly, so that it balances precariously – or so it appears – on one edge. He could not leave it untouched, of course. He pulled down the wall of an old sheep-fold and cleared away other debris, so that it could be seen more clearly, placed a ladder against one side so that visitors could clamber on to the top, set up a chapel and a druid stone to multiply the sense of mystery, then built Bowderstone Cottage so that he could install a guide. In one of his *Letters from England*, Southey's alter ego, Don Manuel Alvarez Espriella, condemned the additions:

> Another mile of broken ground, the most interesting which I ever traversed, brought us to a single rock called the Bowder Stone, a fragment of great size which has fallen from the heights. The same person who formerly disfigured the island in Keswick Lake with so many abominations, has been at work here also; has built a little mock hermitage, set up a new druidical stone, an ugly house for an old woman to live in who is to show the rock, for fear travellers should pass under it without seeing it, cleared away all the fragments round it, and it rests upon a narrow base, like a

ship on its keel, dug a hole underneath through which the curious may gratify themselves by shaking hands with the old woman. The oddity of this amused us greatly, provoking as it was to meet with such hideous buildings in such a place – for the place is as beautiful as eyes can behold or imagination conceive.[10]

Unlike the job of hermit, the position of guide was subject to no onerous conditions, so Pocklington was able to fill it. By the time William Green published his *Tourist's New Guide* in 1819, the old woman had been replaced by a man called John Raven who was happy to trot out facts and figures about the stone, but was 'blind to all the images of surrounding nature, and to all nature's images'. However, 'the movement of the hand towards the pocket, is an act John understands as well as any member of the fraternity to which he belongs', Green observed wryly.[11] The tradition of guides continued throughout the nineteenth century and the Stone was a big draw for Victorian tourists.

It could be argued that Pocklington did much to put the Lake District – and particularly Keswick – on the tourist map, but his sort of jolly exuberance would never endear him to those whose communion with the Lake District was more spiritual. He sold his island to Lieutenant Colonel (later General) Peachy in 1796, retiring to Barrow House. Peachy removed most of the follies and planted more trees to soften the outline of the house, earning praise from Wordsworth, who wrote in his guidebook: 'The taste of a succeeding proprietor rectified the mistakes as far as was practicable, and has ridded the spot of its puerilities.'[12]

Pocklington had no qualms about adapting nature for the sake of entertainment. It was an attitude which the Romantics found not merely tasteless, but immoral.

For all his paranoia and self-inflation, Peter Crosthwaite genuinely was the first local man to see just how lucrative the tourist trade might become and to invent attractions specifically tailored for the visitors. He created a forerunner of the interpretation or visitor centre by recognising that tourists would welcome edifying indoor activities to complement their pursuit of beauty and sublimity among the fells and lakes, especially when they were drenched in rain. His notebooks reveal him to have been an obsessional individual, unable to ignore slights and grievances and preoccupied with his own reputation, but perhaps it was this terrier-like tenaciousness that made him an excellent and accurate observer of natural phenomena, a sort of flamboyant Cumbrian version of Selborne's Gilbert White.

Crosthwaite's erratic notebooks are sprinkled with his observations and measurements. He listed levels, taken 'with good instruments and greatest care', noting that Bassenthwaite was 70 yards, 0 feet and 4 inches above sea level, while Derwentwater was 75 yards, 2 feet and no inches above the same. He recorded the population of Keswick to be 1,078 persons on 1 January 1787. He paced out the distance between the door of Crosthwaite church and the middle of his own museum, noting that it was 1,000 yards. He recorded the way in which 'to take the impression of any leaf or small plant to perfection' and 'how to clean a chimney of soot'.

In addition to offering services as a guide, Crosthwaite capitalised upon his nautical, observational and surveying skills by producing maps of the various lakes, adding the description 'hydrographer' to his many self-declared titles. Even Gell remarked that these had 'the nicest accuracy in every respect'. At that time it was still the lakes themselves, rather than the surrounding mountains, that were the biggest draw. By 1783 Crosthwaite had mapped three of the principal lakes – Derwentwater, Windermere and Ullswater – and drawn a plan of Pocklington's Island. Later he added Bassenthwaite Lake, Coniston Water and Buttermere to the set. Most were drawn to a scale of three inches to the mile and included the sort of information which tourists might find interesting or useful: roads, hotels, prominent houses, landmarks, natural features, currents and the depths of the lakes in

Crosthwaite's Museum in Keswick (1819), detail from
Peter Crosthwaite's map of Buttermere

fathoms. They also marked West's viewing stations. The maps sold well and Crosthwaite maintained his income by regularly updating them.

With his flair for self-publicity, Crosthwaite was almost his own caricature. One contemporary described him as 'a little, purple-faced pig of a man' and he seems to have boiled with an energy which was expressed sometimes in creativity and inventiveness but otherwise in hostility and competitive rancour.

As his business grew, Crosthwaite was able to build a new premises on the south side of Keswick's main street. This three-storey building, opened in 1784, protruded into the road, which gave its large first-floor windows an excellent view of all the coaches that came into town. Playing on his nautical associations, he called his new enterprise 'the Quadrant, Telescope and Weathercock', and it was open to the public every weekday between the hours of 7.00 a.m. and 10.00 p.m. He charged 'Ladies and Gentlemen' one shilling to enter, but 'Country People' got in for sixpence, a principle of differential pricing which now seems to apply in many tourist traps around the globe.

The kernel of his exhibition was the assortment of curiosities he had brought back from the East Indies, to which he added objects of local interest. The exhibits were animal, vegetable or mineral, man-made or natural, and the owner recorded significant gifts and acquisitions in his memorandum books. They included a mammoth's tooth 'sound and entire' for which Crosthwaite paid 3½ guineas, part of the head of a large animal 'not unlike a Bullocks or Bufiloes' found in a marl pit near Wigtown Bay, which was a gift from a Mr Woodal of Hensingham; a tiny stuffed hummingbird, 'weighing only 15 grains Troy or Silversmiths', from Mr Joseph Fisher and a giant turnip, with a greater circumference of thirty-eight inches, presented by his friend Pocklington.

It is easy to smile at the eccentricities of this collection, and of its owner, but bear in mind that the British Museum was, at this time, in its infancy.[13] Crosthwaite's Museum was sufficiently successful for its creator to hand it on as a going concern to his son Daniel. When the latter died in 1847 he left the museum to his widow, but it was kept going for another twenty-three years by his son, John Fisher Crosthwaite. Only in 1870 did the family decide to sell up. To keep any sort of business going for three generations is an achievement, but the museum's endurance also says something about the quality of the collection, which was far from a joke.

Of more curatorial interest than the outsized vegetables were: various Roman artefacts, a collection of Greek and Roman coins, a wide variety of ethnographic objects, zoological specimens such as the heads of a walrus and a babirusa, and a Brigantian sword from Embleton. Peter Breaks, who has studied the museum's catalogues in depth, concludes that Peter Crosthwaite's venture was 'one of the finest museums in the provinces'.[14] Crosthwaite's notebooks, for all their jumbled oddness, reveal their writer to have been a man of keen intellect and curiosity with a wide range of enthusiasms. He was not solely interested in profit, which explains why so many local people were willing to donate exhibits. In one instance a number of them even clubbed together to help him purchase a 'Prodigious great Lobster claw'. On the other hand, he was a shrewd businessman and knew something about marketing. One of his exhibits was the supposed rib of the giant Cor, the legendary founder of Corbridge. It was more likely the fossilised remains of a mammoth.

One of the museum's visitors was Captain Budworth, author of *A Fortnight's Ramble to the Lakes in Westmoreland, Lancashire and Cumberland*, who was impressed by some of Crosthwaite's mechanical inventions and thought that the proprietor possessed some 'valuable curiosities'. Gell was more critical: 'his collection chiefly consists of mineral productions and those Indian bows, caps, and ornaments which are to be found in every museum'.[15] He was unenthusiastic about the Crosthwaite family's unseemly efforts to get customers into their establishment:

> His daughter seems an elegant woman, and more worth seeing than anything else in the house, as to himself he is seated in a gouty chair and drums in one corner of the room, like a fool, to the noise of a barrel organ. While he has mirrors in every direction at the windows, by which he instantly sees every carriage that comes from any of the neighbouring towns . . . The organ strikes up if anyone passes, and his horrid drum is thumped, at the same time that the old woman runs upstairs and rattles away at the gong, in a manner that cannot fail to attract the notice of the unfortunate strangers in the street . . .[16]

The drum mentioned here might have been the tom-tom which Crosthwaite made himself, in imitation of those he had seen in the East Indies, while the organ was a large barrel organ made in London by Joseph Beloudy of Drury Lane, which could play a great variety of marches, minuets and reels. The gong originated in Canton: it was a metal plate, pierced with holes, which could be heard four miles away on a still day. As if all this were not enough, Crosthwaite also installed an Aeolian harp in one of the windows, so that the breeze would vibrate its strings, producing an interesting, if not entirely musical, sound. But the most unusual instrument in the museum was surely Crosthwaite's set of musical stones. These were bars of hornfels which he picked out from the bed of the River Greta. Noting that they rang with a clear note when struck, he assembled a sort of outsized xylophone – or lithophone, to call it by its proper name. He collected enough stones for two full octaves, set them on a frame and invited his visitors to play tunes on them. Only the profoundly deaf could fail to miss the museum's presence at the bottom of Keswick's market place.[17]

A later resident of Keswick, the stonemason Joseph Richardson, refined Crosthwaite's musical invention. It took him thirteen years to produce an instrument with an eight-octave range. When it was finished in 1840, he and his three sons began to give local concerts which featured not only popular waltzes, gallops and polkas but even pieces by Handel, Beethoven and Mozart. To increase the range and repertoire they added steel bars and Swiss bells, and the entire ensemble became known as 'Richardson & Sons, Rock, Bell and Steel Band'. This same instrument was donated to Keswick Museum and Art Gallery in 1917 by Joseph Richardson's great grandson, and it still stands just inside the front door, where visitors can bash away on it.

Crosthwaite nursed grievances. It seems likely that he left the East India Company amid some acrimony – the company certainly owed him pay and were reluctant to part with it. He claimed to have invented a cork-lined lifeboat while at Blyth, and believed that the idea had been stolen from him by Henry Greathead, the South Shields shipbuilder who won a government prize of £1,200 for his design. In Keswick this prickliness continued. He denounced James Clarke's *Survey of the Lakes*, published in 1787, as a 'shameful Imposition upon the Public' which 'will withal if not Exploded hurt the Touring business', by which he meant, no doubt, 'Admiral' Crosthwaite and his various enterprises. He referred to those who had the temerity to set themselves up in competition as 'an ungrateful Junto of impostors'.

He saved his greatest enmity for a hand-loom weaver called Thomas Hutton, who worked as a guide and boatman to visiting gentry during the summer. Many visitors and residents thought highly of Hutton. The *Lonsdale Magazine* of 1822 even sang his praises in verse:

By my button, this Hutton
Is an excellent Guide,
A Horseman, a Footman, a Boatman beside:
A Geologician, a Metaphysician,
Who searches how causes proceed,
A system inventor, an experimenter,
He'll raise Epimedium from seed.
Each Rock and each Dell, he knows it full well,
The Minerals, and Fossils therein;
Each Mountain, and Fountain, the Lakes and the Brakes,
Every Town, every Village, and Inn.
Take him for your Guide, he has often been tried,
And was always found useful when needed:
In fair or foul weather, you may travel together,
And shake hands, at parting, as we did.[18]

These lines show that Hutton and Crosthwaite had many interests in common and, had their personalities not clashed, it is possible to see how they might have collaborated. James Plumtre, who was a visitor to both and counted himself a friend of the 'Admiral', certainly thought so. In his journal he wrote: 'There is another Museum in Keswick, kept by Hutton, the Guide and Botanist, who has a very good collection of the Plants and fossils of the country. It is a great pity that the Admiral and he are bitter enemies. Though of the same trade I see no reason but they might agree well. Both Museums are worth seeing and each might do a good turn and recommend the other.'[19] It was not as if Crosthwaite was incapable of friendship. Out of loyalty for Pocklington he refused to stock any guidebooks which criticised his ally's taste. Crosthwaite also got on with the Keswick watchmaker Jonathan Otley and lent him books, even though the latter was, among other things, a guide, map-maker, amateur scientist, natural historian and guidebook writer, and thus, at first sight, an apparent rival.

One of Tom Hutton's talents as guide was the ability to tell a good story, and sometimes he allowed his gift as a raconteur to overcome any pretensions he might have had towards scientific objectivity. Crosthwaite, who was not immune to exaggeration himself, entered some of the more outrageous incidents into his notebooks. On 31 June 1788, Hutton is said to have pointed out Ireland and the German Ocean from the summit of Skiddaw to a party of visitors from Lancashire and Leeds. The day was too hazy for

Ireland to have been visible, Crosthwaite complained, while seeing what we now call the North Sea was an impossibility given the intervening distances and topography. On 26 June 1801 Crosthwaite noted that Hutton had told a Mr and Mrs Fletcher of Liverpool and their company that he had sounded two places in Leathes Lake (now Thirlmere) and could find no bottom. On 2 August 1787, if Crosthwaite is to be believed, his rival told Miss Dixon of Leeds 'that sometimes the Wind whirreled the sheep high into the air and dashed their Brains out against the Rocks in Borrowdale & Gasgarth'. For all his failings, Crosthwaite had a cartographer's love of accuracy and he felt that his fellow guide's tall tales were a sort of dishonesty which brought the whole profession into disrepute. The quarrel became even more bitter when Hutton decided to open a museum of his own.

Hutton's museum was certainly on a smaller scale than Crosthwaite's, but it was not without interest. One of the most unusual exhibits was a model of a slave ship with its human cargo packed as close as herrings in a barrel. This was a donation from William Wilberforce, who had displayed it when speaking against the slave trade in parliament. Wilberforce employed Hutton as guide on his Lake District tour of 1779 and the two became firm friends. The politician was a frequent visitor to the area and leased a house called Rayriggs on the shore of Windermere from 1780 to 1788.

Hutton's clients seem to have found him amiable and entertaining, which makes the enmity with Crosthwaite difficult to understand, but jealousy and paranoia can become self-confirming. It was inevitable that Crosthwaite's constant complaints would turn other members of the community against him. Sarah Mayson, a shopkeeper, and Mrs Southward, the widow who ran the Royal Oak hotel, steered their customers away from Crosthwaite's Museum and towards Hutton's. In his journal Crosthwaite railed against the Junto which was 'Ruining the man who first taught them to know what the word Museum meant'. He accused Hutton and his associates of hijacking visitors who were looking for the Crosthwaite museum. It seems that Hutton might have stooped to intercepting exhibits which were intended for Crosthwaite. An entry for 1784 reads:

Mr Stamper the Tinman sent me a Present of a most curious East India Hat but the Junto got hold of it and then it was lost to me without Redemption, as what one said another would swear.

There was also a long-running dispute about the pulling down of advertisements, theft of handbills and some instances of vandalism. On 22 May 1786

Crosthwaite recorded that 'Envy' had stolen away 'my two wall props of my Whale Jawes which left them in great Disorder' and on 22 March 1794 that 'some Villain or Villains attempted to knock a hole in the NE end of my house . . .'

Crosthwaite had gone to some effort to construct a zigzagging tourist path up Latrigg, but this too was vandalised:

> December 8, 1786: This day discovered some unhuman dung deposited upon my Latrigg Guide post three of costly stone have been pulled up & carried of since I made the road the last weighed about 500 Pounds and was Boulted down to the world with a stake of Oak drove through it & several other stout stakes were drove round it so that the strength of a bull would seem to have removed it.

In the notebooks, Crosthwaite wrote ruefully that 'the author of every new invention is treated as a Fool or a madman'. He was an engine for ideas, many of which had practical merit. One of his proposals was for the draining of part of Derwentwater to create new agricultural land. He claimed he had the support of two philosophers, 'both poets too'. They were Wordsworth and Coleridge, both of whom had bought his pamphlets. This was perhaps the same project from which Pocklington dissented, according to Coleridge's journal, because 'it would join his kingdom to England'.[20] Another scheme involved placing white painted boards to mark the locations of West's stations. It is easy to see how this would have riled the rest of the guides had Crosthwaite gone ahead.

At times the dispute even spilled into violence. According to Crosthwaite, he was stoned by a gang in the street in April 1794, and in January 1787 his two children, Mary and Daniel, were physically bullied by youngsters from the other camp, or, as Crosthwaite termed them, 'the Junto tribe or the dark Sons of Envy'.

Despite all this hostility and friction, Crosthwaite continued to run his museum until his death in 1808, appropriately enough from apoplexy. Throughout seemingly endless years of war with France, the gentry contin-ued to come to Keswick and more than a hundred a week, in the summer months, could be persuaded to part with a shilling to see the showman's five rooms of curiosities. Though he fought his rivals in Keswick, he was willing to cooperate with others further afield, such as William Todhunter, a hatter and bookseller of Kendal who opened a small museum behind his shop. He left copies of his maps for Todhunter to sell, allowing the bookseller to keep a generous 25 per cent commission. The enterprise of men like Crosthwaite, Hutton and Todhunter reveals the ways in which the local population was influenced by the burgeoning tourist trade. New occupations – guide, map-maker, museum proprietor – flourished, but so did new rivalries, the enmity between the Hutton and Crosthwaite families giving the lie to the myth of a harmonious mountain Arcadia of simple, unaffected souls.

The feud between Crosthwaite and the Junto lasted beyond the deaths of the original protagonists. Crosthwaite's headstone suggests that the industrious but irascible explorer finally found some peace. It reads: 'After many dangers, I have found a port.' But the stones which attend the graves of the Huttons, on the north side of Crosthwaite church, state unequivocally that here lie the proprietors of '*the* MUSEUM' in Keswick.

Overleaf: Keswick and Derwentwater from Latrigg

View of Goslar in the Hartz Mountains (undated) by W. Ripe

5

Wandering Lonely

Wordsworth Leaves the Lake District

I T HAS BECOME ALMOST impossible to consider Wordsworth apart from the Lake District, the landscape in which he spent most of his life. He resembles one of those hefted Herdwick sheep, knowing by instinct where it is most at home. But Wordsworth did not always live in Lakeland: he was a drifter in his youth, wrote important poems inspired by other places, and might conceivably have settled elsewhere.

Only eight years after the death of his mother, his father too met an untimely end. The official cause of death was 'dropsy', the name then used for pulmonary oedema, but he had been confined to bed with a severe chill brought on by an unplanned night outdoors on the aptly named Cold Fell, when he got lost on the way back from Broughton-in-Furness. Although there is nothing to show that father and son were close, John Wordsworth's death severed William's remaining connection with Cockermouth, and had dire implications for his prospects in life, for 'Wicked Jimmy' had been slow to reimburse his agent's expenses, and most of the wealth that should have been divided between the orphaned children was tied up in a debt of £4,265 (equivalent to about £250,000 today) which Lowther refused to honour. Despite litigation which dragged on for decades, they were unable to force him to pay and were thus thrown upon the charity of a grumpy grandfather and two less than pleasant uncles who muttered about them openly in front of the servants. William's brother Richard entered the law and much of his early career was spent in a protracted attempt to extract payment from Lowther. It is a tale worthy of Dickens.

All of this left its mark on William. His passage into adulthood was complicated by his lack of funds, while resentment at his family's mistreatment by someone with status, money and power tilted him towards radicalism. Having known hard times, he remained frugal all his life, and sympathetic towards those who, through no fault of their own, found themselves marginalised, displaced or dispossessed.

One of William's uncles, William Cookson, his mother's younger brother, was supportive at first. He had earned a Fellowship at Cambridge and was established in a clerical career that would, by 1792, see him appointed to the eminent position of Canon of Windsor. Surely the young Wordsworth could be steered along a similarly successful track. William went to Cambridge as a sizar – a sort of charity boy – but he did not take to his studies. This is perhaps not so surprising, since Cambridge placed great emphasis upon mathematics, not the most obvious choice for a future poet. His first published poem, a sonnet, appeared during in 1787, his first year at St John's College, then two years later he completed *An Evening Walk*, a much longer poem which describes a late afternoon walk around Esthwaite Water.

In his first summer vacation, the hefted sheep headed straight back to Hawkshead, which had become his home turf. He was overjoyed to be back in the pleasant valley where he had been reared and welcomed at the domestic table of Ann Tyson, his 'old Dame, so motherly and good'. Wordsworth went off to Cambridge as a mountain youth, a northern villager, and for a while, as he admitted in *The Prelude*, he turned into a dandy with silk hose and hair so powdered that it glistened like a tree in winter. But the artificiality of the life did not appeal, nor did the jealousies that surrounded the competitive examination system. He was filled with melancholy thoughts about his future and did not thrive. He had the feeling that he 'was not for that place, not for that hour'.

At the same time, there was a conviction growing within him that he had a destiny, and this thought was liberating. The crisis came in the vacation of his final year. Ignoring family pressure to study hard for his final examinations, he went on a trip to France with another undergraduate, a cheerful Welshman called Robert Jones. It was a sort of poor man's Grand Tour, conducted on foot, rather than by coach, and with the Swiss Alps as the ultimate destination, rather than Rome or Florence. It is not hard to see why the Alps might have appealed to a lad raised among mountains, but Switzerland had an additional attraction for the radical young poet, for Geneva had been the birthplace of Jean-Jacques Rousseau, whose political philosophy had prepared the ground for the French Revolution, which was already underway when Jones and Wordsworth disembarked at Calais.

Believing that humankind was at its best when living a primitive life close

to nature and at its worst when 'civilised' in cities, Rousseau was one of the
forerunners of Romanticism, and largely responsible for the cult of walking which was then sweeping England. In his autobiographical *Confessions*,
published posthumously in 1782, he wrote:

> Never did I think so much, exist so vividly, and experience so much,
> never have I been so much myself – if I may use the expression – as in
> the journeys I have taken alone and on foot. There is something about
> walking which stimulates and enlivens my thoughts. When I stay in one
> place I can hardly think at all: my body has to be on the move to get my
> mind going.[1]

The *philosophe*, like the young poet, often had to walk because he could
not afford a carriage, but both men turned this necessity into a virtue.
Walking was, after all, the oldest form of locomotion, the most primitive
or natural in Rousseau's terms. Walking was available to anyone who was
able-bodied, so it was about as democratic as it was possible to get. It was
particularly popular with penniless students and poorly paid clergymen.
Solitary walking provided an opportunity for contemplation, for reverie and
for communion with nature. Rousseau's many followers associated it with
wellbeing, freedom, self-expression and virtue.

The familiar accoutrements of the hiker had not yet evolved. Wordsworth
and Jones set off without rucksacks, carrying what they needed, which must
have been remarkably little, tied up in their pocket handkerchiefs. They had
about £20 apiece in their pockets. The pair made their way along public
roads, through towns and hamlets garlanded to celebrate the first anniversary of the fall of the Bastille. It was a jubilant, optimistic France through
which they passed, and Wordsworth felt that they were present at the dawn
of a social vision that was something new in history. He tells us that theirs
was 'a march of military speed' and the companions must have covered some
thirty miles a day to reach Switzerland in the time available.

Maybe they were walking too fast. The friends got lost on the Simplon
Pass and soon found they were descending without having noticed that they
had reached the summit, which must have been an anticlimax. *The Prelude*
does not gush with enthusiasm about Alpine scenery. Perhaps Wordsworth
had built up these mountains so much in his imagination that the reality was
a disappointment. When he came to write his *Guide to the Lakes* he devoted
several pages to a defence of the Lake District against the supposedly

superior attractions of Alpine scenery. He admitted that Swiss mountains were higher, but argued that, above a certain altitude, the sense of sublimity depended more upon the relationship of forms than upon brute size.

To say that Wordsworth discovered himself or found his vocation on this long, adventurous journey would be to go too far, for there were troubled years ahead, but he certainly made a break with family expectations that he might become a lawyer or a clergyman. When he returned to Cambridge, it was to take an unimpressive pass degree, which effectively blocked any prospect of becoming a Fellow. Next he was drawn to the spectacle and bustle of London, so unlike anything he had hitherto experienced, and spent a few aimless months there, drinking it all in, while flirting with radical politics. In spring 1791 he linked up in Wales with his old walking companion Jones and they climbed Snowdon together by night in order to experience dawn from the summit.

Now Wordsworth was tugged back towards France, where he fell in love with Annette Vallon, a young woman four years his senior. His idealism stumbled over the very corporeal problem of Annette's unplanned pregnancy. This episode reflects rather badly on Wordsworth, so it is not surprising that he omitted it from *The Prelude*, or that his family hushed the whole story up for generations. He set off back to England, ostensibly to raise money or find a position so that he could look after his new family, and was not present at the birth or christening of his daughter Caroline. On the first day of February 1793, France declared war on England. The international situation dismayed Wordsworth, who found it almost impossible to bear the thought of his own nation at war with the country which had come to represent his most optimistic ideals. It would be another ten years before Wordsworth returned to see his daughter. The next three years were the most difficult of his life. He had no career and no income, he was racked with guilt for abandoning Annette and his child, and the poetry was only stuttering along.

Wordsworth's youthful wanderings then led him to Stonehenge, where he toured the prehistoric remains with an old schoolfriend called William Calvert. This visit gave him the material for a stormy poem, *Salisbury Plain*, in which a vagrant woman from Keswick tells how she was turned out of her pleasant cottage on the banks of the Derwent and lost her soldier husband and three infant children 'by sword and scourge of fiery fever'. It is a poem against war and is usually taken to reflect both Wordsworth's own sense of loss and separation, and his emotional turmoil at finding his own country in arms against his beloved France. But he represented all that was good and wholesome and worth hanging on to by descriptions of the simple life of the Lake District.

Wordsworth's friendship with Calvert turned out to be his financial salvation, although the circumstances of this deliverance were emotionally uncomfortable. Calvert's younger brother Raisley had a life-threatening tuberculosis. A plan to accompany him on a trip to Portugal, where, it was hoped, the warmer air might revive him, had to be abandoned when Raisley's health deteriorated before they had got as far as Penrith. Raisley had heard about Wordsworth's ambition to become a poet and about his struggles to support himself. Whether he lived or died, he wanted to help, but soon it seemed that the most likely form of succour would be a legacy. Wordsworth spent several depressing months waiting by the young man's bedside. He was supposed to provide companionship, but he must have felt like a vulture. This vigil took place at Windy Brow, the Calverts' house in Keswick, and it was so oppressive that Wordsworth even dreamt of flight from his beloved Lakes. 'I begin to wish much to be in town,' he wrote. 'Cataracts and mountains are good occasional society, but they will not do for constant companions; besides I have not even much of their conversation and still less of that of my books as I am so much with my sick friend and he cannot bear the fatigue of being read to.'[2]

Raisley Calvert died in January 1795 and in his will he left Wordsworth £600,[3] a generous sum which freed the poet from immediate financial anxiety. Even though Wordsworth recognised that the Lake District was 'a country for poetry',[4] his first inclination, once he knew the money was coming, was to head back to London. He was eager to establish himself in literary circles and to build his reputation. But then, through his radical connections, he was offered the use, rent-free, of a cottage in Dorset called Racedown Lodge, and went there with Dorothy, though initially both he and his sister found Dorset an isolated and backward county. Things were much better in the Lake District, they thought, the people somehow more self-reliant. Wordsworth sometimes compared the Lake District to Switzerland, an exemplary republic for all lovers of liberty; he believed that the challenging terrain of mountainous regions brought out the vigour and independence of their inhabitants. But it was while in the West Country, through the Unitarian publisher and bookseller Joseph Cottle, that Wordsworth first met Robert Southey and Samuel Taylor Coleridge.

Coleridge, like Wordsworth, was a Cambridge student, but they just missed being contemporaries. Coleridge went up in 1791, at which time Wordsworth was in France, witnessing a revolution and getting entangled with Annette Vallon. Like Wordsworth, he began well at Cambridge, but soon faltered. His political views put him out of favour and badly in debt. In desperation he enlisted in a regiment of light dragoons. He was a hopeless soldier and his brothers had to buy him out – his official discharge said that he was 'insane'. He returned to Cambridge but would never graduate. In June 1794, he set out with a companion to make a walking tour of North Wales, but his progress was arrested when, stopping off in Oxford, he was introduced to Southey, who was then at Balliol. There was a streak of self-doubt in Coleridge which could turn him into the acolyte of men he perceived as less wavering than himself. Southey had this effect on him, and so in time would Wordsworth.

Southey and Coleridge cooked up the idea of emigrating to Pennsylvania and founding a commune on the banks of the Susquehanna River. After a truncated tour of Wales, Coleridge met up with Southey again in Bristol, eager to pursue this project. Their ideal community would be founded by twelve couples, although it seemed that the free-thinking Coleridge entertained the idea of sharing sexual partners along with everything else.[5] Southey was more strait-laced and already engaged to Edith Fricker, one of the daughters of a local manufacturer. It seemed that the easiest way for Coleridge to find a wife willing to go along with their idealistic venture would be to marry Edith's older sister, Sarah (or Sara, as Coleridge always wrote her name). This wedding took place in October 1795, a month before Southey and Edith tied the knot, but then the poets began to squabble. First they decided to set up their commune in Wales, rather than risk the colonial wilderness; then the whole project fell to pieces, with Coleridge accusing his brother-in-law of being too pragmatic. Thus, when Coleridge first met Wordsworth, there was a vacancy for a hero figure to replace Southey.

William and Dorothy, correspondingly, were so taken with their new friend that they decided to move closer to him, renting Alfoxden House on the edge of the Quantock Hills. Coleridge had a cottage at nearby Nether Stowey. It was here, under the stabilising influence of his sister and with the creative spur of his friendship with Coleridge, that Wordsworth's talent began to flourish. Coleridge supplied a breadth of philosophical vision, while Dorothy's keen eye for detail and her painstakingly kept diaries were one of his principal sources. In 1798 the two poets published *Lyrical Ballads*, a bombshell of a book which blew apart conventional notions of poetic language, although it was not an immediate commercial success. While the collection contained poems which have become much-loved classics of English literature, such as Coleridge's *Rime of the Ancient Mariner* and Wordsworth's *Tintern Abbey*, the verses were experimental for their times, speaking a simple language close to that used by ordinary people in ordinary life, rather than using a high-flown poetic idiom.

Nowadays it can be difficult to see Wordsworth as a radical and a mould-breaker, but that is certainly what he was. Writing plainly was to be preferred to writing in a contrived way, just as travelling on foot was better – more moral – than riding in a contrivance. And rather than write about kings and queens, lords and ladies or gods and goddesses, Wordsworth chose his subjects from the opposite end of the scale. He had sympathy for the simple man and saw virtue in marginalised figures such as beggars, crippled veterans and the very old. The reader is drawn into recognising bonds of common humanity and in this respect Wordsworth's poetry is levelling. Wordsworth is sometimes described, dismissively, as a 'nature poet' but his poetry is about the organic relationship between human beings and the natural world, a pressing theme for the twenty-first century, when this relationship seems to be breaking down everywhere we look. In *The Prelude* we learn that Wordsworth, as a boy, saw the Cumbrian shepherd in his domain as 'a Lord and Master; or a Power, Or Genius, under Nature, under God, Presiding'.[6] He was glad that his first experiences of mankind were among the dignified, hard-working people of his native region. It was because he had this view of the world, formed in childhood, that he was so receptive to the ideals of the French Revolution and so appalled by its aftermath. Even in later life, when his political views had changed, he did not believe that wealth or birth guaranteed ability or worth in a person.

Melvyn Bragg has suggested that the Quantocks and other southern landscapes 'provided all the background and foreground Wordsworth needed for the *Lyrical Ballads*'.[7] In fact the geographical scope of the collection extends into Wales; in addition to poems set in Dorset and at Richmond-upon-Thames, there are others that feature the landscapes of Monmouthshire and Cardiganshire. But the Lake District still exerted a powerful influence, even at this remove. Two poems, *Lines left upon a Seat in a Yew Tree* and *Expostulation and Reply*, are expressly located on the shores of Wordsworth's favoured Esthwaite Water, while *The Thorn* and *The Last of the Flock* are set in a non-specific mountainous country. Wordsworth also reworked the central story of *Salisbury Plain* to write *The Female Vagrant*.

Grasmere (1802) by William Green

Throughout this productive period in the lives of the two poets, the political situation in the country remained tense. With England at war with France, those who had professed democratic or republican sympathies fell under scrutiny. The poets and their entourage attracted suspicion, taking frequent excursions into the countryside, having earnest camp-stool conversations and jotting things down in notebooks. Word got around that a dangerous group of radicals had moved into the area, but in truth both Wordsworth and Coleridge were more interested in writing poetry than in fomenting revolution, and both were already having misgivings about their former views.

This idyllic and fertile period in the lives of the two poets came to a close when the lease on Alfoxden ran out. Seldom averse to mind-broadening travel, the friends decided that they should all go to Germany. Coleridge, however, wanted to study German philosophy, so he headed for the town of Ratzeburg, while the Wordsworths, less certain of their purpose, thought that they should settle in a village near a university, preferably in a pleasant, mountainous landscape. These criteria led them toward the Hartz Mountains of Lower Saxony, where they rented cheap lodgings in

the provincial town of Goslar. They did not enjoy themselves. Isolated by
language from such society as Goslar possessed, and prevented from taking
their customary long walks by a winter so cold that the River Elbe froze
over, they languished for five months before heading home as soon as the
weather improved. Returning, they made for Sockburn-on-Tees, where
their childhood friend from Penrith, Mary Hutchinson, and her brothers
and sisters now lived. The one indisputably positive thing to come out of
this German incarceration was the progress that William made on his autobiographical poem *The Prelude*, but linked to this was another: after such a
long period of feeling isolated, it was natural that Wordsworth should seek
to reconnect with the place where he felt most at home. Germany primed
Wordsworth for Grasmere.

In Sockburn they were eventually joined by Coleridge, who had come
north with Cottle upon hearing news that Wordsworth was seriously ill.
It was a journey that would change Coleridge's life in many ways, not
all to the good. For one thing, he first laid eyes on Sara Hutchinson and
was immediately smitten. Such chemistry is often a mystery, even to those
involved. Sara was plain and dumpy, an unlikely love object perhaps, but she
had a lively mind and could be entertaining. Her namesake, Sarah Coleridge,
lacked these attributes, and was generally considered shallow and dull by
the Wordsworth circle.

William had fully recovered by the time Coleridge and Cottle arrived, and
he was eager to show his friends the North Country, so a walking tour was
quickly planned. This was to be a hearty male-only expedition, although
Dorothy could certainly have matched the pace. Indeed, Cottle was in the
poorest shape and rode on the back of a mare called Lily, 'his legs hugely
muffed up', while the two poets strode along on foot. Their route lay across
the Pennines via Greta Bridge near Barnard Castle, where Cottle sensibly
dropped out. Wordsworth and Coleridge caught the mail coach to Temple
Sowerby, where, by chance, they met William's younger brother John, who
was now a naval officer in the service of the East India Company. He was
between voyages and decided to join the walking party.

In the course of the tour Wordsworth succeeded in introducing his
friend to the two places which had been most significant in his childhood,
Cockermouth and Hawkshead, as well as showing him the three most celebrated lakes, Windermere, Derwentwater and Ullswater. Their route was
convoluted. First they made their way down the eastern shore of Haweswater,
but low cloud persuaded them to abandon the direct course over Kirkstone

Pass to Ambleside. Instead they headed south via Longsleddale to Kentmere and from there to the shores of Windermere, where they took the ferry. Wordsworth was displeased by some of the new houses built around the lake and in Hawkshead he regretted the 'great change among the people since we were last there'.

In Grasmere they stayed at Robert Newton's. Coleridge was much taken with 'the divine sisters, Rydal and Grasmere'.[8] It must have been hugely gratifying for Wordsworth to observe the effects of his native scenery upon his closest friend. He had already decided that he needed to move back to the area and wrote to Dorothy suggesting two possibilities, the first of which was to build a house on the shores of Grasmere. He had discussed the possibility with John, who was willing to help out financially. The alternative was to lease a cottage: the former inn known as the Dove and Olive in Townend, a hamlet just outside Grasmere, was available unfurnished. This is better known to the world as Dove Cottage (a name it did not receive until a century later) but the decision to rent it was not taken until William returned to Sockburn for a discussion with his sister.

Next came some mountaineering, the ever-observant Coleridge recording in his journal 'a host of little winged flies on the snow mangled by the hail storm, near the top of Helvellyn'.[9] Shortly after this climb John left them for Penrith, Wordsworth and Coleridge going north via Derwentwater to Keswick. Coleridge was tremendously stirred by everything he had seen, but his letter to Dorothy Wordsworth, written from Keswick on 10 November 1799, reveals that he was dwelling upon another recent encounter:

> You can feel what I cannot express for myself – how deeply I have been impressed by a world of scenery absolutely new to me. At Rydal and Grasmere I received I think the deepest delight, yet Hawes Water through many a varying view kept my eyes dim with tears, and this evening approaching Derwentwater in diversity of harmonious features, in the majesty of its beauties and the beauty of its majesty – Oh my God! and the black crags close under the snowy mountains, whose snows were pinkish with the setting sun and the reflections from the sandy rich clouds that floated over some and rested upon others! It was to me a vision of a fair country. Why were you not with us, Dorothy? Why were not you, Mary?[10]

Coleridge's finances, like Wordsworth's, were precarious, so it could be that the careful notes he made were material for a *Tour* which he never came to write. 'Sheep will not eat larches,' he noted at one point, adding, 'Eat everything else. Only two funerals in the whole year in Wastdale. Something affecting may be made of it.'[11] As most of us do when we see a new place for the first time, we seek to understand it in terms of somewhere more familiar. For Coleridge it was a comparison with Devon:

Arrive at Matterdale and are struck as by a flash with its similarity to the Devonshire cleaves: bare green hills, the knobs of them black moss, so cleft, so slop'd, so coomb'd, so cottag'd – and the cottages so the sole tree-possessor – all as between Maniton and Ashburton. The stream is quite a Devonshire brawling brook.[12]

The northern part of the excursion took in Cockermouth, then Lorton, Crummock Water and Buttermere, then Ennerdale, Wasdale, Borrowdale, a return to Keswick, Thelkeld, Patterdale and finally Pooley Bridge, where they parted. In the course of the tour, Coleridge realised that he could never lure Wordsworth away from the Lakes: 'he will never quit the north of England – his habits are more assimilated with the inhabitants there – there he & his sister are exceedingly beloved, enthusiastically. Such difference do small Sympathies make – such as Voice, Pronunciation, &c – for from what other Cause can I account for it –.'[13] He valued Wordsworth's company above that of anyone else. The upshot was clear; if he wanted to retain the closeness they enjoyed, he too would have to move north.

In December 1799 William and Dorothy set out from Sockburn, riding as far as Richmond, then took to foot through the soft snow which coated the road through Wensleydale. After spending the night in Askrigg, they set out in the orange light of morning to walk twenty miles in a short winter's day, but still found time to admire the lofty waterfalls along the way. With the wind at their backs they covered the next seventeen miles to Sedburgh in under four hours, an extraordinary feat. The next day their pace slackened a little, although they still managed over 3½ mph, along the up-and-down road to Kendal. After stopping there to buy and order furniture, they took a post chaise to Grasmere. The Wordsworths were home.

Overleaf: The Middle Reach of Ullswater

The Lake Poets: *William Wordsworth* (1818) by Richard Carruthers, *Samuel Taylor Coleridge* (1804) by James Northcote, and *Robert Southey* (c. 1818) by Thomas Phillips

6

The Lake Poets

Wordsworth, Coleridge and Southey

O<small>N THE LAST</small> C<small>HRISTMAS</small> Eve of the eighteenth century, William Wordsworth sat with his sister in their new home at Grasmere and wrote to their mutual friend Coleridge. Both of them had colds and Dorothy also had a toothache which was interfering with her needlework as she prepared soft furnishings for the cottage. One of the upstairs rooms was unusable, Wordsworth wrote, because of a fireplace that smoked like a furnace, but the other was suitable for a sitting room. Dorothy was very pleased with the house and its appurtenances, especially the orchard: 'in imagination she has already built a seat with a summer shed on the highest platform in this our little domestic slip of mountain'.[1]

Compared with the family home in Cockermouth or the handsome proportions of Alfoxden Lodge in Somerset, Dove Cottage was a very humble dwelling. Visitors today are often taken aback by the dark and poky rooms on the ground floor, but though the accommodation was not generous, the cottage did enjoy a favourable location. The view from the top of the garden encompassed two-thirds of the vale, including the lake, the church and a distant view of Helm Crag with its distinctive outcrop of summit rocks. The Wordsworths were back in the midst of the landscape that they loved, and they were also happy to be together.

Through years of separation, Dorothy had imagined – at least since early womanhood – that they would someday live with one another, while Wordsworth was the sort of reclusive poet who liked to have people around, particularly if they were women and devoted to him. Dorothy was her brother's amanuensis, which is to say that she copied down the poems he composed out loud while pacing up and down, but she also cooked and mended for him, dealt with his correspondence, nursed him when he was sick and comforted him when he was unhappy. On the paper mountain of

Wordsworth studies, a cairn-sized pile of books and essays has been built by biographers and psychoanalytically inclined critics hoping to understand this complex relationship, which some have seen as sexually charged and even teetering on the brink of incest. There is no hard evidence for any physical relationship, but their emotional bond did resemble a marriage – at least until an actual wife came along, at which point the dynamics had to change entirely. But there was a third party in this relationship, even before Wordsworth married, and that was Coleridge.

In the Quantocks Coleridge had grown so close to both of the Wordsworths that he thought of William as a brother and wrote of Dorothy as 'our sister'. The trio had a free-flowing and reciprocal understanding, or, as Coleridge succinctly put it, they were 'three people, but one soul'.[2] When the Wordsworths settled in Grasmere, he found it almost impossible to be apart from them. By April he was visiting them in the Lake District, which prompted his London friend Charles Lamb to write, wryly, that 'Coleridge has left us to, to go into the North, on a visit to his God, Wordsworth'.[3]

The Wordsworths looked out for a house for him and found Greta Hall, just outside Keswick. When Coleridge wrote to William Godwin on 21 May 1800, he explained that if he could not find another house at Nether Stowey, he would settle at Keswick, 'in a house of such a prospect, that if according to you and Hume, impressions and ideas *constitute* our being, I shall have a tendency to become a god, so sublime and beautiful will be the series of my visual existence'.[4] By July the move was settled. On the 15th of that month he wrote to his friend Humphry Davy (the chemist and inventor) saying:

> We remove to our own house in Keswick on Tuesday week – my address is, Mr Coleridge, Greta Hall, Keswick, Cumberland. My dear fellow, I would that I could wrap up the view from my house in a pill of opium, and send it to you! I should then be sure of seeing you in the fall of the year. But you *will* come.

So thrilled was Coleridge with the view from his study window that he could hardly stop mentioning it. On 29 July 1800, revelling in his new status as a country gentleman, he wrote to Samuel Purkis, a London friend, describing himself as 'S. T. Coleridge, Esq., Gentleman-Poet and Philosopher in a mist'. The cottage at Nether Stowey had been tiny; Greta Hall was large and well situated.

Yes – my dear Sir! here I am – with Skiddaw at my back – on my right hand the Bassenthwaite Water with its majestic case of mountains, all of simplest outline – looking slant, direct over the feather of this infamous pen, I see the sun setting – my God! what a scene! Right before me is a great camp of single mountains – each in shape resembles a Giant's Tent; and to the left, but closer to it far than the Bassenthwaite Water to my right, is the lake of Keswick, with its islands and white sails, and glossy lights of evening – *crowned* with green meadows.[5]

The view was never far from his mind. It did not matter what time of day it was or what he was doing. In November 1803 he recorded in his notebook that while emptying his urine pot out of the window at midnight he had wondered at the grandeur of the view, the quality of the darkness, the steely-blue glimmer of the River Greta and the gloominess and sullenness of the moon-whitened, cloud-blackened sky. Coleridge combined the vision of the poet, the curiosity of the scientist and the analytical acuity of the philosopher and he was seldom off duty.

Greta Hall is less than a mile from Windy Brow, where Wordsworth attended the failing Raisley Calvert. The owner was a successful carrier named William Jackson, who retained an apartment at the back. Even so, it was a large property, big enough for two families. One of the possibilities dangled before Coleridge to persuade him to relocate was that the Wordsworths might join the Coleridges in Keswick, though, as things worked out, it would be the Southeys who came to share Greta Hall. It was Sarah Coleridge's fate always to be on the edge of things. She had not gone on the German trip; now she was expected to move to Keswick, although she had little taste for walking or views and would have been happier in a larger town. Once the family had moved in, she found that her husband was often out of the house, roving the surrounding hills and valleys or walking the thirteen miles to Grasmere to spend more time with the Wordsworths.

Coleridge had patched up his quarrel with Southey and sought to persuade his old friend to bring his family to live with them, an arrangement that would provide Sarah with sisterly support. When the Southeys arrived in 1803 the trio that became known as the 'Lake Poets' was complete, but this was not a name that Wordsworth, Coleridge and Southey thought up for themselves; it was applied in retrospect, and its origins were hostile. In November 1814, Francis Jeffrey, the editor of the *Edinburgh Review*, wrote a savage review of Wordsworth's poem *The Excursion* (he opened with the

Robert Southey's study at Greta Hall (1841) by Caroline Bowles

words 'This will never do!'), which also criticised 'the peculiarities of his former writings'. Jeffrey disliked Wordsworth's use of plain diction and his inclination to put important truths into the mouths of poor shepherds and itinerant pedlars. The article was a full-scale assault on Wordsworth's central principles and on everything he had written over twenty years. In his *Literaria Biographia* (1817) Coleridge complained that when Jeffrey visited Keswick, he and Southey 'treated him with every hospitable attention' and received many high-coloured compliments in return; yet the next article that Jeffrey wrote castigated 'the School of whining and hypochondriacal poets that haunt the Lakes'.[6] And Coleridge was adamant that the three poets did not form a school. How could they, he protested, when their writing was so different? A series of accidents had brought them together as neighbours; none of it had been planned.

Southey was never at the emotional heart of the group. In the years before he arrived with his family, the core had five members. William, Dorothy and Coleridge, the original band from Alfoxden, who were joined in their walks, their writing and their philosophising by Mary and Sara Hutchinson, who often came to stay. This grouping produced a cat's cradle of relationships, for not only did Dorothy dote on her brother, she was also close enough to Coleridge, in her impulsive, energetic way, to arouse the jealousy of his wife. Coleridge, meanwhile, was obsessed with Sara Hutchinson – and guilt-ridden too because he firmly believed in the sanctity of marriage – but Sara managed his attentions skilfully.

Like a sect or secret society, they had their own language, their own jokes and their own special places. In October 1801 they built a sod seat on White Moss Common between Grasmere and Rydal Water and called it 'Sara's Seat' because she had chosen the spot. There was also 'Sara's Crag' or 'Sara's Rock' which stood beside the road at Wythburn above Thirlmere, and marked the place where meetings and leave takings often occurred. The walk between Greta Hall and Grasmere could take five hours, but the hosts would often accompany the visitors part way home. The friends carved their initials here and came to know it as the 'Rock of Names'. The initials were: WW, MH, DW, STC, JW and SH. JW was John Wordsworth, the sailor brother who could seldom be with them but was nevertheless an honorary member of the group. William called him 'a Poet in every thing but words'.[7] What bound them together was their quasi-religious attitude towards poetry and nature, but anyone who could not share this was excluded and it is noticeable that Sarah Coleridge's initials were never inscribed there. Coleridge's marriage was in danger of coming apart, and his friends would take his side, even though his behaviour was increasingly erratic. Sarah got much of the blame. Dorothy, at her fiercest, wrote in a letter to Mary Hutchinson, 'She would have made a very good wife to many another man, but for Coleridge!! Her radical fault is want of sensibility and what can such a woman be to Coleridge?' Sarah fussed too much over her children and was altogether a 'sad fiddle-faddler'.[8]

We might be inclined to be a lot more sympathetic to Sarah Coleridge. She certainly had a lot to contend with. Their eldest son, Hartley, born in 1796, was already a precocious child of nature who was encouraged to run wild, and a second boy, Derwent, was born at Keswick on 14 September 1800. The family was short of funds and although her husband had journalistic work which might pay some bills, he seemed unable to meet his deadlines. He would rather tramp the fells or go off to his friends in Grasmere. When he was at home, he often complained that he was ill and took to his couch. It was part of his tragedy that the Cumbrian landscape, which so enthused him, was inseparable from the Cumbrian weather, which did not suit his constitution at all. He had suffered rheumatic fever as a boy, and ever since had endured asthmatic symptoms and a twitchy stomach whenever the barometer was low. In a letter to Thomas Poole, written from Keswick on 7 July 1801, Coleridge denied that the rainfall was any worse in Keswick than it had been in Devon, yet the following year he penned the lighthearted *Ode to Rain* which mentioned both his sickening stomach and his swelling knees and closed with the line 'Do go, dear Rain! Do go away!'[9] He might have joked about it, but the damp climate was making him ill, and his condition was aggravated by his reckless excursions in all weathers.

The charge that Coleridge and Wordsworth were both hypochondriacs has some substance. Dorothy's journals are full of anxious concern for William's health. The effort of composition seems to have given him grievous headaches. Coleridge, meanwhile, could hardly begin a letter without giving a full account of his various ailments, which included boils, swollen eyes, rheumatic pains and spasms of the bowel. We might wonder, in the case of both poets, whether many of their complaints were psychosomatic. Writing poetry involved an almost physical effort for Wordsworth as he strode up and down in deep concentration. Writing also came fitfully to Coleridge and he had the additional pressure of feeling hopelessly trapped in a bad marriage. He believed that he was suffering from a form of gout and this was one of the reasons he took such long walks – there was a theory that vigorous exercise could force the gouty material to the body's extremities.

His resort to opium has become a central part of his legend, but laudanum, a tincture of opium in alcohol, was an almost universal analgesic at the time. The highly principled abolitionist William Wilberforce took it for forty-five years and so did Dorothy Wordsworth whenever she had toothache. Coleridge was using laudanum before he settled in the Lakes; but sometime in 1801 or 1802 he graduated to the Kendal Black Drop, a much stronger concoction dispensed by a Quaker called Mrs Braithwaite, who presumably thought she was doing more good than harm.[10] Thomas De Quincey, a latecomer to Wordsworth's Lake District circle, was another addict and left the most graphic descriptions of the consequences of the drug. Its worst effect was that it robbed its user of restful sleep. Opium brought Coleridge lethargy mixed with restlessness and agitation mixed with melancholy. It made him pity and loathe himself. He complained that he had been 'seduced into the ACCURSED Habit ignorantly',[11] and by 1803 he was utterly dependent on the drug. When his addiction reached its peak, he was drinking a pint of laudanum every day.

In 1801 Coleridge could write to Godwin, 'The Poet is dead in me – my imagination (or rather the Somewhat that had been imaginative) lies, like a Cold Snuff on the circular rim of a Brass Candle-stick, without even a stink of Tallow to remind you that it was once cloathed and mitred with Flame.'[12] His London friends thought he should return to the metropolis, as his 'rural retirement' was clearly doing him no good, but Coleridge would have none of it. Living in the countryside was not the problem, he thought; indeed, his surroundings were his principal consolation.

While Coleridge's life was falling apart, Wordsworth's was becoming more and more settled. In April 1802 William and Dorothy went to stay with Thomas Clarkson, a prominent opponent of the slave trade, at Eusemere Hill, his house near Pooley Bridge on the eastern side of Ullswater. During the visit, William rode over to County Durham to see Mary Hutchinson to arrange an autumn wedding. In July he and Dorothy went to Calais to settle matters both financially and emotionally with Annette and to meet his daughter Caroline for the first time. Having cut free of this previous entanglement, he married Mary Hutchinson at a church near Scarborough on 4 October 1802. Presumably in an attempt to lessen the emotional pain involved, William allowed Dorothy to sleep with the wedding ring on her finger on the night before the wedding. Even so, she could not bring herself to attend the ceremony, preferring to stay in her bedroom. Mary and Dorothy had been friends for a long time, however, considering one another sisters, and both still had William's best interests at heart. At this juncture the possibility of Wordsworth living outside the Lake District arose again, because Mary would have been happy for them to set up home in Yorkshire, but Dorothy was resolved to stay in Grasmere and William could not leave her. So Mary joined them both at Dove Cottage and the well-known ménage came into being.

Wordsworth's financial situation was also about to improve. The old Earl of Lonsdale died in May 1802 and his successor, William Lowther (a fourth cousin once removed) decided to settle all his predecessor's debts. The new earl was an altogether more likeable man and in time became one of Wordsworth's principal patrons.

Coleridge, conversely, had little to celebrate. He had interrupted an interlude in London on hearing news that Sara Hutchinson was ill and stayed with her at Gallow Hill in Yorkshire for ten days before returning to Greta

Hall. Whatever passed between Coleridge and Sara (or 'Asra', as the poet called her in his notebooks) it seems that it was decisive. Their intense platonic relationship was not going to turn into a sexual one and Coleridge was not going to desert his wife. It made him miserable and he poured his feelings into a verse letter to Sara, dated 4 April 1802, which contained the following lines:

> These Mountains too, these Vales, these Woods, these Lakes,
> Scenes full of Beauty and of Loftiness
> Where all my Life I fondly hope to live –
> I were sunk low indeed, did they *no* solace give!
> But oft I seem to feel, and evermore to fear,
> They are not to me now the Things, which they once were.[13]

We often think that pleasant surroundings can elevate mood, indeed scientific research has proved the point, but, as these lines show, Coleridge recognised limits to the efficacy of a good view. In his misery he could see the beauty, but not *feel* it. Indeed, he saw that in the depths of his depression he was likely to project his unhappiness on to the landscape and see it differently. In order to experience the real, independent joy that was to be found in nature, you need to be able to find inner springs of joy. This was something which Coleridge, in the trough of his own self-contempt, was unable to do. In late summer he set off on his longest and most strenuous solo walk around the Lakes (we will accompany him on it in Chapter 13). He hoped that it would prove cathartic and cure not only his gout but also his troubled soul. It was only a partial success. He reworked the verse letter to Sara as *Dejection: An Ode* and the poem was published on Wordsworth's wedding day, which also happened to be the seventh anniversary of Coleridge's union with Sarah. It served to underline the differences in the two poets' fortunes.

On their walk back from Eusemere Hill in April, William and Dorothy had been obliged to battle against a blustery wind strong enough to trouble the surface of the lake. In her journal Dorothy noted the primroses, wood sorrels, violets, strawberries and celandines that she saw on the roadside, but it was the lakeside belt of daffodils, 'about the breadth of a country turnpike road', that made the greatest impression upon her:

> I never saw daffodils so beautiful they grew among the mossy stones about & about them, some rested their heads upon these stones as on

a pillow for weariness & the rest tossed & reeled & danced & seemed as if they verily laughed with the wind that blew directly over the Lake to them.[14]

Dorothy's prose account of the daffodils was written soon after the walk and has a sense of immediacy and veracity. William wrote his famous poem – which is also his most critically maligned – two years later. It is popularly known as *The Daffodils* but this was not a title that Wordsworth chose for it, indeed it is unlikely that the poet would have wanted to advertise his theme in advance, because his poem is about a sudden vision of something joyful – 'all at once I saw a crowd'. Pamela Woof has studied the differences between Dorothy and William's accounts of this celebrated scene:[15] William simplified the view and tidied it up for a public audience, while the gusty wind became a breeze, and colour was added to the view – his daffodils are 'golden'. Above all, he lightened the mood, emphasising the fluttering, sprightly dance of the flowers and eliminating the threatening, elemental quality of the weather. But William's poem is as much about the nature of memory and the role of the imagination as it is about a particular day on the shores of Ullswater.

In August 1803 William and his sister went on a tour of Scotland with Coleridge, but the trip was not a success. Coleridge was still in bad spirits and Wordsworth was getting tired of him. They split up at Loch Lomond, the Wordsworths continuing to Glencoe, while Coleridge set off on another marathon walk during which he covered 263 miles in eight days, passing through the Great Glen to Inverness, then returning via Loch Tay, Perth and Edinburgh, walking some of the way barefoot after he burned his shoes while drying them by the fire.[16] Whatever hopes he had for this journey it did not restore his health, and returning to Keswick he decided that his only hope was to seek recuperation in a warmer climate. Leaving his family in the care of the Southeys at Greta Hall, on 9 April 1804 he sailed from Portsmouth for Malta where he would remain for two years.

Southey had not particularly wanted to come to the Lakes. At the time of Coleridge's death he wrote: 'Forty years have elapsed since our first meeting – and one consequence of that meeting has been that I have resided during the last thirty in this place, whither I first came with no other intention than that of visiting him.'[17] He did not share the intimate connection with the natural world that was the source of creativity for Wordsworth and Coleridge, and was happiest when surrounded by books rather than by mountains. His reputation as a poet rests on five epic poems which were admired in his day but are now hardly read, but he was also a diligent book reviewer, a translator and a regular contributor to the *Quarterly Review*. He also wrote non-fiction, including a history of Brazil, a history of the Peninsular War and a life of Nelson which did much to establish the admiral as a national hero. All this brought its rewards; Hunter Davies estimated that Southey earned around £2,000 per annum from his literary endeavours, as compared with the meagre £20 a year that Wordsworth made from his poetry.[18] Harriet Martineau thought well of him: 'It should never be forgotten,' she wrote, 'that Southey worked double-tides to make up for Coleridge's idleness. While Coleridge was dreaming and discoursing, Southey was toiling to maintain Coleridge's wife and children.'[19]

This industry, placed alongside his moral rectitude and a certain stiffness and reserve in his character, have left Southey with a reputation for dullness, particularly when compared with the wild roving of Coleridge or the self-centred intensity of Wordsworth, but anyone who has dipped into Southey's *Letters from England*, written under the guise of Don Manuel Alvarez Espriella, will know what a witty and entertaining writer he could be. It is an inventive sort of travel book, written as a money-making venture shortly after he arrived in Keswick. By assuming the persona of a Spaniard, he could poke fun at the English through the eyes of an imaginary tourist, while playing some ironic games at the expense of the Spanish. In the following extract he grumbles about the weather on the shores of 'Winandermere', which might well reflect its author's own feelings about the climate:

> The morning threatened rain, luckily, as it induced us to provide ourselves with umbrellas, a precaution which we might otherwise have neglected. They make these things in England to serve as walking-sticks, by which means they are admirably adapted for foot travellers. Much rain has fallen lately in the neighbourhood: and the influx of such visitors as ourselves is so great, that the person of whom we purchased these umbrellas told us, he had sold forty in the course of the week.[20]

Although he spent most of his life in the Lake District, Southey never became part of the place. His son Charles, who became a local vicar, wrote a memoir in which he remarked that his father only ever recognised about twenty Keswick residents by sight. One of the favoured few was Jonathan

Otley, the geologist, clockmaker and guidebook writer, who enjoyed visiting rights to Southey's library.

During the long winter months Southey kept to his studies, but 'with the swallows the tourists began to come, and among them many friends and acquaintances, and so many strangers bearing letters of introduction, that his stores of the latter were being continually increased, and sometimes pleasing and valuable additions made to the former class'.[21] During his time there, Greta Hall received visits from, among others, Charles Lamb, William Hazlitt, Percy Bysshe Shelley and Walter Scott. Southey was, by all accounts, a very gracious host and clearly willing to vary his rigorous routine in order to organise excursions for his guests.

Southey had his favourite spots. He liked to take visitors up Skiddaw or Blencathra for the views, but he also arranged mutton pie picnics at Brandlehow Park on the shores of Derwentwater, while his favourite walk with his children was up the path beside the waterfall in Cat Gill to the top of Walla Crag, a route that he thought had just the right amount of difficulty and excitement without being dangerous. Though they shared an occupation, had mutual friends and lived in the same sequestered part of the country, Wordsworth and Southey did not have much in common and – initially at least – did not warm to one another. De Quincey tells us that Wordsworth thought Southey's poetry was shallow, while Southey disliked Wordsworth's haughty dogmatism.

Coleridge was not particularly happy during his stay on Malta. He thought it was a barren rock, devoid of rivers, brooks, hedges and trees, and he was homesick for the landscape he loved. The trigger for his return was a piece of tragic news. While at the Governor's Palace in Valletta, he collapsed when he heard that Wordsworth's brother John had been drowned in the wreck of the *Earl of Abergavenny* in a storm off the Dorset coast.

John had hoped to make enough money out of his investments in this voyage to retire from the sea and settle close to his brother and sister. On the day he received the news, Wordsworth wrote to Sir George Beaumont, a friend recently made, 'from a house of mourning'. Dorothy and Mary, he said, 'were in miserable affliction which I do all in my power to alleviate', adding 'heaven knows I want consolation myself'.[22] While Coleridge made arrangements to return, friends closer to hand rallied round and Southey came over from Keswick, which marked the beginning of a more amicable relationship between the two households.

Coleridge put off his return to Greta Hall for several months, having already decided that he must live apart from his wife. Southey held the Wordsworths responsible for the deterioration in the Coleridges' marriage. 'His present plan,' he wrote in a letter, 'is to live with the Wordsworths – it is from idolatry of that family that this has begun . . .'[23] The Wordsworths were about to go off to stay for six months in a roomy house on Beaumont's Leicestershire estate, so Coleridge joined them there. They were worried about him. His eyes seemed sunken in a face that had grown fat, he was still hooked on opium and he looked desperately unwell. This is another point in the story where the bond between the Wordsworths and the Lake District might have been broken. Dorothy wrote to a friend in February 1807 worrying about where they might all live. William and Mary's third child had been born the previous summer, so Dove Cottage would be too small if Coleridge were to come with his two boys.[24] She also thought that it might be indelicate for Coleridge to live so close to Mrs Coleridge so soon after the separation. There was also Coleridge's health to consider. He really ought to live in the driest part of the country, so they were willing to say farewell to their beloved vales and mountains to be near him. With help from their new friend Lord Lonsdale the Wordsworths had bought property in Patterdale, but it seemed possible that they might find themselves living in Kent.

It was during this period that De Quincey arrived in the Lake District. As a shy undergraduate he had written to Wordsworth in the spring of 1803 to express his admiration for *Lyrical Ballads* and to ask permission to visit. Wordsworth had sent him a polite but hardly effusive reply. De Quincey was so in awe of his literary hero that on two occasions he got as far as the inn at Church Coniston before he was unmanned by nerves at the prospect of a meeting. Indeed, in 1806 he managed to get to the Gorge of Hammerscar, where the view opens out over the Vale of Grasmere, and could see the Wordsworths' little white cottage, 'just two bowshots from the water', before he retreated faintheartedly to Coniston and scuttled back to Oxford. Eventually he met Wordsworth in 1807 and found him a little stiff, although he was an immediate hit with Dorothy and the children. He wrote one of the most detailed physical descriptions of the poet, condemning his legs as unornamental, his body as ill made and his shoulders as drooping, but saying that his face, with its large nose, expansive forehead, deep, solemn eyes and firm mouth, more than compensated for his lack of a

good figure. He thought that Mary was ladylike and made up for her plain-
ness by an angelic charm and simplicity, while Dorothy's dark complexion,
ardent and sympathetic manner, quickness of movement and lively intellect
all made a strong impression upon him.

On this first visit he stayed a week, but when the question of the
Wordsworths' new domicile was settled, he took over the tenancy of Dove
Cottage. He lived there until 1820 and continued to rent it, using it mostly as
a place to store his books, until 1835. De Quincey was friendly with Charles
Lloyd, another poet who had made his home in the Lake District in 1800.
He was in a lower literary league than Coleridge, Wordsworth or Southey,
though he knew them and had indeed been a lodger and disciple of Coleridge
in Bristol and Nether Stowey. Lloyd had been prone to seizures and had been

Thomas De Quincey with His Daughters and Granddaughter (1855) by James Archer

an irksome house guest, so Coleridge did not anticipate his former protégé's arrival with any glee, but as the son of a successful Midlands banker Lloyd enjoyed independent means and shortly after his marriage in 1799 he bought the large house at Low Brathay, near Ambleside. This was a sunny interlude in a life clouded by mental illness. De Quincey, who became a close friend, wrote that Lloyd 'stood in the very centre of earthly pleasures' with a secure income, an excellent wife and an elegant mansion which cost so little to run that there was plenty of money left with which to throw parties. But De Quincey was also aware of Lloyd's lack of self-confidence and his mental and physical symptoms, which he tried – rather as Coleridge had done – to assuage with opium and vigorous walks. Ultimately his derangement became so severe that he was admitted to a lunatic asylum near York, from which he escaped in 1818, seeking temporary shelter with De Quincey. He recovered sufficiently to be reunited with his wife and enjoyed a brief flourish of creativity before the illness returned. He died in an asylum near Versailles in 1839.

It was at one of the Lloyds' dances that De Quincey first saw John Wilson, another eminent arrival in Lakeland society, though they were not introduced until they met at the Wordsworths'. Wilson was the heir to a fortune made by his father through the manufacture of cotton gauze in Paisley, and, like De Quincey, he was a youthful admirer of Wordsworth's poetry and had written to his hero before attempting to make his acquaintance, but the resemblance does not go much further. Wilson was a powerfully built, leonine, larger-than-life individual, who could mix with all levels of society and had been gifted with intellect and charm as well as physique. While at Oxford he had won a 100-guinea wager by leaping across the River Cherwell, but he had also been the first to receive the Newdigate Prize for Poetry. In Martineau's opinion 'the very spirit of the moorland, lake, brook, tarn, ghyll, and ridge breathes from his prose poetry'[25] and she thought that he did much to convey the character of the district to foreigners and the 'untravelled English', but nowadays his prose seems mannered and his poetry is forgotten.

He is remembered mostly for his energetic sporting pursuits. He liked to ride, row, hunt, shoot, walk and fish and he even enjoyed taking on the local wrestlers. He was the first to recognise that the Lake District could be a gigantic playground or gymnasium, and thus was the forerunner of every climber who has clung to a ledge, every mountain biker who has juddered down a track and every paraglider who has leapt off a crag.

Wilson added to his many blessings by marrying Jane Penny, 'the leading belle of the Lake country', and enlarged a cottage at Elleray on the slopes of

Professor John Wilson (undated) by Sir Henry Raeburn

Orrest Head as a family home, but then things went wrong. An uncle who had been responsible for managing his fortune succeeded in ruining him and he was forced to take his family to live with his mother in Edinburgh; but this exuberant man soon bounced back, becoming not only one of the principal writers (under the pseudonym 'Christopher North') for the popular *Blackwood's* magazine, but also being appointed to the chair of Moral Philosophy at Edinburgh University. He kept his house at Elleray and for thirty years he oscillated between Edinburgh and the Lake District.

*

When the Wordsworths finally decided to move, they did not go far, just to the western side of the village, where a Liverpool merchant called John Crump was prepared to lease them his recently built house, Allan Bank. It was ironic that they should find themselves occupying this house, because William had excoriated Crump – 'a wretched creature, wretched in name and nature' – and his house, which he had called 'a temple of abomination', believing that it would be visible from every part of the vale, 'and entirely destroy its character of simplicity and seclusion'.[26] Large and architecturally undistinguished, the house sat in an elevated position beneath the slopes of Silver Howe, and it had been built to take advantage of fine views over the lake, but without much consideration of the effect it would have upon views from elsewhere; this was at the heart of Wordsworth's objection, although he also saw Crump as a harbinger of worse to come. The Wordsworth family stayed at Allan Bank for three years. The place was hardly finished, the fireplaces smoked badly and workmen were often on the premises trying to remedy the faults. The Wordsworths moved to the Parsonage in Grasmere, but this was to be a scene of tragic loss. Two of William and Mary's children – Catherine, who was three, and Tom, who was six – died in the course of 1812.

While still at Allan Bank, Coleridge was given room to embark on a new literary venture, an uncompromisingly highbrow and hopelessly uncommercial journal called *The Friend*. At times the house must have been an emotional pressure cooker, because Sara Hutchinson was also there and agreed to help Coleridge with his venture, and from time to time Mrs Coleridge and their daughter (yet another Sara) would also be guests. It is surprising that Miss Hutchinson was willing to help with *The Friend*, because Coleridge was as infatuated with her as before. They worked well together, though, and kept *The Friend* going for nine months before Sara decided she had had enough and left Grasmere to stay with her brother Tom in Wales.

If Coleridge had been a taxing house guest while *The Friend* had been a going concern, he became impossible once it had folded. Even Dorothy, always his staunchest supporter, was despairing. On 12 April 1810 she wrote to Catherine Clarkson: 'We have no hope of him – none that he will ever do anything more than he has already done. If he were not under our Roof, he would be just as much the slave of stimulants as ever; & his whole time and thoughts, (except when he is reading and he reads a great deal), are employed in deceiving himself, and seeking to deceive others.'[27] The portents were ominous, and the Wordsworths must have been very relieved when their friend decided he would move back to Greta Hall to live again with his wife and children and the Southeys.

Basil Montagu, one of William's oldest friends from his days in London and the West Country, came to stay at Allan Bank in September. He had heard about Coleridge's sorry condition and thought he might be able to arrange medical treatment for his opium addiction, if he would agree to accompany him to London. Coleridge assented and departed with the visitor, but the warning Wordsworth felt obliged to give Montagu would cause a deep rift between the two poets. Having had recent experience of Coleridge as a house guest, he cautioned the teetotal Montagu not to lodge him under his own roof. According to Dorothy, William had intended to give Coleridge corresponding advice about lodgings, but the opportunity had not arisen during the latter's brief stop in Grasmere en route to London. Montagu saw enough of Coleridge's habits on the journey to see the wisdom of Wordsworth's warning, but later made the ruinous mistake of telling Coleridge everything that Wordsworth had said about him. It later emerged that Wordsworth had said that Coleridge was a 'rotten drunkard' in the habit of running up debts 'at little Pot-Houses for Gin' and that he had been 'an absolute nuisance in the family' – or at least that was what Coleridge thought he had heard. In a letter to Dorothy, written from London after an attempt at reconciliation with his old friend, William denied that he had ever used such words, and lamented that Coleridge had somehow mistaken the spirit of his remarks to Montagu.

Wordsworth and Coleridge never regained their old intimacy and Coleridge would never live in the Lake District again. On his last visit to Keswick, he drove through Grasmere without stopping, something previously unheard of; and when young Tom Wordsworth died, his grieving parents felt sure that their old ally would come to the succour of the family – but he set off for Margate instead. In the following year, 1813, the Wordsworths left Grasmere, but only to move a few miles down the road to a handsome house called Rydal Mount. It would be home to William, Mary and Dorothy for the rest of their lives.

Overleaf : Head of Ullswater

Julius Caesar Ibbetson (1804) by J. C. Ibbetson

7

Artists among the Lakes

A New Aesthetic Frontier

I F EIGHTEENTH-CENTURY RESIDENTS OF the Lake District were nonplussed to find a coterie of poets in their midst, they must also have wondered why their paths were overrun by outsiders lugging sketchbooks and easels. Though the Lake District was opened up by a vanguard of literati, the visual artists were not far behind, indeed the first print-makers to visit the area were active in the 1750s and 1760s.

There was never a Lakeland School of painters in the way that there was an identifiable group of Lake Poets. With some notable exceptions, artists came to the District for a stay of just a few days or weeks, often as part of a larger tour through northern Britain that might include Derbyshire, Yorkshire, Durham, Northumberland and the Scottish Borders. Compared to Wordsworth or Coleridge in the literary sphere, the painters who settled in the Lake District were of lesser standing, and art historians have tended to be dismissive, yet there were substantial figures among the short-term visitors; indeed, Turner and Constable both spent time in the Lakes, each producing significant work.

To make their reputations, artists had to exhibit in London, and from a metropolitan perspective the Lake District must have seemed mysteriously remote. A visit to the North Country was still an adventure, perhaps more so than crossing the Channel. We are now so accustomed to the idea of landscape as an artistic category that it is difficult to imagine how new all of this must have seemed in the eighteenth century, when the most well-established genres were portraiture and the painting of great historical scenes. Back then there was an excitement about the northern landscape; it represented a new aesthetic frontier.

One of the trailblazers was William Bellers, whose *Six Select Views in the North of England* of 1752 contained the first published images of

Sir George Beaumont and Joseph Farington Sketching in Oils (1777) by Thomas Hearne

Derwentwater, Ullswater and Windermere. Though the subject matter was exceptional for the period, Bellers imposed a stereotypical Arcadian vision upon the Lake District and failed to convey any real sense of place. His foregrounds included elegantly dressed visitors who looked as though they had just left the ballroom to climb fences and sit on rocks. In the next decade Thomas Smith of Derby, who was self-taught, helped to establish a market for souvenir prints of famous houses and views of wild countryside. Smith's Lake District scenes were outlandish fantasies, but in his defence it could be argued that techniques for depicting mountain scenery were still in their infancy. If his view of Derwentwater resembles anywhere on the planet, it is probably China, and it has been suggested that Smith's rounded lumps of mountains might have been an attempt to pander to the fashionable taste for chinoiserie. The islands in the lake look like giant lily pads, while the fore-ground is dominated by grotesque stumps (the remnants of the Greenwich Hospital's oaks) and a spindly tree. His view of Windermere is a little tamer, though Melvyn Bragg nonetheless compared it to a failed volcanic lake.[1] There was no attempt at verisimilitude, and, rather than presenting a comforting pastoral, as did Bellers, Smith amplified the drama and over-egged the strangeness.

The Trustees of Dove Cottage own a painting by Thomas Hearne entitled *Sir George Beaumont and Joseph Farington Sketching a Waterfall.* It is dated 1777, only five years after Gilpin made his visit to Borrowdale. Wordsworth was still a boy in Cockermouth at the time, but his future patron Beaumont was already an enthusiastic amateur artist and connoisseur, having stud-ied landscape painting at the Royal Academy under the Welshman Richard Wilson, who is often regarded as the first British landscape painter of any distinction. In the early 1750s Wilson had taken the Grand Tour to Venice and Rome and his paintings of subjects in North Wales, such as Snowdon and Cader Idris, are bathed in the light of the Roman *campagna*. His bucolic vision owed much to Claude and Poussin, and, like Gilpin, he was prepared to recompose nature if he felt it necessary. Although Wilson was one of the first to paint bare mountains, he never visited the Lake District, yet his influence on other painters was profound. The first wave of artists to visit the Lake District saw it through an imaginary Italian heat haze.

The artists in Hearne's painting are sheltering under large umbrellas beside the rock-strewn torrent of Lodore Falls. With their cumbersome easels, wigs and frock coats they seem to be uncomfortably perched among the boulders, not part of the place at all, although their devotion and concen-tration are evident.

Farington was a North Countryman whose father was the vicar of Leigh in Lancashire, and he had studied in Manchester before going to London. He was sufficiently at home in the north to become a Keswick resident between 1775 and 1781. His decision to move north was influenced by his read-ing of Gray;[2] he even arranged to arrive in October, the same month that the poet's Lake District tour had begun. Farington later became a hugely influential member of the Royal Academy, elected an Associate in 1783 and a full Member in 1785, and serving on the powerful Hanging Committee. His reputation as an artist rests largely on his *Twenty Views of the Lakes* published between 1784 and 1789. He was friendly with William Cookson,

Wordsworth's uncle, who agreed to write the descriptive notes to accompany the *Views*. Of all the artists who had visited the Lakes by that time, Farington was the most accurate topographical draughtsman; his sketches of cottages and villages have an intimacy which perhaps only a resident could achieve.

Between them, Beaumont, the influential patron, and Farington, the pillar of the artistic establishment, were able to establish the status of the Lake District as a northern Arcadia, so that while the Grand Tour had once been *de rigueur* for any artist hoping to attract wealthy clients, now a trip to the Lake District was essential for anyone who aspired to establish a metropolitan reputation. Throughout the 1780s and 1790s painters continued to come, but there was a gradual migration in taste, reflected in Beaumont's own work, away from Wilson's brand of Classicism towards the wilder shores of the Picturesque. The ludicrous side of Gilpin's dogmatism was becoming easy to see, and the early babbling about stations and prospects had subsided. Uvedale Price had rescued the Picturesque from absurdity by concentrating on qualities rather than formulaic composition, with a greater emphasis upon the close-up and upon the results of natural processes. Roughness, shagginess, irregularity and sudden variation were in vogue, while Arcadianism was on the wane.

Philip de Loutherbourg exhibited paintings of Patterdale and Skiddaw in the Royal Academy exhibition of 1784. He was a talented and innovative stage designer who in 1781 opened a mechanical theatre called the Eidophusikon in London's Leicester Square, where three-dimensional sets, lighting and sound effects were used to represent stirring scenes and natural wonders, including shipwrecks, the fiery lakes of Hell, the Bay of Naples and Niagara Falls. Always with an eye for the dramatic, he easily lost touch with the reality of the place he was painting. The Abbot Hall gallery in Kendal holds two large paintings of Belle Isle on Windermere by Loutherbourg which encapsulate the shift in taste. Intended to be seen together, one shows a scene of Arcadian tranquillity, the mirror-like lake untroubled by the merest breeze. The other shows Windermere tossed by a storm as wild as any that sank ships for audiences at the Eidophusikon.

Other artists who made the pilgrimage to the Lake District included Thomas Gainsborough, who came in late summer 1783, and the Exeter watercolourist Francis Towne, who visited in 1786. John Laporte followed

Belle Isle, Windermere, *in a Calm* (1786) by P. J. De Loutherbourg

in 1790, Paul Sandby in 1793 and Joseph Wright of Derby made several visits between 1783 and his death in 1797.

Thomas Girtin, another significant watercolourist, painted a number of Lake District subjects – but without ever visiting. He had formed an evening sketching club in London in 1799 and Beaumont enrolled as a member. It seems that Sir George lent Girtin some of his own Lake District sketches, which the latter worked up into watercolour paintings. He must have felt, as did Gilpin, that nature – or perhaps Beaumont – was not sufficiently skilled in composition and needed a little assistance, because he made some 'improvements' to the originals.

Whereas artists like Smith or De Loutherbourg are criticised for fantasy, falsification and exaggeration, others such as Wilson and Girtin are rarely taken to task for their alterations, and this raises all sorts of philosophical questions about the purposes and qualities of art. There is a long tradition, going back to Plato, which suggests that a good work of art is one which accurately represents its subject and it is this belief which laymen invoke when they praise a good likeness. On the other hand, when critics say that someone like Farington was a good draughtsman, there is usually a disparaging subtext – 'that's all he was', for example – so there must be more

Borrowdale (*c.* 1801) by Thomas Girtin

to art than mere accuracy. Perhaps art is concerned with something else altogether, such as the artist's own emotional responses, or the revelation of a truth which is not otherwise apparent. Those who could be true to themselves might break through to some kind of transcendental reality. The danger in this is that the imagination runs wild and loses any connection with the world as it is. As we survey the range of artists who have painted and drawn the Lake District, we find examples from the full spectrum of these tendencies.

Joseph Mallord William Turner came to the Lake District in 1797 at the outset of his career. At the age of twenty-one, this son of a Covent Garden barber had exhibited his first oil painting at the Royal Academy the previous year. He arrived in Keswick – which he made his base for the first four days – from Jedburgh in the Scottish Borders, in the course of a northern tour of over a thousand miles, which he completed within eight weeks.[3] Turner would remain a prodigious traveller throughout his life, later visiting France, Switzerland, Savoy and Italy. He developed the practice of making sketches in the summer, which he would work up into paintings once he returned to the studio. On his way north in 1797 he had concentrated on castles, abbeys and antiquities, but in the Lake District, one of the principal objectives of his journey, he encountered nature in the raw and in this process was transformed from a painter of architecture into one concerned with the elemental stuff of the world – rock, water, air and light. Here in the north he found landscapes that were more rugged, more imposing, more expansive than any he had previously seen.

In order to cram in as much experience as possible, Turner planned his tour carefully, probably taking advice from his friends Hearne and Girtin. He was careful to save plenty of space for Lake District drawings in the largest of the two sketchbooks he carried with him. He took no notice of West's stations, nor indeed of any viewpoints suggested by Gray, Gilpin or Pennant, preferring to make his own discoveries.

Although he arrived in the first week of August, it rained for much of his stay, but while poor weather might ruin a picnic or a boat trip, it is not necessarily bad news for an artist, particularly one such as Turner, who was developing a gift for the changing conditions of light and atmosphere. Arguably a fortnight of clear blue skies would have been far less welcome, although Turner had to omit the mountain tops from many of his sketches because they could not be seen for cloud. Even this apparent disadvantage could be turned around, however. It gave him more scope for creative invention once he began to develop ideas in the studio. Turner's Lake District paintings are not topographically accurate in the manner of a Farington, but they have what Ruskin would later call their 'mountain truth'.[4] Turner took tremendous liberties, inventing ridgelines and conjuring rainbows, but his paintings captured the authentic mood, essence or spirit of the Lake District in a way that mere depictions never could.

Having sketched a little in the environs of Keswick, Turner made his first excursion, to Lodore Falls, not much more than a trickle despite the murky weather, and then to Borrowdale, where he sketched a view towards Skiddaw with Longthwaite Bridge and Castle Crag in the foreground. Next came a trip to Crummock Water and Buttermere. The fruit of this outing was the spectacular oil painting produced for exhibition at the Royal Academy the following year. Now in the Turner Collection at Tate Britain, it bears the title *Buttermere Lake, with Part of Cromackwater, Cumberland, a Shower*. A sombre venture towards the Sublime, the picture is brought alive by its invented rainbow. In the sketch made on site, there was only a lightened sky.

Quitting Keswick, Turner made his way through St John's Vale and Dunmail Raise to Grasmere, where he worked up a sketch towards Rydal

Buttermere Lake, with Part of Cromackwater, Cumberland, a Shower (1798)
by J. M.W. Turner

in watercolour, but still had to imagine the tops of the surrounding fells. Next came a trip over to Patterdale, where he sketched Aira Force in pencil and watercolour and attempted to draw the mountains around Ullswater. He was hampered once again by low cloud. In a sketch looking south from Aira Park, Place Fell is shown, but the great hump of St Sunday Crag, which would dominate the view in clearer weather, is nowhere to be seen. This did not prevent Turner from creating two shimmering, ethereal versions of the scene in later years, one of which, *Ullswater, Cumberland* (*c.* 1835), has recently been purchased by the Wordsworth Trust.[5]

Though Turner did not seek out established viewing stations, he accepted the convention that the Lakes were best seen from a modest elevation and he made no drawings on the high fells. Perhaps the persistently inclement weather or the thought of carrying a heavy sketchbook deterred him, but it might simply never have occurred to this young city-bred man that there was anything worth drawing on the ridges. In other respects, however, he tore up the rule book, overthrowing all the polite Arcadian conventions. There are no elegant frock-coated figures in Turner's sketches and no improbably ornamental trees.

Kirkstone Pass brought Turner back to the central area of the Lakes, where he made studies of the rickety watermills at Stock Ghyll in Ambleside, one of which was developed into a watercolour entitled *Ambleside Mill, Westmoreland*, for exhibition at the Royal Academy in 1789. Like Wordsworth, Turner had a keen eye for human involvement in the landscape and he was attracted by scenes of small-scale industry. While at Grasmere he had sketched a nearby lead mine; now at Waterhead, at the northern end of Windermere, he drew men loading slates on to a barge from a horse-drawn cart.

Heading south, Turner arrived at Coniston, where the weather seems to have been a little better. It was here that he gathered sketches for the finest of the paintings to come out of his 1797 tour, *Morning amongst the Coniston Fells*, a work in oil exhibited the following year. It was shown at the Royal Academy accompanied in the catalogue by lines adapted from the Morning Hymn in Book V of Milton's *Paradise Lost*, in which Adam and Eve call upon the elements of the natural world to praise the creator. Turner's response to the Arcadian dream of the Lake District was to go even further and evoke Eden. The shepherd and his wife who gather their flock in the centre of this immense landscape are surely to be taken for a Cumbrian First Couple, and it is interesting to reflect that Turner painted this while Wordsworth was still in Germany remembering his own childhood paradise at Hawkshead.

The painting, based upon a view of the Coppermines valley with Wetherlam in the distance, is composed with an almost Manichaean dualism. A dark, brooding, rain-soaked and entirely believable foreground leads to luminous, sunlit uplands where the clouds are clearing. It could be heaven, except that there is a little wisp of smoke at the crest of the track to remind us that this is a real valley with real inhabitants engaged in industry.

From Coniston, Turner made his way to Furness Abbey, then crossed the sands to Lancaster to continue his tour through Yorkshire, Lincolnshire and Cambridgeshire, but he did not forget the Lake District. There were later visits in 1801 and 1831 and notable paintings, such as his glowing watercolour of *Winander-Mere, Westmoreland* (*c*. 1835) which, in its depiction of boats full of happy pleasure-seekers, along with crowds of equally hedonistic holidaymakers on the shore, captures a moment in the growth of tourism. Ruskin would later call Turner 'a wild meteoric phenomenon' who, in the midst of tamer, less adventurous artists could seem 'lawless alike and scholarless'.[6] He was clearly a man of enormous energy and resilience, who was excited rather than daunted by the vicissitudes of the Cumbrian weather. Of all the painters to visit, Turner was the closest in spirit to Coleridge, sharing his passion, his recklessness and his insatiable curiosity.

For more pragmatic souls not touched with genius, art could still provide a comfortable living. William Green was a Manchester surveyor who got his first glimpse of the Lake District in 1778, while still in his late teens, when working on a survey of 'Lancashire North-of-the-Sands'.[7] Green seems to have been happy enough in his work, but, perhaps like others who have seen the Lake District for the first time, he recognised the possibility of a better existence. On a visit to Ulverston he met Thomas West, who encouraged him to develop his embryonic talent as an artist. He began publishing aquatints of the District in 1795, yet he did not take the decision to settle in Ambleside until 1800, following a commercially unsuccessful map-making venture in Manchester and a lacklustre period of hob-nobbing in artistic circles in London. This move north, at around the same time as the Wordsworths' decision to take Dove Cottage, was a gamble for a middle-aged man with a pregnant wife, but it turned out well.

Miss Ellen Weeton, a waspish spinster and journal-keeper who knew Green well, described him as 'a man of good size, rather inclining to corpulent, and good, solid, thick legs'.[8] Green flattered himself that he had come to Ambleside to contribute to the improvement of the arts, Weeton remarked unkindly, when in fact this was 'a great big lie – he came solely to get a living for himself and his family'.[9] But this does not seem ignoble, especially when we learn that when Green died twenty-three years later, possibly from overwork, he was survived not only by his wife, but by four daughters and six sons.

Green took a cottage in the very centre of town, on Market Square, but he was frequently not at home. He would often go off into distant valleys, lugging his heavy artist's equipment with him, and sometimes staying away for several days. Whenever possible he liked to complete his drawings in situ and would therefore work throughout the hours of daylight, even if the weather was unfriendly, and he sometimes lit a fire to warm him as he sketched.

In contrast to Turner, whose first tour of the Lakes predated Green's arrival by only three years, he is at the other end of an emotional and creative spectrum. Turner combined close observation with intuition and

Wyemart Ltd
Unit 4D Tom Head Ind. Est
Ramsden Road
Hereford Herefordshire
HR2 6LR
UNITED KINGDOM

Order Date: 03/08/2014

Order Number: 1033770

Marketplace: Amazon UK

Marketplace Order #: 205-9433755-3005135

Ship Method: Standard

Items:

Qty	Item	Locator	Condition	Price
1	The English Lakes: A History Thompson, Ian SKU: mon0000021953 ISBN: 074759838X - Books	4D -1-S -003-001-41	Very Good	£2.29

Notes:

If you have any questions or concerns regarding this order, please contact us at wyemart@sky.com

Thank you for your order!

In the event of a return, **please indicate your reason for return below and mail this packing slip and book** to the address listed above. If you should need additional assistance with your return, please contact Customer Support by email at wyemart@sky.com, or by telephone at 01432 343317.

emotional empathy in pursuit of a deeper reality: Green was the objective observer who could only draw what he saw. Surveying and cartography were highly esteemed activities during the Enlightenment, but in the age of Romanticism they would come to seem prosaic, unimaginative and lacking in feeling. Turner had little interest in topography: Green recorded it painstakingly. Turner could work confidently on an immeasurable scale: Green was at his best when drawing things that were close to hand, like rocks and old buildings. His black and white etchings are better than his watercolours, for here there was some technical innovation. He used his thickest lines for objects in the foreground, with lines of diminishing weight for objects further away. This gave his work a sense of depth, but also focused attention on foreground detail which other artists would have missed.

As an artist Green had much in common with Farington, who left the Lakes the year after Green arrived. Neither man was a great artist, but there is a place for the faithful representation of topography and architecture. His work sold well to the growing numbers of moneyed tourists who came from Manchester, Liverpool and the Midlands and wanted authentic reminders of their travels. Green thought he was doing the Lake District a

Bridge House, Ambleside (1821) by William Green

service by recording it as it was. As one who loved vernacular buildings, he was afraid that rapid changes in Lake District society were likely to sweep them away, a concern that has echoed over the intervening years and is still voiced today. Green complained that 'modernising has, however, recently spoiled many of these buildings, and a few years more will probably see them pared and plaistered into all the monotony of the erections of the present day'.[10] Architectural conservationists still value the information captured in Green's close studies of farms and villages.

In all, Green produced more than a thousand unique images. With some help from his daughters he engraved and published his own prints, and every year there would be an exhibition in Ambleside, for which the two main rooms of his house had to be prepared. It must have been an exhausting life, but it supported the family and gave Green something else he would have craved – entry into polite society. Though he sometimes complained that he had remained an off-comer, he seems to have been welcome, not only in the dale farmhouses he so often sketched, but also in the drawing rooms of the gentry. It seems that he compensated for his long days of artistic solitude with a very active social life. He could play the flute and the fiddle and recite Shakespeare. He was friendly with the Wordsworths, sometimes joining William and the local doctor at cards. There were invitations to musical soirées with the Harden family at Brathay Hall. In addition to being charming and wealthy, John Harden and his wife Jessy were both talented amateur musicians and artists and many gifted visitors benefited from the open house they kept. Through such connections, many well-established local families became Green's patrons. Southey and Lloyd both subscribed to his collections of etchings, as did Wordsworth, and his social circle extended to De Quincey and Thomas Arnold. John Wilson (Christopher North) was another admirer, while Hartley Coleridge wrote of him that 'he knew trees and waterfalls as well as he knew his own children'.[11]

Knowing the success of West's *Guide*, the entrepreneurial Green often thought of writing one of his own, but misgivings about his ability to produce the text led to procrastination. In the preface to *The Tourist's New Guide*, which was finally published in 1819, he says that he decided to write his own 'short essay' to accompany sixty etchings in 1814, but the idea could have been in gestation for much longer. Green complains that 'a number of journies were made for the express purpose of procuring materials which have been collected, arranged, and combined, with infinite labour, at a very heavy expense, and to the great inconvenience of the author's practice as an artist'.[12]

Elterwater 'light from left hand' (1786) by Francis Towne

Knowing his limitations, Green commissioned his friend Jonathan Otley to write a section on geology and John Gough to add notes on botany. In one significant respect, Green's book was an advance on West's. As Green explained, West 'contented himself by speaking of the scenery of easy access from the public roads, for he has entirely omitted the vast and romantic wilds which lie between the sea and the chain of lofty mountains, beginning at Coniston and ending at Lows Water – who shall traverse Seathwaite, Eskdale, Wastdale, Ennerdale, and Ennerdale-dale, and not be ready to acknowledge that the western side of his tour, though probably less beautiful, is infinitely more magnificent than the eastern side?'[13]

One of Green's friends was the Yorkshireman Julius Caesar Ibbetson, another painter of note, who first came to the Ambleside area in 1798, married a local girl in 1801 and lived both at Clappersgate and Troutbeck before departing for his home county in 1805. The two men drank and dined together when Ibbetson came to town and sometimes went off sketching around Ullswater, Brother's Water and Haweswater. Ibbetson produced mellow representations of Ullswater and Castle Crag in Borrowdale, but is better remembered for a delightful picture of his own home, surrounded by pigs and cows, and for a lively portrayal of community life in Ambleside's Market Square. He was an amiable rough diamond with a drink problem, not always welcome in polite society. The Wordsworths stopped taking tea with the Ibbetsons and, when writing to Lady Beaumont, Dorothy passed on the opinion that the artist's conversation in the company of women was 'unbecoming and indecent'.[14]

*

By the beginning of the nineteenth century a Lake District tour was obligatory for any self-respecting artist. John Constable came in 1806, at the age of thirty, staying at Storrs Hall on Windermere, which his uncle, David Pike Watts, had acquired in 1804, and spending time with the Hardens at Brathay Hall, before moving on to Borrowdale, where he spent three weeks. It seems likely that Beaumont, to whom Constable had been introduced as a boy, would have encouraged him to make this trip, but the young artist had not yet established his reputation and seems to have been depressed.

While in the Lakes he was introduced to Southey and also to Wordsworth, who told him that as a boy his mind had been so 'lost in extraordinary conceptions' that he was once 'held by a wall not knowing but he was part of it'.[15] This mystical memory did not impress Constable, who thought Wordsworth too full of himself, although in time the two men became friends, brimming with mutual admiration.

C. R. Leslie, Constable's friend and biographer, later wrote: 'I have heard him say that the solitude of mountains oppressed his spirits. His nature was particularly social and could not feel satisfied with scenery, however grand in itself, that did not abound in human associations.'[16] Although the Lake District was never an unpeopled wilderness – indeed, it abounded in the farms, villages and mills that Constable loved to paint – Leslie dismissed the significance of the artist's Lake District journey, and this opinion has taken hold, even though there is much evidence to the contrary. Constable was very productive while in the Lake District, producing a stack of studies in pencil and wash, investigating clouds, meteorological effects, light and shade and the changes of mood associated with different times of the day.[17] For an artist interested in changeable skies the variable weather of the Lake District would have been a gift. It may be true, as Leslie suggested, that Constable's 'mind was formed for a different class of landscape' – the Suffolk countryside he had known all his life – but if he had been unhappy in the Lakes, why did he stay for seven weeks, working with such industry? Why should he have inscribed, on the back of his sketch of Esk Hause, 'the finest scenery that ever was'?[18] And it simply cannot be true that he produced no work of consequence; indeed, as far as mountain subject material is concerned, the critic Charles Rhyne has compared this body of sketches and watercolours favourably with anything produced by any European artist by that date, 'even the precocious Turner'.[19] In fact the sketches he made propelled his exhibited work for the next three years. In 1807 he showed *A View from Westmorland*, *Keswick Lake* and *Bow Fell*,

Cumberland at the Royal Academy and he told Farington that in one of them 'he had got something original, while in 1808 he sent *Windermere Lake, Borrowdale* and *A Scene in Cumberland* and planned to send another view of Borrowdale the following year, but was advised against it by Farington, who thought it unfinished.[20] Almost all of this work has been lost,[21] so we can only guess at its quality. Unfortunately the public were becoming sated with Lake District images, and Constable's efforts were not a commercial success. What is clear, though, is that Constable's visit to the Lake District was not a time-wasting diversion from his true vocation, but an important stage in his development.

The Lower Falls, Rydal (1806) by John Constable

Saddleback and Part of Skiddaw, Stormy Day – Noon (1806) by John Constable

In this chapter a selective approach has been unavoidable. So many artists have painted in the Lake District that any attempt at a comprehensive list would make dull reading, so the focus has necessarily been upon those with the biggest reputations or the strongest connections by dint of residence. Artists who painted in the age of the snapshot and the picture postcard have generally been omitted. But many readers will be aware that the most popular Lake District image-maker of the twentieth century was William Heaton Cooper (1903–95), the climber-artist whose studio in Grasmere sold almost 90,000 prints and postcards a year, and that William was the son of Alfred Heaton Cooper, the most commercially successful Lake District artist of his own day and the founder of a dynasty of talented watercolourists.

After training in London, Alfred set off to the Norwegian fjords to make his livelihood as a landscape painter. He married Mathilde, a local girl, but found that he could not make an adequate living, so he returned to England with his bride, eventually settling in Coniston in 1894, where his studio was a red-roofed log cabin which he had shipped especially from Norway. When he discovered that wealthy art-buying tourists were more often found in Ambleside, he upped the cabin and took it there, where it can still be seen on Lake Road.

At the time of Alfred's death in 1929, William was living in a bohemian commune in the south of England, but he returned to take over the Ambleside studio. As his reputation grew, he decided to move to Grasmere, where he began to build a home in 1938. It was during the Second World War, in which he served as a camouflage officer, that he saw a way in which to secure his family's finances. Producing a constant supply of original paintings was a precarious livelihood, but the arrival of improved colour-printing techniques prompted him to sell reproductions as well, pricing them so that they could be afforded by the Lake District's thousands of tourists. This unashamedly commercial approach brought him huge success, though the art world could be sniffy. Well-observed, technically accomplished, atmospheric and generally serene, Heaton Cooper's prints found a ready market. They have always been popular with climbers and walkers. His Lake District is a calming one, where rocks and summits are often bathed in the light of evening or of dawn. It is a comforting vision of the landscape which must, by now, have found its way into hundreds of thousands, perhaps even millions, of homes.

Overleaf: Watendlath Bridge

A Cumbrian Girl (*c.* 1806) by John Constable

8

The Buttermere Beauty

Mary Robinson, Captain Budworth
and the Keswick Impostor

THE MOST CELEBRATED MENU in the literature of the Lake District must be the breakfast served to Captain Joseph Budworth by Robert Newton of Grasmere in 1792. It included: a stuffed roast pike, a boiled fowl, veal cutlets and ham, beans and bacon, cabbage, pease and potatoes, anchovy sauce, parsley and butter, cheese, wheat bread and oat cakes, followed by three cups of preserved gooseberries and a bowl of rich cream. All of which could be had for a mere ten pence per head. How much of this the enthusiastic Budworth was able to scoff we do not know, but he did note that it was a 'complete bellyful'. After which he set out to climb Helm Crag, a modest hill by Lake District standards, but steep enough with so much cargo on board.

Unlike the very first tourists, Budworth was not content just to stay in the valleys, admiring static views across still lakes from West's various stations. He was a man of action who wanted to be among the hills. The fact that he only had one arm, having lost the other at the siege of Gibraltar, did not deter him. He had two good legs. He published his travels as *A Fortnight's Ramble to the Lakes in Westmoreland, Lancashire and Cumberland*, under the pen name 'A. Rambler'.

Nowadays descriptions of the vale containing the lakes of Buttermere, Crummock Water and Loweswater routinely use words like *lovely* and *secluded* and stress the contrast between the fertile fields of the valley floor and the steep fellsides with their tumbling waterfalls, but eighteenth-century depictions placed greater emphasis on the wildness of this remote place; the waters of Buttermere were 'deep and sullen' and the 'barrier mountains, by excluding the sun for much of its daily course', strengthened this gloomy impression. Budworth's landlady in Buttermere had 'never seen but one chaise in the valley, which came from Cockermouth and left it at the Keswick-road; she spoke of it as a phaenomenon'.[1] Budworth may have been attracted to the isolated village by its reputation among fishermen. The lake was deep enough to contain char, a salmon-like fish related to those in the Arctic; in Britain it can only be found in a few upland lakes and is thus much prized.[2] Perhaps Budworth was drawn by the prospect of this delicacy, but what he found at the village's Fish Inn turned out to be even more enticing. When Budworth and his companions arrived at the tavern, it was the landlord's teenage daughter who made the strongest impression.

> Her mother and she were spinning woollen yarn in the back kitchen. On our going into it the girl flew away as swift as a mountain sheep, and it was not till our return from Scale Force that we could say that we first saw her. She brought in part of our dinner and seemed to be about fifteen.[3]

When Budsworth's account of his travels was published it included a poignantly sensual description of the girl:

Inn at Buttermere (1809) by William Green

Her hair was thick and long, of a dark brown, and though unadorned with ringlets, did not seem to want them; her face was a fine oval, with full eyes, and lips as red as vermilion; her cheeks had more of the lily than the rose; and, although she had never been out of the village (and I hope she will have no ambition to wish it), she had a manner about her which seemed better calculated to set off a dress, than dress *her*. She was a very Lavinia 'Seeming, when unadorn'd, adorn'd the most.' When we first saw her at her distaff, after she had got the better of her first fears, she looked like an angel; and I doubt not that she is the reigning Lily of the Valley.[4]

Lavinia's real name was Mary Robinson. Curiously, considering the impression that Mary clearly made upon the middle-aged Budworth, he called her 'Sally of Buttermere' in the first two editions of his book. This was, perhaps, a deliberate attempt to protect her identity, either for her own sake or to safeguard a middle-aged author's private fantasies, but in any case it was ineffective. When *A Fortnight's Ramble* was published Mary seemed to be the embodiment of so much that the Lake District tourists were seeking – natural beauty united with a guileless innocence – that a visit to the Fish Inn became obligatory on any itinerary and Mary was soon plagued by attentions that were uninvited and unwelcome.

Once fixed in Budworth's pages, Mary became fair game for any young buck with a sketchbook who took up lodgings at the Fish, and she must have had a hard time keeping them off. Her admirers were the sort of educated young gentlemen who, but for the Napoleonic Wars, might have sampled the delights of Europe on exuberant Grand Tours. After taking a few pints of the strong home-brewed beer served by Mary's father, such young visitors, we can imagine, lost their inhibitions and flirted openly with the long-suffering serving girl. Some of them left poetic tributes to Mary, written on the walls, not just in English but in French, Latin and Greek. On one occasion an admirer left a pair of stockings in her empty shoes, but when he came back the following year he found she had not worn them.

Budworth, it seems, became concerned that, by promoting Mary as one of the attractions of the Lake District, he might have done her a great disservice. In the winter of 1797–8 he decided to visit Buttermere again. Unsure perhaps of his own motives, he justified this second journey by claiming a wish to see the 'incomparable Scale Force waterfall bound up with icicles', but admitted that his 'grand intention' was 'to settle an account with my own mind and do away with any false pride which the handsome things said of a young creature at Buttermere might have disordered her with'.[5] His account of this second visit was published in the *Gentleman's Magazine* in January 1800.

Budworth's attempt to climb the 'glassy hill' to view the waterfall was unsuccessful: 'although I had sharp nails in the balls of my shoes, and large stubbs to the heels, with a pike to my hazel stick, my efforts were useless; I tumbled twice, and slid bodily down the hill again'.[6] His feet slipped through a crust of melting ice into the freezing water below – 'I soon got over my shoe-tops and up to one knee' – and he felt himself conquered. He returned to the Fish Inn, where he had taken lodgings, and Mary, who was then nineteen, endeared herself to him still further by bringing him warm water to wash his legs and even a pair of her old father's shoes and stockings to use while his own were drying.

By Budworth's own account neither Mary nor her parents recognised him from his previous trip, and he took great delight in observing Mary incognito. The captain, we might think, was being honest neither with himself nor with his readers when he claimed to have Mary's welfare uppermost in his mind. There was to be a dance that evening at the Fish Inn, and Budworth was clearly excited by the preparations and by the prospect of seeing more of the landlord's daughter.

> Mary's hair, so ornamental when we before saw her, was folded under her cap; she went out to prepare for the dance; on my calling suddenly, she instantly came in; her hair was down her back, rather darker coloured, remarkably thick, and a near yard long; and I regretted it was going to be concealed under a cap.[7]

Budworth himself sat in a corner, puffing his way through the last tobacco to be found in the house, watching Mary pruriently from beneath his self-generated smokescreen. 'I never saw more graceful dancing, or a woman of finer figure to set it off, than in Mary of Buttermere,' he wrote later.[8] The dance continued until two in the morning, and Budworth, overstimulated by all he had seen, could not sleep. The following morning the weather was louring and the visitor, not wishing to get snowed in, decided to leave but not before having a heart-to-heart with Mary. Taking her by the hand he confessed that he was the author of *A Fortnight's Ramble* and that he had been watching her behaviour throughout the previous evening. He was pleased, he told her, that she conducted herself with such propriety. Then he launched into a little lecture:

You may remember I advised you in that Book, never to leave your native valley. Your age and situation require the utmost care. Strangers shall come, and have come, purposefully to see you; and some of them with very bad intention. We hope you will never cease to be upon your guard. You really are not so handsome as you promised to be; and I have long wished, by conversation like this, to do away what mischief the flattering character I gave of you may expose you to. Be merry and wise.[9]

We can never know what Mary really thought of this speech and its revised estimate of her charms. Budworth claimed that she thanked him sincerely, reassuring him that 'I ever have, and trust that I always shall take care of myself.' He, at least, was satisfied that he had rectified any harm he might have done and 'toiled out of the valley of Buttermere', never to be seen there again. In writing about her again he had done nothing to diminish Mary's celebrity and she would soon be much in the public eye, and under regrettable circumstances.

On 3 September 1803 a carriage clattered through the Scotch Gate of Carlisle accompanied by the town's full complement of yeomanry. It was a short journey down to the sandy island in the River Eden where, the previous evening, a gibbet had been erected. As the escorts formed a ring around the scaffold, the prisoner, one John Hatfield, alias the Honourable Alexander Augustus Hope and also known to the press as the 'Keswick Impostor', stepped down from the coach and mounted a short ladder to the platform, where he untied his neckerchief and covered his eyes with it. Although Hatfield had presented his executioner with a bag of silver in the hope of an efficient dispatch, the hangman was no expert and the noose slipped twice before Hatfield dropped to his death.[10]

Hatfield had been found guilty on several charges – of assuming a false name and title, of passing himself off as a Member of Parliament, of forging bills of exchange – but the reason for his conviction was the franking of a number of letters to avoid paying postage, a crime that was taken much more seriously at the beginning of the nineteenth century than it is today. Another charge that might have been brought against him was bigamy, and it is arguable that it was this transgression, rather than anything which appeared on the charge sheet, that sealed his fate. The members of a Cumberland jury had no mercy for a man who had so grossly deceived a daughter of their own county. A year before,

Alexander Hope had confirmed all of Captain Budworth's worst fears by marrying the famous Buttermere Beauty.

Coleridge was living in Keswick when Hatfield, alias Colonel Hope, first checked into the Queen's Head Hotel on 19 or 20 July 1802. Though enslaved to his drug addiction, Coleridge found time to submit articles to the *Morning Post* and was about to be presented with a scoop. He wrote of Keswick that for one-third of the year the town swarmed 'with Tourists of all shapes & sizes, & characters – it is the very place I would recommend to a novelist or a farce writer'. Mary Robinson and John Hatfield were soon to provide this northern correspondent with a 'novel of real life'[11] and he would break the story.

Coleridge has provided some of the best physical descriptions of 'the pretended Alexander Augustus Hope'. He was an imposing figure, rather stout with a striking countenance, but what 'added to the power of large bright eyes was the blackness of his eye-brows and eye-lashes, contrasted with his complexion and the light colour of his hair'. Coleridge wondered whether this effect had been produced by artificial means, 'but if it was indeed done for the purposes of disguise, it was a trouble thrown away: there were too many other peculiarities of look and limb, which it was not in his power to hide or alter'.[12]

His 'handsome equipage' drew admiring glances, and his visiting cards designated him 'The Hon. Augustus Hope', a brother of Lord Hopetoun. What really took the townsfolk in was that this patrician Scotsman franked his own mail, a mark of high social status. De Quincey tells us that 'All doors flew open at his approach: boats, boatmen, nets, and the most unlimited sporting privileges, were placed at the disposal of the "Honourable" gentleman.'[13] According to the *Newgate Calendar*, where his crimes were later described with relish, 'his manners were extremely polished and insinuating, and he was possessed of qualities which might have rendered him an ornament of society'. Everyone seems to have been impressed by his manners and the smoothness of his conversation. Coleridge described it thus:

> He has an astonishing flow of words, and his language, to the generality of men, would appear as choice and elegant as it was undoubtedly fluent and copious. Add to this, that his conversation is of that sort, which is generally most delightful: inexhaustible in anecdotes, he knows everything of every body, and more particularly . . . of all persons distinguished by splendour of situation, birth or military exploit.[14]

Mary Robinson, Maid of Buttermere, artist unknown

If Budworth had been drawn to the Lake District by its scenic reputation, Hatfield was attracted by the prospect of mingling with well-heeled tourists. No doubt, too, he chose a part of the country suitably remote from both London and Tiverton, where he was well known. The bogus Colonel Hope, happy to strut among the unsuspecting but wary of critical scrutiny, did his best to avoid Coleridge. Whenever there was to be company at the Fish Inn, the distinguished guest was found to have gone fishing, and he only once attended the church at Keswick.

He married Mary just three months later, rapid work for any suitor, but she had clearly not been Hatfield's target when he first arrived in the area. There was a something parasitic to his villainy, and he was looking for someone suitably young, wealthy and unattached. Indeed, he seems to have swiftly fixed his sights on a rich, beautiful and well-born young woman called Miss Amaryllis D'Arcy, who was travelling in the company of an Irish gentleman, Colonel Nathaniel Moore, and his wife. De Quincey tells us that Hatfield 'was wooing a young Irish lady at the very time when the Buttermere girl became his victim'.[15]

After a few days in Keswick he made his first excursion to Buttermere, where, we may assume, he first met Mary, but then he took off to

Grasmere, where he lodged in a small public house behind the churchyard and made the acquaintance of the Liverpool lawyer and businessman John Crump, the same man who, in 1808, became Wordsworth's landlord at Allan Bank. Crump took exception to the tone of the articles which Coleridge wrote in the *Morning Post*, thinking that they made him look gullible, and it did not help that Coleridge included a swipe at his taste in architecture. Coleridge thought that Hatfield and Crump were both intruders in their own ways. According to De Quincey, this quarrel endured for ten years, until the two men met by accident at Allan Bank, the 'very nuisance of a house' which had first turned Coleridge against the Liverpool man.[16] Wordsworth and his friends got over their snootiness in time; Coleridge would refer to the merchant as 'my friend Mr Crump' and Wordsworth would invite him to family picnics on Grasmere Island. Perhaps the fact that he was one of Hatfield's victims softened their hearts towards him.

Hatfield was an impulsive man, unable to bridle his amatory urges. While in Grasmere, says Coleridge, the bogus Hope made eager and repeated attempts to debauch a beautiful girl who was staying there, but was thwarted by the watchful care of her worthy mistress. After a stay of three weeks, he returned to Keswick, where he remained for a day or two, amusing himself with fishing expeditions, chiefly in the company of a local man called Birkett who supplied the tackle. According to the account in the *Morning Post*, Hope made a promise of marriage to Birkett's daughter and also 'something very like a promise of marriage' to one of the maids at the Queen's Head. It was all sport to John Hatfield.

Mary was hardly likely to ease the fraudster's financial problems, but marriage to an heiress like Miss D'Arcy could have dissolved them in an instant. Despite other distractions, Colonel Hope was assiduously paying court to Miss D'Arcy when he first encountered Mary, but it is doubtful that he would have been successful in his suit. Although Amaryllis had accepted his proposal, those around her had their misgivings. Colonel Moore affronted him by asking him to 'write to certain Noblemen and Gentlemen both in Ireland and England, whose names and addresses he would furnish him with, and obtain from them every necessary information respecting himself and the young Lady under his protection'.[17] Hope was being asked for references, and he must have known that this particular game was up, but then to rush headlong into marriage with Mary confirms the impetuousness of his nature.

Mary did not succumb at once. Sometime during the last ten days of August 1802 the adventurer arrived again in Buttermere and, according to Coleridge, 'attempted without delay, and by every artifice of looks and language, to conciliate the affections of the young woman'. He proposed in the first week of September, offering to whisk Mary over the border for a quick marriage – Gretna Green was only fifty-five miles away. Mary, we are told, refused him, pointing out, reasonably enough, that she had not known him very long. Coleridge, who was always firmly on Mary's side, remarked that 'her natural good sense informed her, that strange events are seldom happy events'.[18] Yet a week or two later the suitor tried again, this time sending a written proposal of marriage, which she also turned down. There is nothing to show that Mary thought Colonel Hope was anything other than what he claimed to be, but her reluctance to be plucked from the comforts of family and familiar surroundings, even for such a socially advantageous match, is entirely understandable.

Mary was aware that Hope had paid addresses to Miss D'Arcy, and must have thought such a union more socially appropriate, but Hope claimed that it had all been an artifice designed to provoke her jealousy and make her reconsider his proposal. Before condemning Mary for her lack of judgement, it is worth remembering that most of her supposed social superiors were also taken in.

The wedding took place on Saturday 2 October, in the little church of St Cuthbert, which sits among tidy green fields midway between the villages of High and Low Lorton on the road between Keswick and Cockermouth. Such a marriage would still sell newspapers today. Here was the distinguished brother of an earl marrying a famous beauty of humble origins after a whirlwind romance. To add further spice, Alexander Hope was almost twice the age of his bride. News of the event was carried back to Keswick by George Wood, the landlord of the Queen's Head, but it soon became a national story, largely through the report published on 11 October in the *Morning Post* under the headline 'Romantic Marriage'. It was written by Coleridge, who had, it seems, been paying attention to the worries of Colonel Moore, for it raised some doubts about the true identity of the groom:

His marriage, however, with a poor girl without money, family or expectations has weakened the suspicions entertained to his disadvantage. But the interest which the good people of Keswick take in the welfare of the Beauty of Buttermere has not yet suffered them entirely to subside, and they await with anxiety the moment when they shall receive decisive proofs that the bridegroom is the real person whom he describes himself to be. The circumstances of his marriage are sufficient to satisfy us that he is no impostor, and therefore we may venture to congratulate the Beauty of Buttermere on her good fortune.[19]

This sort of attention was the last thing the charlatan needed. Charles Hope, the authentic Earl of Hopetoun, now wrote two letters to the *Morning Post* accusing Mary's new husband of being a fake and pointing out that the real Alexander Hope had been in Germany all summer and was currently residing in Vienna. Mary, too, must have been growing suspicious. Her new husband had promised her a visit to his brother's estate at Hopetoun near Edinburgh. He bought her no new clothes for this auspicious journey, apart from a pair of gloves, but promised that they would obtain some in the first decent-sized town they stopped in. But they only got as far as Longtown on the Scottish border before Alexander said they must go back to Buttermere, mysteriously cutting short their honeymoon.

Hatfield's problems deepened with the arrival in Keswick of a Welsh judge named George Hardinge, described by Coleridge as 'a very singular gentleman', who was determined to get to the bottom of the rumours. When confronted by the judge, Hatfield had the nerve to say that although his name was Hope, he had never claimed to be the brother of the Earl of Hopetoun, nor the MP for Linlithgow, but when the evidence of the franked letters came to light a warrant was issued against him and Hatfield was committed to the care of a constable, who was soft-hearted enough to allow his prisoner to go fishing upon Derwentwater, where he enlisted the help of a friendly fisherman, probably Birkett, who put him ashore and then guided the absconder through Borrowdale. To heighten the drama, Coleridge added that Hatfield 'probably escaped over the Stake, a fearsome Alpine pass, over Glaramara into Langdale'.[20] According to the *Newgate Calendar* the fugitive 'took refuge for a few days on board a sloop off Ravenglass, and then went in the coach to Ulverston, and was afterwards seen in Chester'. A wanted notice was printed in the papers:

Notorious Impostor, Swindler, and Felon.
John Hatfield, who lately married a young woman, commonly called the Beauty of Buttermere, under an assumed name; height about five feet ten inches, aged about forty-four, full face, bright eyes, thick eyebrows, strong but light beard, good complexion with some colour, thick but not

very prominent nose, smiling countenance, fine teeth, a scar on one of his cheeks near the chin, very long, thick, light hair, with a great deal of it grey, done up in a club, stout, square shouldered, full breast and chest, rather corpulent and stout limbed but very active, and has rather a spring in his gait, with apparently a little hitch in bringing up one leg; the two middle fingers of his left hand are stiff from an old wound and he frequently has the custom of pulling them straight with his right; has something of the Irish brogue in his speech, fluent and elegant in his language, great command of words, frequently puts his hand to his heart, very fond of compliments and generally addressing himself to persons most distinguished by rank or situation, attentive in the extreme to females, and likely to insinuate himself where there are young ladies.[21]

A fifty-pound reward was posted for information that might see him 'safely lodged in one of his Majesty's gaols'. By the time the Bow Street officers reached Chester, Hatfield had slipped away to Wales. He was ultimately apprehended about sixteen miles from Swansea, and committed to Brecon gaol. There he tried to convince his captors that he came from an old Welsh family, but the men from Bow Street took him to London for further interrogation.

In his rapid flight from Keswick, Hatfield had abandoned his carriage and in it was found a handsome dressing box. It contained an assortment of toiletry trinkets, all silver, and a pair of elegant pistols. There was also a cash book which showed that he had deposited considerable sums in various banks. Mary herself then discovered that there was a false bottom in the travelling trunk which Hope had left at Buttermere. Beneath it was a large mass of letters and papers, including some addressed to him from his legitimate wife and his children.

Soon the extent of Hatfield's villainy was revealed. In London he had already spent time in the King's Bench prison for debt, and he had also been gaoled in Dublin and Scarborough. During this last incarceration he had somehow managed to seduce Michelli Nation, a rich twenty-three-year-old from Devon, who paid his debts and agreed to marry him. Through this connection he was able to swindle some Devon merchants and go back up to London in fine style, but his creditors soon discovered the true state of his finances and leaving his family in Tiverton he fled north. His dramatic appearance in Keswick as the Honourable Alexander Augustus Hope was the last episode in a career of deception.

John Hatfield, artist unknown

The trial of the Keswick Impostor took place at the Cumberland Assizes on
15 August 1803 before the Honourable Sir Alexander Thompson. Two of
the indictments concerned 'false, forged and counterfeit' bills of exchange,
both drawn upon one John Crump, Esquire. One of these was for £30 which
Hatfield had used to pay his hotel bill in Keswick, the other was for £20 and
was payable to Nathaniel Montgomery Moore; serious enough offences, but
it was the third charge that carried the harshest penalty:

> With having assumed the name of Alexander Hope, and pretending
> to be a member of Parliament of the United Kingdom of Great Britain
> and Ireland, the brother of the Right Honourable Lord Hopetoun, and
> a Colonel in the Army, and under such false and fictitious name and
> character, at various times in the month of October, 1802, having forged
> and counterfeited the handwriting of the said Alexander Hope, in the
> superscription of certain letters or packets, in order to avoid the payment
> of the duty on postage.[22]

There was no mention in any of the charges to Hatfield's bigamous marriage to Mary Robinson, the law placing more weight upon property than upon broken hearts and ruined lives. Hatfield pleaded 'Not Guilty' but the evidence of his guilt was conclusive. Wordsworth and Coleridge were both in Carlisle on the last day of the impostor's trial. Coleridge alarmed the whole court by 'hallooing' the word 'Dinner!' to Wordsworth, who was sitting on the opposite side of the hall. Then, 'impelled by Miss Wordsworth', the friends obtained a last interview with the condemned psychopath. They found him a vain hypocrite. 'It is not by mere Thought,' wrote Coleridge, 'that I can understand this man.'[23] Mary was pregnant at the time of the trial and gave birth to a son in June 1803, but the child died of pneumonia within three weeks.

Coleridge obtained the mass of letters concealed in the bottom of Hatfield's trunk and planned to write an epic novel which would have told the whole story, not just the events in Buttermere, but also Hatfield's earlier crimes. The poet had been deeply affected by the scandal, but the book never materialised. The articles in the *Morning Post*, supplemented by the trial records, did, however, furnish the material for the anonymous *Particulars of the Life of John Hatfield*, published in 1803 in two numbers of R. S. Kirkby's *Wonderful and Scientific Museum; or Magazine of Remarkable Characters*. A novel, *James Hatfield and the Beauty of Buttermere: A Story of Modern Times*, by Henry Colburn, was published in 1841 with illustrations by Robert Cruikshank. Versions of the story were represented as melodrama and farce, these productions often bearing little relation to the facts, but keeping the sensation of the scandal alive. Southey, along with Charles and Mary Lamb, went to see a play called *Mary of Buttermere* not long before Hatfield's trial. Mary Lamb found the whole thing laughable, not least the stage set, which depicted 'mountains very like large haycocks, and a lake like nothing at all'.[24]

Book VII of Wordsworth's *The Prelude* describes the time the poet spent in London after his return from France. He recalled visits to shows where he saw 'Singers, Rope-dancers, Giants and Dwarfs, Clowns, Conjurors, Posture-Masters, Harlequins'. Poetic licence allowed him to include one performance that he could not have seen during this first youthful spell in London, since the events upon which it was based had not yet occurred. But it seems likely that at some point in his life Wordsworth did see performed:

> ... a Story drawn
> From our own ground, the Maid of Buttermere,
> And how the Spoiler came, 'a bold bad Man'
> To God unfaithful, Children, Wife and Home,
> And wooed the artless Daughter of the hills,
> And wedded her, in cruel mockery
> Of love and marriage bonds.[25]

The most recent fictional treatment of the story is Melvyn Bragg's 1987 novel *The Maid of Buttermere*, which is closely focused upon Mary's relationship with Hatfield, followed by the latter's denunciation and trial. When Coleridge wrote his articles for the *Morning Post*, the story of the Buttermere Beauty slipped the ropes which tethered it to a particular time and place. The story of an innocent beauty and a deceitful swindler could be played out against almost any backdrop. On the other hand, the most successful versions of the tale, including the novels by Colburn and Bragg, evoked the glassy expanses of the Cumbrian lakes and the mist-shrouded beauties of the enclosing fells. The landscape had been part of the story from the outset. As Norman Nicholson observed, the Buttermere story retained its appeal because it was an allegory in which Mary stood for both naturalness and beauty and also for uncorrupted human nature. The landscape in which she lived took on the aura of a classical Arcadia. Hatfield seemed like the harbinger of the new way of life, driven by economic imperatives, that would soon be disrupting lives, destroying old certainties and despoiling the landscape.

Hatfield's sort could only succeed in a society which was shot through with artificiality and mendacity. He seduced gullible women and flattered status-conscious men into lending him money which he never had any intention of repaying. Though he liked to cut a dash in Keswick, Scarborough or Tiverton, he was happiest in the coffee-houses of London, which were for him a sort of spiritual home. Significantly, when he was undergoing examination at Bow Street, his cause was taken up by the dandies known as the Bond Street Loungers, who affected admiration for his large black eyebrows, rolling eyes and ruddy complexion, and even tried to imitate the curious hitch in his walk. While Hatfield was condemned by many, there were others, not only in the fashionable clubs of London but even in the streets of Keswick, who were prepared to see him as a colourful adventurer and even as a champion of liberty.

The Lake District meanwhile was confirmed in its role as a national Eden. The ordinary countryfolk were seen as almost a race apart, as if they were Rousseau's noble savages and the 'impassable' hills had barricaded them against the vices of civilised society. The picturesque and the morally incorruptible were imaginatively entwined and Mary Robinson became a symbol of all that was pure, beautiful and wholesome.

In the 1810 edition of his *A Fortnight's Ramble*, Budworth added a note regretting that he had ever brought Mary into the public eye. 'We have heard that she is greatly altered in appearance,' he wrote, 'a careworn countenance depicting the agonies she had laboured under.' People in the area respected the dignified way in which she had dealt with her troubles and four years after Hatfield's hanging she married a farmer called Harrison from Uldale. By all accounts they lived a contented life, away from the glare of celebrity, and raised four children. Mary died in 1837 and is buried in the churchyard at Caldbeck.

Overleaf: Shafts of light, with a view towards Helm Crag and Easedale Tarn in the middle distance and the Langdale Pikes in the far distance

Brathay Hall (1808) by John Harden: an example of the
sort of architecture Wordsworth disliked

9

'Let Nature be all in all'

Wordsworth and the Origins of Landscape Conservation

'A SWEET MORNING,' DOROTHY WROTE in her journal on 6 May 1802, 'we have put the finishing stroke to our Bower & here we are sitting in the orchard. It is one o'clock. We are sitting upon a seat under the wall which I found my Brother Building up when I came to him with his apple . . .' As she sat in this cool, shady spot she noticed the lambs bleating in nearby fields, a cuckoo calling, the sounds of a neighbour chopping wood, the cackling of hens and the conversation of women at their doors. The plum and pear trees were in blossom, the stitchwort was just coming out, but the primroses were already past their prime. The setting Dorothy described so closely was the steep and stony little orchard garden which rose up the hillside immediately to the rear of Dove Cottage. Gardening was integral to the Wordsworths' lives there, and typically, in this snapshot, William is found in the middle of a construction project, while Dorothy's attention is drawn to the plants and flowers.

William and Dorothy were committed gardeners, whose shared philosophy reflected their approach to living appropriately within the landscape. In modern-day parlance they believed in 'treading lightly' upon the earth. This is nowhere more clear than in Dorothy's journal entry for 31 January 1802, where she describes the discovery of a wild strawberry growing from a rock. Dorothy was in the habit of gathering wild plants to embellish the garden, which included daffodils, daisies, primroses, lesser celandines, heartsease, marsh marigolds, purple and spotted orchids, snowdrops, geraniums and various mosses, lichens and ferns. The material was free, easy to look after and guaranteed the harmony of the garden with its environs. However, on this occasion she was overcome by guilt, not because she was taking anyone's property, but because the strawberry had an intrinsic right to remain: 'I uprooted it rashly, & felt as if I had been committing an outrage, so I planted it again – it will have a stormy life of it, but let it live if it can.'

The word 'ecology' could not have been part of the Wordsworths' vocabulary, since it was not coined until 1866 by the German biologist Ernst Haeckel. Nevertheless, their live-and-let-live approach to the natural world has strong resonances with ecological thinking today. It is significant that the Wordsworths did not enclose their garden at Dove Cottage, though De Quincey decided to put a stone wall around it during his later tenancy. He also chopped down the orchard, but otherwise the garden today closely resembles the one which William and Dorothy made, thanks to the restoration undertaken by the late George Kirkby, who was gardener and chief guide at the Wordsworth Trust from 1971. Their garden was contiguous with nature, not a place set apart. Pantheistic by inclination, Wordsworth saw something at work in both nature and the human mind and strove to express this harmony in his gardens as well as his poetry. Unlike 'Capability' Brown and his followers, his purpose was not to improve nature. Nature was her own best designer, and should be regarded as a teacher or mentor. Small adjustments might be needed to make a garden more accommodating to its human users, but these should be made 'in the spirit of Nature, with an invisible hand of art'. And the garden was a microcosm of the wider landscape, in which nature could also teach us how to dwell.

The case for Wordsworth as a landscape gardener was persuasively made in *Wordsworth and the Art of Landscape* (1968) by an American scholar called Russell Noyes.[1] Landscape gardening was the precursor of landscape architecture, a profession for which Noyes trained before turning to English literature, but to claim Wordsworth as a landscape architect would be an anachronism, since the first people to call themselves by this title professionally were Calvert Vaux and Frederick Law Olmsted, who used it in 1858 when submitting their winning entry for the competition to design New York City's Central Park; this was eight years after the poet's death. Nevertheless, I think Wordsworth was one of the spiritual and intellectual precursors of the modern profession, and that this view is supported by the range, scale and depth of his interests in landscape, which were never confined to the boundaries of a garden. Wordsworth's forays into gardening and travel writing reveal what can only be described as ecological insights, and this makes him a figure of considerable contemporary relevance. The importance of the Lake District to students of Romanticism is well established, but it was also the cradle for nascent ideas in landscape conservation and environmentalism.

Wordsworth's principal essays in gardening were the orchard garden he created at Dove Cottage, the terraced garden he developed at Rydal Mount and the winter garden that he designed in 1806 for the Beaumonts in a disused quarry in the grounds of Coleorton Hall in Leicestershire.[2] In their own gardens, he and Dorothy seem to have worked intuitively, making improvements as they went along, with William doing much of the physical work himself. At Coleorton, however, he worked more in the manner of a present-day landscape architect, producing a plan for others to follow, accompanied by a detailed written description sent in a letter to Lady Beaumont.

For all his originality of mind, Wordsworth's opinions about landscape were influenced by the dominant aesthetic of the day, which was the Picturesque. In 1810 Wordsworth and Beaumont paid a visit to one of the most influential gardens of the eighteenth century, the Leasowes, near Halesowen in the Midlands, which had been laid out by another poet, William Shenstone, between 1743 and his death in 1763. Shenstone's garden, the remains of which are now part of a public park, was one of the most visited and discussed gardens of the eighteenth century. Wordsworth was following in the footsteps of Gilpin and Gray and a host of other literary visitors. What made the Leasowes so significant was that it was a departure in taste, albeit one that had been initially forced upon Shenstone through lack of funds. Abandoning thoughts of making a formal garden, Shenstone turned his estate into a *ferme ornée*, an ornamental farm, by adding temples, statues, decorated urns and verses pasted on to screens. The whole thing grew gradually in response to the existing landscape. Features were linked by a circuit path and seats were placed strategically to take advantage of views within the estate and to the countryside beyond. Wordsworth was also influenced by two Hereford squires, Richard Payne Knight and Uvedale Price, who developed the theory of Picturesque gardening on their estates at Downton Castle and Foxley. Price, whom Wordsworth visited in 1810, thought that intricacy and variety were the hallmarks of Picturesque landscapes, and that they should also possess the objective qualities of roughness, irregularity and sudden variation.

By the time the Wordsworths moved to Rydal Mount, William was thoroughly steeped in Picturesque theory through his contact with Beaumont and Price, and at last the family had a garden of sufficient size to bring out their talents. They were still reeling from the deaths of Catherine and Tom, so the garden became a therapeutic focus offering meaningful labour,

Rydal Mount (1821) by William Green

healthy exercise and a creative venture in which everyone could share. In a letter to Mrs Clarkson, Dorothy wrote:

> We are all gardeners, especially Sara, who is mistress and superintendent of that concern. I am content to work under her – and Mary does her share, and sometimes we work very hard, and this is a great amusement to us though sad thoughts often come between. Thomas was a darling in a garden – our best helper – steady to his work – always pleased. God bless his memory.[3]

The overall plan was William's, though he never committed it to paper. A design in the mind is more flexible than one that has been set down. Steep slopes can often seem like a constraint, but here they offered Wordsworth the opportunity to construct long terraces, supported by little walls of native stone. The web of interconnected terraces at Rydal Mount made it the ideal place for the poet to walk and compose. Canon Rawnsley collected reminiscences of Wordsworth from elderly inhabitants who had once known him. One left an unforgettable description of the poet's practice:

I think I can see him at it now. He was ter'ble thrang with visitors and folks, you mun kna, at times, but if he could git awa fra them for a spell, he was out upon his gres walk; and then he would set hie heäd a bit forrad, and put his hands behint his back. And then he would start a bumming, and it was bum, bum, bum, stop; then bum, bum, bum, reet down till t'other end, and then he'd set down and git a bit o' paper and write a bit; and then he'd git up, and bum, bum, bum, and goa on bumming for long enough right down and back agean. I suppose, ya kna, the bumming helped him out a bit. However, his lips were always goan' whoale time he was on the gres walk.[+]

Wordsworth was considered a local authority on gardening matters and gave advice to various neighbours concerning their grounds, including Dr Thomas Arnold, the headmaster of Rugby School, who had bought a small property called Fox How to make into a summer home. He also assisted Mrs Eliza Fletcher, the widow of an Edinburgh lawyer, who bought the small farm of Lancrigg, beneath the slopes of Helm Crag, and Harriet Martineau, who took up residence at The Knoll in Ambleside and asked Wordsworth about the planting of her grounds. He was considered knowledgeable about the planting and maintenance of trees; famously, he set out the eight yew trees, transplanted from Loughrigg, in the churchyard at Grasmere, where they are still growing close to his grave. This informal consultancy appears to have been offered in a spirit of neighbourliness and friendship. Wordsworth did not see landscape design as a commercial enterprise.

All of this indicates an interest in the design and management of land which went well beyond the concerns of the domestic garden, but surprisingly it is in his *Guide through the District of the Lakes in the North of England*, first published in 1810, that Wordsworth revealed the depth of his concerns for the landscape and its management. It was originally written to accompany Joseph Wilkinson's *Select Views in Cumberland, Westmoreland, and Lancashire*, but was subsequently revised by the author to be published alone. Ultimately the *Guide* ran into five editions, each revised by Wordsworth, the last of which appeared in 1835. Its title page is addressed 'for the use of Tourists and Residents', which provides a clue to Wordsworth's motivation. The initial impulse to link with Wilkinson's collection of engravings might have been pecuniary, but Wordsworth's other reasons for wanting to write a guidebook become very clear in Section Three, which is subtitled 'Changes, and Rules of Taste for Preventing their Bad Effects'. Wordsworth claimed that in preparing the *Guide* 'it was the Author's principal wish to furnish a guide or companion for the *Minds* of Persons of taste, and feeling for Landscape, who might be inclined to explore the District of the Lakes with that degree of attention to which its beauty may fairly lay claim',[5] but he was equally concerned with the consequences of the Lake District's growing popularity. Many visitors wanted to build houses there and settle, at least for part of the year, on an island or a site overlooking a lake. Wordsworth deplored the taste of some of these settlers and wrote sections of the *Guide* in a defensive spirit.

Wordsworth would have understood the concept of 'environmental impact assessment', now a routine part of the planning process in Britain, which generally includes an assessment of the visual impact of new buildings and structures. There are many passages in the *Guide* where Wordsworth refers to the inappropriateness of some of the changes he has noticed. The two matters that irritated him most were unnatural plantations and incongruous architecture. For example, when describing St Herbert's Hermitage on Derwentwater, he complained that the whole island had been 'planted anew with Scots firs, left to spindle up by each other's side – a melancholy phalanx, defying the power of the winds and disregarding the regret of the spectator'.[6] By 'Scots firs' Wordsworth would have been referring to what we now call Scots pine (*Pinus sylvestris*). According to Richard Mabey's *Flora Britannica*, the Scots pine has not been native in England for about four thousand years. Nevertheless, Scots pine were frequently planted and often grew self-sown.[7] Wordsworth found the Scots pine unattractive in its youth, but admitted that when full grown it could become a noble tree and even planted some at Rydal Mount. Away from the immediate surroundings of a house, however, he thought that they were uncharacteristic aliens.

He saved his deepest opprobrium for the larch (*Larix decidua*), a tree introduced to Britain as long ago as 1620, and widely planted in the eighteenth century on Scottish estates. Although the larch has almost as much right to be considered native as the sycamore (*Acer pseudoplatanus*), also introduced from central Europe, though in the fifteenth or sixteenth century, Wordsworth could not abide it. 'In spring,' he grumbled, 'the larch becomes green long before the native trees; and its green is so peculiar and vivid, that, finding nothing to harmonise with it, wherever it comes forth, a disagreeable speck is produced. In summer, when all other trees are in their pride, it is of a dingy lifeless hue; in autumn of a spiritless unvaried yellow, and in winter it is still more lamentably distinguished from every other deciduous tree of the forest, for they only seem to sleep, but the larch appears absolutely dead.'[8]

Wordsworth's objections to the larch and to other exotics were aesthetic rather than scientific. His feelings about the larch become easier to understand when one considers that it was the species most associated with commercial forestry in his day. Many of his criticisms concern the unnatural shapes and textures of plantations. Commercial plantations do not have the age structure of native woodlands; the trees of the 'artificial planter . . . however well chosen and adapted to their several situations, must generally start all at the same time; and this necessity would of itself prevent that fine connection of parts, that sympathy and organization, if I may so express myself, which pervades the whole of a natural wood'.[9]

De Quincey recorded an occasion when Wordsworth, not knowing he was being observed by a group of forest labourers, got so worked up at the sight of larches planted when birches had been grubbed up that he poured out 'a litany of comminations and maledictions' and threw his hat at the odious intruders.[10]

There were other species which Wordsworth loved and hated to see go. In a letter to Beaumont, dated 10 November 1806, he railed against 'the barbarisers of our beautiful Lake-region' among whom was 'the extirpator of this beautiful shrub, or rather tree the Holly!'. He took some comfort that this man was not one of the locals, but a man from outside the area whose business was to make birdlime. 'You probably know,' he added in parentheses, 'that bird-lime is made of the bark of the Holly.'[11]

In the *Guide* Wordsworth was affronted by the 'gross transgressions' of the foresters, though he understood how a human inclination towards 'distinct ideas, and from the perception of order, regularity and contrivance' led them astray. He gave an example of that which he deplored, the hill of Dunmallet, at the foot of Ullswater, which

was once divided into different portions, by avenues of fir-trees, with a green and almost perpendicular lane descending down the steep hill through each avenue: – contrast this quaint appearance with the image of the same hill overgrown with self-planted wood, – each tree springing up in the situation best suited to its kind, and with that shape which the situation constrained or suffered it to take.[12]

His concern was shared by William Green, who wrote an eight-page discourse entitled 'A Few Observations with respect to the mode in which

Plantations ought to be Conducted', published in 1809. In his own guide-book Green complained angrily about the damage which bad planting could do, such as the 'frightful plantation of firs blotting out the pass on Wrynose'.[13] In remarks such as these Wordsworth and Green prefigured twentieth-century battles over afforestation.

Though Wordsworth had no access to the technical vocabulary of an ecological science yet to be invented, he demonstrated a pre-ecological understanding of natural processes (such as colonisation and succession) and an unerring eye for the patterns of nature. Contrasting the 'small patches and large tracts of larch plantations that are over-running the hillsides' he described the process by which woods and forests are formed in nature:

> Seeds are scattered indiscriminately by winds, brought by waters, and dropped by birds. They perish, or produce, according as the soil and situation upon which they fall are suited to them: and under the same dependence, the seedling or the sucker, if not cropped by animals, (which Nature is often careful to prevent by fencing about with brambles or other prickly shrubs) thrives, and the tree grows, sometimes single, taking its own shape without constraint, but for the most part compelled to conform itself to some law imposed upon it by its neighbours. From low and sheltered places, vegetation travels upwards to the more exposed, and the young plants are protected, and to a certain degree fashioned, by those that have preceded them. The continuous mass of foliage which would thus be produced, is broken by rocks, or by glades or open places, where the browsing of animals has prevented the growth of wood. As vegetation ascends, the winds begin also to bear their part in moulding the forms of the trees; but, thus mutually protected, trees, though not of the hardiest kind, are enabled to climb high up the mountains. Gradually, however, by the quality of the ground, and by increasing exposure, a stop is put to their ascent: the hardy trees only are left: those also, by little and little, give way – and a wild and irregular boundary is established, graceful in its outline, and never contemplated without some feeling, more or less distinct, of the powers of Nature by which it is imposed.[14]

Although Wordsworth was under the sway of Picturesque theory, he frequently transcended the purely visual fixations of the movement's principal adherents. It is true that Wordsworth, like Price, admired the Picturesque qualities of roughness, irregularity and sudden variation. What is abundantly clear from the passage just quoted, however, is that Wordsworth understood the processes through which such qualities came into being. The treed landscape described by Wordsworth is not a static scene, but a living community of plants and animals interacting in ways that are both competitive and cooperative. The wild and irregular treeline, so different from the straight edge of an artificial plantation, is the result of complex interactions between soils, ground conditions, altitude and microclimate, not just the sort of artful effect that might be dreamed up by a painter.

Wordsworth understood the limitations of the Picturesque and could be scornful of 'picturesque travellers' and 'scene hunters'. As he explained in a letter to Jacob Fletcher, his purpose was to teach the Tourists 'to look through the clear eye of understanding as well as through the hazy one of vague Sensibility'.[15]

Wordsworth also avoided another Picturesque trap, which was the urge to depopulate the view. The idea of landscape improvement had not stopped short of removing entire villages if they detracted from a prospect or pricked a landowner's pride of ownership. On the other hand, a dilapidated hovel or two might add to the picturesque qualities of a scene, so that poverty became an aesthetic bonus. Wordsworth, to his credit, did not people his poems with marginalised people like gypsies, crippled soldiers and vagrants for mere picturesque effect, but in order to give such people a voice.

One of the problems faced by ecologically inclined designers today is that true ecosystems are often too messy for the public taste. Wordsworth seems to have run into the same attitude. A respectable neighbour at Rydal Mount once told him that he should 'sweep all that dirty black stuff from that wall'. The dirty black stuff in question was actually a bank of earth which the poet describes as 'exquisitely decorated with ivy, flowers, moss, and ferns, such as grow of themselves in like places; but the mere notion of fitness associated with a trim garden prevented, in this instance, all sense of the spontaneous bounty and delicate care of nature'. Wordsworth also mentions a beautiful rock immediately below his house, adorned with ancient oaks, flowers and shrubs. He pokes fun at the Manchester tradesman who told him 'What a nice place this would be, if that ugly lump were out of the way.'[16]

When discussing his own gardens, or giving advice to others about landscape design, Wordsworth was happy to invoke the hand of nature. His advice to those who owned or designed ornamental grounds was 'to keep as much out of sight as possible; let Nature be all in all, taking care that everything done by man shall be in the way of being adopted by her'.[17]

Later in life, Wordsworth's pantheistic tendency gave way to a more conventional Christianity, in which nature is seen as the handiwork of God. When the invisible hand of Art is following Nature, it is also emulating the work of the Creator. In this way Wordsworth could claim an ultimate transcendental authority for his opinions on the aesthetics of landscape.

Believing, as he did, that nature was her own best designer, he had a particular dislike of artificially engineered lake shores. In the *Guide* he wrote:

> Winds and waves work with a careless and graceful hand: and should they in some places carry away a portion of the soil, the trifling loss would be amply compensated by the additional spirit, dignity and loveliness, which these agents and powers of nature would soon communicate to what was left behind.[18]

Once again Wordsworth's comments have contemporary resonance. Natural forces, left to their own purposes, generally produce landscapes which human beings find aesthetically satisfying, but the environment also constrains the sorts of human developments that are wise or possible. Wordsworth was aware of the ever-present danger that human interventions or additions were going to spoil the aesthetic produced by natural processes. The risk was at its least in the case of vernacular architecture, whose forms had developed in a gradual evolution which had fitted them to their place in the world. Thus Wordsworth was able to take a positive view of the dry-stone walls that criss-crossed the Lakeland valleys and often climbed high up their sides. 'When first erected,' he wrote, 'these stone fences must have little disfigured the face of the country.'[19] Nowadays we would recognise the walls themselves as part of a cultural landscape, artefacts that have accrued cultural and heritage values and are therefore worth conserving in their own right.

Similarly, Wordsworth admired vernacular cottages, saying that 'these humble dwellings remind the contemplative spectator of a production of nature'. Their design has been refined so slowly over time that they seem to belong entirely to the place in which they were created. The cottages which Wordsworth admired – and we still admire – can be said 'to have grown rather than to have been erected; - to have risen, by an instinct of their own, out of their native rock'.[20]

Gutterscale (1809) by William Green: the type of vernacular
architecture admired by Wordsworth

Wordsworth was most aggravated by human interventions that did not
seem to be subservient to nature. For Wordsworth these were more obvious
when they were additions rather than subtractions. In terms of architectural
additions, he disliked all that was obtrusive or ostentatious. In the absence of
any planning controls, the principal check upon new development was the use
of old manorial powers by existing landowners. Although 'greenfield' projects
were still unusual at this time, houses were often rebuilt on, or adjacent to,
previously occupied sites, but the fashion for grand houses commanding fine
views meant that these stood out in a way that earlier buildings had not.
Wordsworth was well enough versed in the Picturesque to understand 'the
craving for prospect', indeed he expressed surprise that some of those who
built failed to take advantage of the wonderful views available, yet he regretted that this taste had become immoderate and thus 'rendered it impossible
that buildings, whatever might have been their architecture, should in most
instances be ornamental to the landscape; rising as they do from the summits
of naked hills in staring contrast to the snugness and privacy of the ancient
houses'.[21] He not only thought that such ill-sited houses were intrusive, but
also that they would probably be uncomfortable, for unlike ancient cottages
they had not been located in convenient and well-sheltered positions.

Wordsworth was not alone in his opinions. Green loved old buildings and packhorse bridges, and lamented modernisation. Coleridge, on his first walking tour of the District, back in 1799, had been appalled by some of the houses around Windermere, including Brathay Hall, which had been rebuilt between 1794 and 1796 and was the most conspicuous property at the head of the lake. This was the house that the Hardens would take over in 1806, but at the time it belonged to a Mr Law. In his journal Coleridge did not mince words:

> Mr. Law amid the awful mountains with his twenty cropped trees, four stumps standing upend on the trunk of each, all looking like strange devils with perpendicular horns. Head of the Lake of Wyandermere: Mr. Law's white palace – a bitch! Matthew Harrison's house where Llandaff lived – these and more among the mountains! Mrs. Taylor's house! The damned scoundrel on the right hand with his house and a barn built to represent a chapel: his name is Partridge from London and 'tis his Brother's cowpen. This *fowl* is a stocking weaver by trade, have mercy on his five wits.[22]

Dorothy became similarly agitated when writing in her journal about Belle Isle after a boat trip to the island in June 1802:

> The shrubs have been cut away in some parts of the island. I observed to the Boatman that I did not think it improved – he replied – 'We think it is for one could hardly see the house before.' It seems to me to be, however, no better than it was. They have made no natural glades, it is merely a lawn with a few miserable young trees standing as if they were half starved. There are no sheep no cattle upon these lawns. It is neither one thing or another – neither natural nor wholly cultivated & artificial which it was before, & that great house! Mercy upon us! If it could be concealed it would be well for all who are not pained to see the pleasantest of earthly spots deformed by man. But it cannot be covered. Even the tallest of our old oak trees would not reach to the top of it.[23]

Wordsworth and his circle were not large landowners, so their influence upon what might be built or not built was indirect, but they could proselytise their taste through their writings. Their opinion of what was appropriate or inappropriate would become the mainstream view; indeed, it would ultimately be given the backing of the law. At the time, all they could do was exhort, complain and occasionally rant.

House on Belle Isle, Windermere (1783) by Peter Crosthwaite

Wordsworth's dislike of obtrusive additions to the landscape led him to write harshly about the practice of whitewashing vernacular farmhouses (even though Dove Cottage had itself been whitewashed). As before, he was able to understand the motivation of those he criticised. Just as geometrical plantations revealed a love of order, so whitewashed buildings carried associations of cleanliness and neatness. Nevertheless, he argued that 'five or six white houses, scattered over a valley, by their obtrusiveness, dot the surface, and divide it into triangles, or other mathematical figures, haunting the eye, and disturbing that response which might otherwise be perfect'.[24] Natural stone does not, of course, have these disadvantages. If people must apply render to their cottages, Wordsworth argued, they should not paint it white, but use a more muted colour close to that of the native rock. This whole campaign now seems faintly ridiculous, since white cottages have become an accepted part of the cultural heritage, as likely to feature on postcards and in watercolour paintings as those whose walls are green-grey slate, but Wordsworth's objection is still intelligible and there would, no doubt, be an outcry if some residents developed a taste for painting their homes bright pink or lurid yellow.[25]

*

Dove Cottage (1800) by Amos Green

Marxist critics have painted Wordsworth as someone who abandoned the radicalism of his youth to become a crusty bulwark of the Tory establishment, opposed to all social change, someone who was aware of the distress around him, but unwilling to countenance the structural changes needed to provide relief and justice. And it is easy to make a parallel between the political conservatism of his later years and the preservationist mindset which dominated his opinions about the landscape. One of Rawnsley's respondents said of Wordsworth that 'he 'ud never pass folks draining, or ditching, or walling a cottage, but what he'd stop and say, "Eh dear, but it's a pity to move that stean, and doant ya think"'. Rawnsley asked the reason for Wordsworth's opposition. His interviewee replied: 'Well, well, he couldn't bide to see t'faäce o' things altered ye kna. It was all along of him that Grasmere folks have their Common open. Ye may ga now reet up t'sky ower Grizedale. Wi'out liggin' leg to t'fence, and all through him. He said it was a pity to enclose it and run walls over it, and the quality backed him, and he won.'[26]

Wordsworth's ethos would be evoked in later years by those who campaigned for the Lake District to become a National Park and it still underlies the activities of conservation groups like the Friends of the Lake

District, but even lovers of the Lake District sometimes see the poet as tainted by his reactionary politics. Thus, in 1997, Robert Gambles, a member of the Executive Committee of the Friends, could write that Wordsworth's views on the changes taking place in the landscape in his time 'were often no more than prejudices fraught with snobbery, conservatism and inconsistency'.[27]

In the world of literary scholarship, meanwhile, opinion about Wordsworth seems to have shifted again. In 1991 a Professor of English called Jonathan Bate published *Romantic Ecology*, a book which offered another way of reading Wordsworth. It was wrong, Bate argued, to see Wordsworth's attitudes in terms of Red or Blue – politically Wordsworth could be regarded as a Green. Although Bate did not say as much, it might be that Wordsworth's attitudes shifted during his lifetime from 'Red-Green' to 'Blue-Green'. Conservatism has its own internal tensions between those who endorse *laissez-faire* free enterprise, and those, like Wordsworth, who resist what they see as damaging change, but there is force in Bate's contention that the environmentalism of Wordsworth's later years was a continuation of the radicalism of his youth, not a reaction against it.

Overleaf: Blencathra summit

Helvellyn, Striding Edge (1912)

10

'A pleasant sort of fear'

The Birth of Fellwalking

SHEPHERDS HAVE BEEN STRIDING the fells for generations – it was from their ranks that the first guides were drawn – but if we draw a distinction between walking in the line of work and walking for pleasure, it is natural to ask where this recreation came from. Who was the Lake District's first fellwalker?

In this form the question cannot be answered – the earliest walker probably left no traces – but we can pinpoint the earliest documented ascents of particular mountains. The summit that first attracted attention, by virtue of its proximity to Keswick, was Skiddaw. William Nicholson, later Bishop of Carlisle, entered into his diary for 20 May 1684 that he had climbed Skiddaw with some friends and that the top was already a well-known point of view. Five years later the geographer John Adams built a hut on the fell to house his telescopes. By the time Hutchinson climbed the mountain in 1773 there must have been a well-worn path to the crest; nevertheless, he employed a guide who did not distinguish himself by his courage. When a thunderstorm suddenly blew up, he threw himself to the ground in a funk, while the rest of the party revelled in the sublimity of the event. The surveyor John Houseman, who climbed the fell in two hours in 1789, recommended ascending on foot rather than on horseback, and advocated the hire of a guide, though he and his companions did not take one, then got lost and became anxious about their chances of survival if overwhelmed by 'atmospheric obscurity'.[1]

The most celebrated ascent of Skiddaw was undertaken by the gothic novelist Ann Radcliffe in 1794. Provoking a pleasant sort of fear was her stock in trade, so it is not surprising that she found a little terror along the way:

Not a tree, or bush appeared on Skiddaw, not even a stone wall any where broke the simple greatness of its lines. Sometimes, we looked into chasms, where the torrent, heard roaring long before it was seen, had worked itself into a deep channel, and fell from ledge to ledge, foaming and shining amidst the dark rock. The streams are sublime from the length and precipitancy of their course, which, hurrying the sight of them into the abyss, act, as it were, in sympathy upon the nerves, and, to save ourselves from following, we recoil from the view with involuntary horror.[2]

Radcliffe found the air on the summit 'boisterous, intensely cold and difficult to be inspired, although the day was below warm and serene'.[3] The novelist ascended the mountain on horseback, but on the top she met an old farmer who, though he had passed his whole life within view of the hill, had climbed it for the first time. He was sheltering 'under the lee of an heaped up pile of slates, formed by the customary contributions of one from every visitor'.[4] This early description of a cairn suggests a considerable pedestrian traffic on the summit, while the presence of the elderly 'statesman' shows that the taste for views was not confined to educated visitors.

Joseph Budworth's *A Fortnight's Ramble* was the first published pedestrian tour. He was not intimidated by a steep path, although he did have a tendency to exaggerate. He described a descent in the Langdale Pikes 'across a sward nearly perpendicular, and of immoderate height'. Despite the reassurances of his guide, Paul Postlethwaite, a lad of fifteen who said he had been down the path a hundred times, Budworth could only proceed after tying up his right eye so that he could not see the drop. Then he held out his hazel stick to the boy and was drawn across the slope. This graphic episode highlights the disparity between the visitors and the locals. Budworth was braver than most of the tourists, but he was still unmanned by a steep gradient. For the locals, who used the high passes in all but the very worst weather, a rugged path held no fears; indeed, the most popular pastime among them was to follow fox hounds on foot across slopes that would have locked the knees of Budworth or Gray in terror.

Wordsworth's legs, so De Quincey tells us, were 'pointedly condemned by all female connoisseurs' but they were also 'serviceable legs beyond the average standard of human requisition'.[5] De Quincey estimated that Wordsworth must have traversed a distance of 175,000 to 180,000 miles on those legs, though he did not reveal his calculations. This exertion, said the confessed opium-eater, stood Wordsworth 'in the stead of alcohol and all other stimulants whatever to the animal spirits'.

Several of Wordsworth's lengthy walks have already featured in earlier chapters: the excursion to France with Robert Jones and the later trip to Wales, the tour that introduced Coleridge to the Lake District and the epic walk from Richmond to Kendal with Dorothy. There was also an earlier journey with Dorothy, when the pair hiked from Kendal to Keswick via Grasmere to attend to the ailing Raisley Calvert at Windy Brow. Once settled at Grasmere they thought nothing of stuffing a bit of cold mutton into their pockets and setting out over Dunmail Raise to be with the Coleridges and Southeys, or going over Kirkstone to visit the Clarksons at Eusemere. Distance did not daunt them: in her forties Dorothy could walk twenty miles in an afternoon. In 1805 William climbed Helvellyn from Patterdale in the company of Sir Walter Scott and Sir Humphry Davy. In 1830 he was still going strong; he crossed Kirkstone with Mary, who rode up the hill, but, as William wrote proudly to his nephew, 'down hill we tripped it away side by side charmingly. Think of that, my dear Charles, for a Derby and Joan of sixty each!!'[6]

Despite all the evidence in diaries and correspondence showing that Wordsworth liked to get on to the tops, this was not the impression gained by his neighbours in Rydal. When Canon Rawnsley asked the owner of Nab Cottage (where Hartley Coleridge had once been tenant) about Wordsworth's walking habits, he received the following reply: 'Well, well, he was ter'ble fond of going along under Loughrigg and ower by t'Redbank, but he was niver nowt of a mountaineer, allus kep' aboot t'roads.'[7] This impression was confirmed by a sixty-five-year-old half farmer, half hotel keeper from Rydal who, as a boy, had made deliveries of butter to Rydal Mount:

> He was a gey good walker, an' for a' he hed latterly a pony and phaeton, I nevver yance seed him in a conveyance in t'whole o' my time. But he was nivver a mountain man. He wad gae a deal by Pelter-bridge and round by Red Bank, but he was maist terr'ble fond o' under t'Nab, and by t'auld high road to t'Swan Inn and back, and verra often came as far as Dungeon Ghyll.[8]

It is difficult to square these remarks with what we know of the poet. Rawnsley's interviewees were elderly and when young would have known an equally aged Wordsworth, and they would have encountered him more often in the lanes than they ever did upon the fells. They were probably making another point, too – that although Wordsworth lived among them, he was separated by class and occupation; he was never really one of them, not a mountain man.

What all of them agreed was that Wordsworth liked to be outdoors and that his often distant manner had something to do with the way he composed his poems. The lanes and valley paths served Wordsworth, like the terraces of his garden, as an outdoor study. The same respondent observed:

> Noa, noa, he was quite an open-air man was Wudsworth: studied a deal aboot t'roads. He wasn't particlar fond of gitten up early, but did a deal of study efter breakfast, and a deal efter tea. Walked t'roads efter dark, he wad, a deal, between his tea and supper, and efter. Not a verra conversable man, a mumblin' and stoppin', and seein' nowt nor neabody.[9]

Southey liked to walk too, but characteristically the bibliophile claimed that he could walk at 3 mph with his nose in a book, but that his speed went up to 4 mph when he was not reading. De Quincey likewise was a considerable pedestrian in his own right. As a destitute youth he had toured North Wales, often having to sleep under the stars and subsisting for days on berries gathered from the hedgerows.

It was Coleridge, however, lacking the discipline of Wordsworth or Southey, who threw himself into fellwalking with the greatest energy – even, indeed, abandon. Soon after arriving at Greta Hall he launched out upon walks in all directions from his new base. On 14 August 1800 he recorded an ascent of Skiddaw where, while scratching his name on a piece of slate at the summit, he was recognised by a 'lean-expression-faced man' who exclaimed, 'Coleridge! I lay my life that is the *poet Coleridge!*'[10] On 24 August he walked to Latrigg with Sara and young Hartley at sunset with Walla Crag standing out in purple-red, Torrent Crag in maroon and the lake a deep purple-blue. The next day he was up Blencathra (Saddleback, as he called it), lying down to better appreciate the view of Thirlmere (which he knew as Withburne Water). And so it continued. His notebooks from this period are brimful of fresh, accurate and evocative observations which shimmer with colour and atmosphere. Sometimes they are almost scientific in their detail, as in the description of a waterfall on Blencathra: 'For the first eight or nine feet it falls perpendicular, water-colour, then meets rock

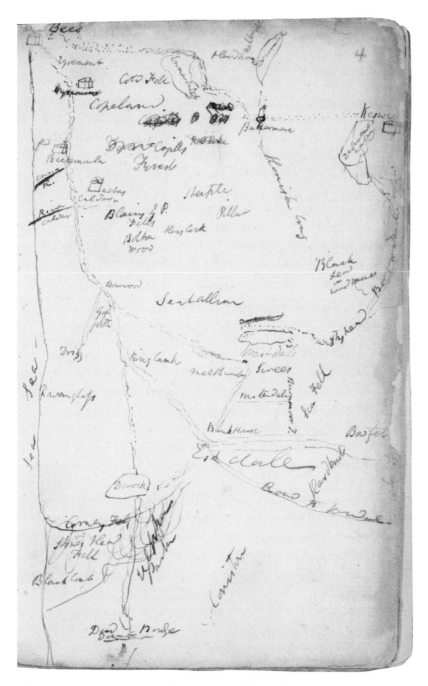

Diary page showing a route taken by Samuel Taylor Coleridge in August 1802

and rushes down in a steep slope, all foam, till the last two feet when the
rock ceases but the water preserves the same colour and inclination as if it
were there.'[11]

Coleridge could be reckless, but he also took his walking seriously. To
be sure that he had well-fitting boots, he had casts made of his feet and
he treated the leather with a mixture of two parts mutton suet, four parts
hog's lard and one part Venice turpentine, which he applied warm so that it
would soak in.[12] Fellwalkers will recognise an ancestor of modern dubbins
and waxes.

On Sunday 1 August 1802 Coleridge wrapped a shirt, cravat, two pairs
of stockings, some paper, half a dozen pens, a book of German poems, his
nightcap and a little tea and sugar in a natty green oilskin, neatly squared,
and put it all into his net knapsack. Then he pulled a broom apart to create
a stout walking stick and set out on his most adventurous solo walk in the
Lake District.

Four days later he sat down on the top of Scafell to put the finishing
touches to a long letter to Sara Hutchinson, describing his route and experiences thus far. He had walked by Buttermere, taking the path by Scale
Force which had thwarted Budworth in winter, then on to Floutern Tarn
and Ennerdale. After visiting St Bees Head, which was a disappointment,
he headed back into the mountains via Wastwater, where he was impressed
by screes 'as steep as the meal new ground from the miller's spout'. From
Wasdale Head he scaled Scafell, 'believed by the shepherds here to be higher
than either Helvellyn or Skiddaw'. At a stone table, sheltering from a fierce
wind, he penned the last sentence of his Scafell letter: 'I must now drop
down, how I may, into Eskdale – that lies under to my right – the upper part
of it the wildest and savagest surely of all the vales that were ever seen from
the top of an English mountain, and the lower part the loveliest.'[13]

These could easily have been the last words that Coleridge ever wrote.
He told Sara the story of his descent from Scafell in a second letter written
from Taw House in Eskdale on 6 August, but an account of this adventure
rightly belongs in the annals of rock-climbing rather than fellwalking and
must be deferred until a later chapter. There was no third letter to Sara
relating the rest of the walk, but the poet's notebooks describe a relatively uneventful passage through Eskdale to Devoke Water, then on to
Ulpha, Torver and Coniston, before completing the circuit via Hawkshead
to Grasmere. By 10 August he was back at Greta Hall writing again to
Sara. He had been away for nine days, spent or given away all his spare

cash, worn out his boots and torn the knee of his pantaloons, which cost sixpence to have patched.

Although Coleridge's health was deteriorating, it does not seem to have stopped him walking. The year 1803 saw his extraordinary breaka-way pedestrian tour of Scotland, and in January 1804 he recorded a walk from Grasmere to Kendal 'through heavy hot air and the latter half of the journey through drizzle', arriving at five o'clock in the evening. He stopped only once, for lunch, and estimated that he had covered nineteen miles in five hours. The distance was actually sixteen miles, but this was still a good pace for an ailing man about to seek restoration in warmer climes.[14]

This was not quite the end of Coleridge's career as a walker. He returned from Malta, no fitter and a lot fatter, but in the interval, while he was lodging with the Wordsworths at Allan Bank and working on *The Friend*, he regularly walked from Grasmere to Penrith over Kirkstone Pass to deliver copy to his printer. After Coleridge's return to London and the rift between the poets we hear no more about him as fellwalker, but for ten years this passionate man had outwalked even Wordsworth.

The Lake Poets were not the inventors of pedestrianism, but they gave it a tremendous boost. Rebecca Solnit rightly traces the origins of the English love of taking a stroll to the landscape gardens of the eighteenth century. She says that Wordsworth was not so much the founding father of walking for pleasure, but that he acted as the fulcrum or catalyst that transformed walking in the park or garden into rambling in the countryside.[15]

From its beginning fellwalking was not a male-only pastime, though William Green expressed his sympathy for women who were forced by 'an excess of outdoor ceremony' to wear cumbersome clothes which prevented them from leaping from rock to rock with the celerity of the indigenous sheep.[16] Dorothy and Mary Wordsworth were both walkers, as was Sara Hutchinson, but they were more than matched by the Smith sisters of Coniston: Elizabeth, Kitty and Juliet.

The Smith family arrived in Patterdale in 1880, but two years later moved to Townson Ground on the north-east shore of Coniston Water. They became friendly with Thomas Wilkinson, a Quaker farmer at Yanwath on the banks of the River Eamont. Wilkinson dabbled in landscape gardening (he laid out many of the paths at Lowther) and agreed to work on their Coniston property. He also liked to walk the fells and he would often go in the company of the Smith girls. It is through his *Tours of British Mountains*, published in 1824, that we know so much about their fearlessness.

Elizabeth is the sister who is most remembered, partly because she was a notable philologist and translator, but also because she succumbed to consumption and died when she was only twenty-nine. She spent her last days in a tent on the lawn to get the benefit of fresh air. Later a house called Tent Lodge was built on the spot and this, in later years, would serve as a holiday home for the Tennysons, where they were visited by Matthew Arnold, Edward Lear and Charles Dodgson, among others.

The Smith girls loved to be out of doors. Elizabeth had mastered the oars and would take sightseeing visitors out on the lake. She was also agile on the mountains. In Patterdale she had once taken her sketchbook and clambered among the rocks beside Aira Force, going a little too far and getting herself cragfast on the brink of a chasm. De Quincey, who milked this story for all it was worth, suggested that she was on the point of leaping when she called upon God and was answered by a vision of her sister, clad in a white muslin morning robe, who guided her to safety. When she got home she found that her sister had not left the house.[17]

Wilkinson climbed the Langdale Pikes with his 'intrepid maids' and confessed that he was the first to show anything like fear, while the adventurous Elizabeth broke away from the rest and 'winding round the corner of a rock, presently ascended out of sight'. Wilkinson was alarmed: 'I knew not whether she might be clambering up the cliffs above us, or falling down the precipices below.'[18] Elizabeth had missed her way again, but with no serious consequences. On another occasion he declined an invitation to climb Helvellyn in winter, fearing 'wreaths of snow and sheets of ice', but the girls laughingly told him that they had already climbed it without a guide. Indeed, they had enjoyed the climb so much that two of them had repeated it the following day.[19]

Elizabeth Smith and Coleridge both had their heart-pausing moments on the fells, but a less fortunate Laker, Charles Gough, met his end on Striding Edge. Gough was a twenty-one-year-old Manchester-born artist who set out from Patterdale on 17 April 1805 and was never seen alive again. His body was found by shepherds three months later, but what captured the public imagination most was that his dog Foxey was found alive beside his body. Initial reports were misleading. The *Carlisle Journal* of 27 July 1805 suggested that Gough had frozen to death while sketching, and that his spaniel bitch had pupped in a furze bush nearby and offered the grisly interpretation that the dog had torn the clothes from her master's body and stripped him to a perfect skeleton.

Wordsworth and Scott, who visited the supposed scene of the tragedy, both wrote poems on the subject, presenting Foxey as a loyal companion who would not leave her master's side, while Christopher North suggested that ravens had been responsible for picking the bones clean. Then, in 1829, Sir Edwin Landseer painted *Attachment*, a typically mawkish portrait of Foxey beside the body on a ledge above a yawning abyss.

In its many iterations the story became more and more contested. Where exactly had Gough died? Had he fallen to his death? Was Foxey a spaniel or, as Landseer depicted her, a terrier? Might Gough even have had two dogs with him that day? Canon Rawnsley, turning sleuth, tried to get to the bottom of the matter, reviewing accounts of the accident and interviewing old shepherds in Patterdale. No one he spoke to thought badly of Foxey – 'a dog wad nivver dea sic a thing' – and it was clear that Gough had slipped to his death. In his pockets were a gold watch, some fishing tackle, a silver pencil and two Claude lenses, the latter proving that he was, indeed, the first martyr to Picturesque enthusiasm. His skull was found yards from his skeleton and there was a hat, split in two by a fall on to rocks. In 1891, under the instruction of Rawnsley, a memorial stone was taken up the mountain on a sledge and erected on the edge of the summit, above the path to Striding Edge.

If the Gough story gave Striding Edge a fearful reputation it did nothing to halt the popularity of walking in the hills. 'I will clamber through the clouds and exist,'[20] wrote John Keats to the artist Haydon before his Lake District visit of 1818. He managed to get up Skiddaw, though – ironically enough – mist prevented an ascent of Helvellyn. Even Charles Dickens and Wilkie Collins, neither of them hearty outdoor types, had a go. In the autumn of 1857 they climbed Carrock Fell, one of the summits 'back o' Skiddaw'. It was so wet that they had difficulty persuading anyone to be their guide, though the innkeeper at Hesket Newmarket ultimately agreed. Collins, 'with nothing but a packet of clammy gingerbread nuts in his pocket by way of refreshment', got wet through and wondered why he had left London, 'where there are nice short walks in level public gardens'.[21]

While literary types strode about the hills of Cumberland and Westmorland entertaining fine thoughts, conditions had become much worse in the cities of the industrial north, where workers were enslaved to the mill hooter

Attachment (1829) by Edwin Landseer

and the factory bell. Working a seventy-hour week gave factory hands little time for any sort of recreation, never mind trips to distant mountains. The stopping up of footpaths and enclosure of much common land also meant that there was precious little recreational space in the towns. In the

1760s, when the first tourists arrived in the Lake District, the population of Manchester was around 18,000. By the turn of the century, when the Wordsworths were settling into Dove Cottage, it had risen to 40,000 and by 1830 it exceeded 180,000. All building was in the hands of the private speculator, and sanitation was still medieval. Among the more comfortable classes there was not just a distaste for the poor, but a real fear of revolution. At the brutal Peterloo Massacre of 1819 in Manchester cavalry dispersed a meeting for parliamentary reform, killing about fifteen peaceful protesters. At the same time, reformers had made the connection between lack of recreational opportunity and the 'debasing pleasures' of the gin parlour and the public house.

In response to these conditions, Parliament set up in 1833 the Select Commission on Public Walks, which surveyed the accessible open space in major towns and cities of England. While London had the Royal Parks, none of these was in the East End or south of the Thames, while the cities of the north had no parks at all. The Commission took a paternalistic view; parks would provide the workers with fresh air and exercise and thus improve their health. Contact with nature would be morally improving and would keep them out of the alehouse. At the same time, a mixing of the classes in outdoor space would help to ease social tensions. If parks could offer all this, some progressive thinkers began to imagine the benefits which excursions into the countryside might bring to people generally confined to the noisesome dirt of the factory and town. The Lake District was suitably located to provide these advantages to the workers of Lancashire.

Overleaf: Morning light on Ullswater from Pooley Bridge

Railway at Grange-over-Sands (1929)

11

'Speak, passing winds'

The Protest over Railways

KNOWING THAT WORDSWORTH COULD be upset by the shifting of a boulder or the felling of a tree, it is not hard to imagine his distress when he first heard of plans to engineer a railway line through the heart of the Lake District. Shares were advertised in the *Westmorland Gazette* of 31 August 1844 for a company that proposed to build a line to Low Wood, at the head of Windermere.

In a letter to the editor of the *Morning Post*, dated 9 December 1844, Wordsworth argued that the area had no need for the railway: 'manufactures are trifling; mines it has none, and its quarries are either wrought out or superseded; the soil is light and the cultivatable parts of the country are very limited; so that it has little to send out, and little has it also to receive. Summer TOURISTS (and the very word precludes the notion of a railway) it has in abundance . . . The staple of the district is, in fact, its beauty and its character of seclusion.'[1]

He argued that access was already easy. There were existing railways within four miles of Ullswater, and if anyone wanted to command a view of the whole of Windermere they only had to climb one of the eminences within eight or nine miles of Kendal.

But the argument which followed is out of step with the democratic kilter of our own times, and a long way from the radicalism of Wordsworth's own youth. 'There is nothing innate about the taste for picturesque scenery,' he asserted, reminding his readers that once no one appreciated mountains. It was a refined taste that had to be cultivated gradually. Wordsworth even dragged his fellow poet Robert Burns into the argument: 'He lived in Nithsdale, where he was in daily sight of Skiddaw, yet he never crossed the Solway for a better acquaintance with that mountain.'[2] If the sight of Skiddaw did not appeal to Burns, what hope was there for a Manchester mechanic?

In a second letter to the same newspaper, Wordsworth elaborated upon his concerns. The railway itself would cause damage by 'its scarifications, its intersections, its noisy machinery, its smoke, and swarms of pleasure-hunters, most of them thinking that they do not fly fast enough through the country which they have come to see'.[3] The second part of this sentence reveals the poet's real fears. He might have felt sympathy for the common man, but when it came to the Lake District he did not want proletarian hordes invading his sanctuary.

In the first letter he worried that the directors of the railway companies would devise entertainments to tempt the humbler classes to leave their homes: 'we should have wrestling matches, horse and boat races without number, and pot-houses and beer-shops would keep pace with these excitements and recreations, most of which might too easily be had elsewhere'.[4]

He was alarmed by reports that some of the 'affluent benevolent manufacturers of Yorkshire and Lancashire' were entertaining 'the thought of sending, at their own expense, large bodies of their workmen, by railway, to the banks of Windermere'. 'Surely those gentlemen will think a little more,' he wrote, 'before they put such a scheme into practice. The rich man cannot benefit the poor, nor the superior the inferior, by anything that degrades him. Packing men off after this fashion, for holiday entertainment, is, in fact, treating them like children.'[5]

Reading these desperately argued letters today, one has the sense that Wordsworth knew that he was on the losing side of the dispute. He was ranged against three sets of opponents: speculators and developers, technologists and believers in progress and 'those persons who are ever ready to step forward in what appears to be the cause of the poor'. He salved his own conscience by convincing himself that excursions to the Lakes would not benefit the industrial classes, because they had not developed the necessary aesthetic sensibilities to be able to appreciate what they might see. Though these arguments now seem insufferably elitist and indefensible, Wordsworth can be given credit for stating succinctly the dilemma presented by all tourism: when many people go looking for beauty and tranquillity, their search can destroy the very qualities for which they are hunting. 'Would not this,' asks Wordsworth, 'be pretty much like the child's cutting up his drum to learn where the sound came from?'[6]

Wordsworth also expressed his opposition to the railway in a sonnet:

On the Projected Kendal and Windermere Railway

Is there no nook of English ground secure
From rash assault? Schemes of retirement sown
In youth, and 'mid the busy world kept pure
As when their earliest flowers of hope were blown,
Must perish; – how can they this blight endure?
And must he too the ruthless change bemoan
Who scorns a false utilitarian lure
'Mid his paternal fields at random thrown?
Baffle the threat, bright Scene, from Orrest-head
Given to the pausing traveller's rapturous glance:
Plead for thy peace, thou beautiful romance
Of nature; and, if human hearts be dead,
Speak, passing winds; ye torrents, with your strong
And constant voice, protest against the wrong.[7]

In August 1845 Wordsworth wrote to his nephew Christopher bemoaning the fact that a railway was being driven past the remains of Furness Abbey. 'Many of the trees which embowered the ruin have been felled to make way for this pestilential nuisance,' he complained, but he was even more worried about the surveyors he had seen in the Vale of Grasmere, who were at work on 'a line meditated to pass through Rydal Park and immediately behind Rydal Mount'.[8]

When it came to railways, landowners carefully balanced their interests. Though many disliked the idea of tracks across their property, there was money to be made through preference shares and hikes in the value of land. Although shares in the Windermere railway were fully subscribed within three weeks of advertisement, strongly supported by the Lancashire businessmen who were moving into the area, reaction rapidly set in and a committee of concerned local landowners was formed, with Professor Wilson of Elleray taking the chair. He stood to lose his sense of rural retirement and tranquillity, as did the owners of several neighbouring villas, including Lord Bradford and Messrs Dunlop of Holehird and Benson of Dove Nest. These men came together to fight for their own interests and Wordsworth added his name to their cause. The objectors complained to the Board of Trade, but were met with a stern rebuke from the Railway Commissioners[9] in their report to Parliament:

Windermere from Orrest Head (1849) by James Baker Pyre

We are precluded from taking into consideration the feelings of individuals who are privately interested. But we must state, that an argument which goes to deprive the artisan of the offered means of changing his narrow abode, his crowded streets, his unwholesome toil, for the fresh air, and the healthful holiday, which sends him back to his work refreshed and invigorated, simply that some individuals may retain to themselves the exclusive enjoyment of scenes which should be open alike to all, appears to us to be an argument wholly untenable.

Opponents of the railway did not occupy morally secure ground, but they did hold the physical ground, so the railway company was forced to back down, deciding to terminate the line at the hamlet of Birthwaite, south of Orrest Head.[10] In the absence of planning controls or a systematic inquiry to weigh the pros and cons of the proposal, one brigade of money and influence had been pitted against another and the defenders had won a significant concession.

Birthwaite was not somewhere that anyone from outside the area was likely to recognise, so the terminus and the town which rapidly grew up around it took its name from the lake, and this has caused confusion ever since, particularly as the new station – in the steam-age sense of the word – was ninety metres above the water and three-quarters of a mile away from the shore, a position which only made sense if the line was to run on to Ambleside. Wordsworth was fearful that the proposal to push it deeper into the Lake District might be revived.

A brass band played as the first train of sixteen fully laden carriages pulled out of Kendal station at 10.00 a.m. on 21 April 1847. At the celebration dinner held that evening in the Crown Hotel in Bowness, Cornelius Nicholson, mayor of Kendal and a director of the company, spoke out against Wordsworth's attack on the railway, pointing out that the operative classes of the manufacturing districts ought to be recognised as intelligent human beings, fully capable of being influenced by the beauties of the Lake District. Richard Monckton Milnes, the Conservative MP for Pontefract and a poet as well as a politician, chose to rebut Wordsworth's protests with a sonnet of his own, published in the *Westmorland Gazette* shortly after the line opened:[11]

> The hour may come, nay must in these our days
> When the swift steam-car with the cat'ract's shout
> Shall mingle its harsh roll, and motley rout
> Of multitudes, these mountain echoes raise
> But thou, the Patriarch of these beauteous ways
> Canst never grudge that gloomy streets send out,
> The crowded sons of labour, care and doubt,
> To read these scenes by light of thine own lays,
> Disordered laughter and encounter rude
> The Poet's finer sense perchance may pain,
> But many a glade and nook of solitude,
> For quiet walk and thought will still remain,
> Where He those poor intruders can elude,
> Nor lose one dream for all their homely gain.

It had come to something when Wordsworth could be so firmly put in his place by the Railway Commissioners and a Tory MP, both sounding far more progressive in their attitudes than the one-time radical, but Wordsworth's political views had been heading to the right for some time. When Lord Lonsdale died in 1802, he was succeeded by his cousin, Sir

William Lowther, who became Viscount Lowther (created Earl of Lonsdale in 1807) and settled all his predecessor's debts, including the long-standing claims of the Wordsworth family. It was the start of a rapprochement with the aristocracy which would lead William to campaign for the Tory cause in the elections of 1818. Wordsworth's growing feeling was that the organic relationships which kept society together were being eroded by commerce and self-interest. Since the Whigs, as the party of 'progress', were clearly implicated in this, he was drawn instead to the paternalism of the Tories.[12]

In 1813 Lowther set Wordsworth up with a job as Distributor of Stamps for Westmorland, essentially a tax collector, a post he kept until 1842 – in Thomas Love Peacock's novel *Melincourt* of 1817 he was satirically portrayed as 'Mr Paperstamp'. Having witnessed the French Revolution at first hand, he became fearful in middle age of all forms of social unrest, an outlook which ultimately led him to favour repression to reform.

Some of the reminiscences collected by Rawnsley suggest that in his pursuit of social position Wordsworth had lost whatever common touch he might once have possessed. He asked one old man who had been in service at Rydal Mount whether Wordsworth had been popular locally and received this reply:

> There's nea doot but what he was fond of quality, and quality was fond o' him, but he niver exed fowk aboot their wark, nor noticed t'flocks nor nowt: not but what he was a kind man if fwoaks was sick and taen badly. But farming, nor beast, nor sheep, nor fields wasn't in his way, he exed nea questions about flocks or herds, and was a distant man, not what you might call an outward man by noa means.[13]

Wordsworth, it seems, would cross the road rather than get tangled up in conversation with his neighbours, but the irony is that this private man, who wrote so much about the virtues of rural retirement, became one of the Lake District's principal draws and was plagued by visitors. According to Martineau, the number of strangers received at Rydal Mount during the later years of the poet's life averaged eight hundred per season.[14] He did not leave the task of greeting visitors to others, but would show them around his garden terraces before wishing them 'improved health and much enjoyment of the lake scenery', then packing them on their way. Even today, the three houses most closely associated with him – Dove Cottage, Rydal Mount and his birthplace in Cockermouth – are bustling tourist shrines.

Another irony is that growth in Wordsworth's fame was accompanied by a withering of his talent. He wrote less and less poetry, which led his wife Mary to joke that Rydal Mount should be known as 'Idle Mount'. Letters, gifts and honours came as thickly as the visitors. Following the death of Southey, he was invited to become Poet Laureate, only accepting after the prime minister, Sir Robert Peel, had reassured him that nothing would be required of him. The appointment confirmed his Establishment status and brought him to the terminus of the political journey he had been making for twenty years.

If Wordsworth had died young, he would have been remembered not as the self-important curmudgeon he became, but as the generous-hearted, iconoclastic radical of his youth. There is, however, a story – possibly apocryphal – which relates how the older Wordsworth, on his way to dine at Lowther Castle, removed an obstruction that had been placed across the footpath. At the same dinner was the landowner, Sir John Wallace, who threatened to horsewhip whoever had broken down the barrier, at which point Wordsworth is reputed to have leapt to his feet and declared, 'I broke down your wall, Sir John, it was obstructing an ancient right of way, and I will do it again. I am a Tory, but scratch me on the back deep enough and you will find a Whig in me yet.'[15]

Harriet Martineau was one of those eminent Victorians who has fallen almost completely out of view, but she was a outstanding woman who deserves to be better known. She held a view of progress which was strikingly at odds with the conservatism of Rydal Mount, and she took a diametrically opposed view of development within the Lake District. The railway, far from being a pernicious evil, was going to open up the dales to new ideas and release communities from their backwardness and ignorance. Before she arrived in the Lakes she was already established in London as a political economist, novelist and journalist. She has been called the first woman sociologist and claimed as an early feminist. For any woman of this period to lead such an independent life would be remarkable enough, but the disadvantages which Martineau had to overcome make her achievements all the more noteworthy, for she had no inherited wealth or position, her hearing was so poor that she had to use an ear trumpet, and she had prolonged periods of excruciating illness. A husband might have lent support, but he could also have been an impediment. She never married.

Martineau first came to the Lake District in 1845 to convalesce. Her health had broken down when she was in her late thirties, and she was found to have an ovarian cyst. She went for treatment from her brother-in-law, a celebrated doctor in Newcastle, then lived for five years in a Tynemouth boarding house before renting a cottage at Waterhead. The illness had broken many ties, so she felt free to choose where she might live and decided that the country would be better for her health than London.

Intending to settle for life, she built a house called The Knoll on a grassy hillock in Ambleside which she was fortunate enough to purchase at a give-away price. Typically, this energetic woman did not wait until the house was finished before she began to lay out the garden. She planted beeches for grand effect, limes with a view to keeping bees and hawthorns and hollies for their winter berries. She wondered how she might get turf for her garden and thought about lifting sods from the fellside, but Wordsworth quickly put her straight. The mountain grass belonged to the statesmen farmers and could not be touched. It could take a hundred years for the denuded area to recover. Martineau was not too proud to accept gardening advice from Wordsworth, who also planted a commemorative stone pine under her terrace wall.

Martineau's arrival must have refreshed the cultured circles based upon Rydal Mount and Dr Arnold's house at Fox How, but it is not difficult to see how her radical opinions might have shaken things up. Arriving in the area at the height of the railway controversy, she found herself out of step with many of her neighbours. 'When I first came,' she later wrote, 'I told my friends that I was alarmed for myself, when I saw the spirit of insolence which seemed to possess the cultivated residents, who really did virtually assume that the mountains and vales were somehow their prop-erty, or at least a privilege appropriate to superior people like themselves. Wordsworth's sonnets about the railway were a mild expression of his feel-ings in this direction.'[16]

When Martineau considered vernacular cottages she did not peer at them through the lens of Picturesque theory. They might be in harmony with the landscape, but were they healthy places to live? Martineau found plenty of evidence to the contrary. They were usually cramped and smoky and she noted that the 'country custom of men sitting bonneted within doors, arose from the need of keeping their heads covered from the soot and draft, and even the dirt of the chimney'.[17] The country way of life which charmed so many visitors struck Martineau as intolerably primitive. She was shocked by the dirt, the overcrowding and the intemperance. Young working men, she observed, hardly ever took a bath, while there was a superstition that if a child had its arms and hands washed before the age of six months, it would grow up to be a thief.

As an active social reformer, Martineau tried to do something about the lack of sanitation in Ambleside by helping to form a building society. Although Ambleside was known for the excellence of its wallers and slaters, who were often sent for from Manchester, Liverpool and even London, the standard of new housing locally was generally poor, and Martineau noted with dismay that even in the burgeoning town of Windermere typhoid fever had killed a schoolmaster and several others 'who could ill be spared', an outbreak which she attributed to insufficient house drainage.[18]

Martineau was aware that radical opinions might prove too strong for polite society in Ambleside and deliberately remained aloof, observing it all with a sociologist's detachment. She noticed that retired merchants and professional men would fall in love with the region, buy a house, spend a few years 'in a transport with what they have done', then move away. She had more time for her fellow intellectuals and took tea frequently with the Wordsworths, even though some of her ideas were a direct threat to the poet's vision of the Lake District as a secluded and sequestered place.

Harriet Martineau (1844) by Augustus Egg

On one such visit, Mary Wordsworth echoed her husband's opinion that green fields with daisies and buttercups would suffice for Lancashire operatives, so there was no need for them to come to the Lakes. Martineau responded that the people should have the opportunity to judge this for themselves, but no one there was sympathetic to her opinion. There was, she recorded, no end of ridicule of 'the people from Birthwaite'. Some had been seen getting their dinner in a churchyard, others had been puzzled about how to get up Loughrigg. Martineau's observation that 'they would know next time' was not well received.

Wordsworth was already old when Martineau came to know him, although his mind was sharp and his voice remained deep and strong. His life had already been punctuated by tragic losses and he was not spared further grief in his later years. His patron Beaumont died in 1827, and he also lost his literary friends: Scott in 1832, followed by both Coleridge and Lamb in 1834.

Meanwhile, in 1829, his beloved sister was struck by an extremely painful physical illness, the nature of which remains obscure, and for two days it seemed as though she might die.[19] She had further attacks; in 1833 she was confined to bed with swollen legs covered in black spots. She complained that she could no longer read – the new ideas pushed the old ones out of her head. Mary believed that Dorothy had walked too much over the years, bringing on the bodily pains that drove her to alcohol and opium for relief, and these in turn overthrew her mind. Then, in 1835, while everyone was anticipating Dorothy's demise, Sara Hutchinson passed away suddenly, without much pain or fuss. Dorothy took it badly and her dementia was soon full-blown, though she lived on for over twenty years. The hardest blow of all came in July 1847 with the death of the Wordsworths' precious daughter Dora, who had married against her father's wishes. William retired to his room and cried incessantly. Mary's grief was more private but she seemed to shrink and grow whiter by the day. She once said that the worst of living in the Lake District 'was that it made one so unwilling to go'. She outlived William, who died at eighty in 1850, and Dorothy, who went five years later.

Had Wordsworth lived longer he would not have liked the changes which the railway brought for it stimulated development in just the way its backers had hoped it would. The new settlement which spread down the hill from the terminus, engulfing the little lake port of Bowness, might not have been the Geneva of the Lakes, but it was a sizeable town almost entirely devoted to the needs of tourists, trippers and commuters. Gothic and Swiss Chalet freely hybridised in the big hotels and tall Victorian lodging houses with their bay windows and high gables, a style which owed more to the suburban villa than to the Westmorland vernacular. In the twentieth century, when Victorian architecture was out of favour, this mixed-up mode provided further ammunition for Windermere's detractors.

A gradient of social class soon became established. Workers' pay packets only extended as far as a trip to Bowness or Windermere, while the middle classes removed themselves to Ambleside or Grasmere and the cotton barons and merchant princes of Liverpool were met by their carriages and whisked away to their villas, strung like a necklace along the eastern shore of Windermere. The wealthiest formed a yacht club with an annual fee equivalent to a worker's salary. Its headquarters were in the Old England Hotel at Bowness, which also offered its guests billiards, hot and cold baths, lawn tennis, excellent char, trout, pike and perch fishing and four-in-hand coaches to Coniston and Ullswater.

Martineau viewed all this with equanimity. Change was merely a social fact and it was likely to bring improved living conditions for many. Not taken in for a moment by the myth of a rural Arcadia, she thought that 'scarcely anything can be conceived more lifeless, unvaried, and unideal, than the existence of the Dalesmen and their families; and where the intellect is left so idle and unimproved as among them, the vices are sure to prevail'.[20] William Green was not worried by the surge in building either; indeed, he thought there should be more of it, since the demand for rooms exceeded the supply of boarding houses. He even anticipated the Garden City movement by suggesting that an 'ideal residential paradise' could be built south of Keswick on land owned by the Greenwich Hospital.[21]

Though snobs would complain that Bowness was as tawdry as Blackpool, the truth – as Norman Nicholson clearly saw in the 1960s – was that the holiday town on the lake, though it might not have the elegance of a spa, was seldom as boisterous as the seaside and had a dignity of its own.[22] It is not so different fifty years on.

Overleaf: Brantwood

Ruskin in His Study at Brantwood, Cumbria (1882) by W. G. Collingwood

12

The Sage of Brantwood

John Ruskin Wrestles the Capitalist Dragon

W HEN WORDSWORTH AND SOUTHEY were at the height of their fame, the precocious son of a London wine merchant was introduced to the beauties of the Lake District by his socially ambitious and aesthetically inclined parents, John James and Margaret Ruskin. Lacking the connections, or the nerve, to call on the poets directly, the Ruskins contrived to be in church at times when these celebrities would be among the congregation. Although only eleven, John Ruskin, a bookworm since the age of five, was well enough acquainted with Wordsworth's poetry to be disappointed by his glimpse of the great man in the chapel at Rydal. He later wrote:

> This gentleman possesses a long face and a large nose with a moderate assortment of grey hairs and 2 small grey eyes not filled with fury wrapt inspired with a mouth of moderate dimensions that is quite large enough to let in a sufficient quantity of beef or mutton & to let out a sufficient quantity of poetry . . .[1]

Southey, on the other hand, when spotted by the family in Crosthwaite church, appeared to be the real deal. He had a beaky nose and 'his dark lightning-eye made him seem half-inspired'. These were John's heroes, but although he attempted to capture his impressions of his three-week vacation in a long mock-picturesque poem titled *Iteriad*, he was not destined to become a Lake Poet. He would, however, become one of the most prominent public intellectuals of his age. To call him an art critic might be narrowly accurate, but it would not capture the breadth of his interests or his influence. Visionary or sage would be better terms, and they seem to fit the image of his later years, when Ruskin sported a beard of biblical proportions. He had a social authority which it is difficult to imagine in our more popularist and democratic times, when the ideas of the great and the good are often debunked in the media and private lives are combed for any trace of scandal. His views on art, craftsmanship, work and society influenced an extraordinary range of people, from writers such as Leo Tolstoy, Marcel Proust and D. H. Lawrence, and artists such as Edward Burne-Jones and Edouard Manet, to social reformers and political activists such as Octavia Hill, William Morris, Peter Kropotkin and even Mahatma Gandhi. Ruskin did not become a Lake District resident until 1871, when he was already fifty-two and exhausted, with most of his achievements behind him and a dark future of mental instability gusting towards him. Yet his whole life and career were shaped by his early encounters with the Cumbrian landscape, and, as Wordsworth had done, he used his position in society to try to defend it.

Ruskin had an aunt on his father's side who lived in Perth, and it became family tradition every other year to take a journey to Scotland, stopping off in the Lake District on the way. His father would combine business with pleasure by calling at country seats to take orders for wine. Ruskin would say that even on the earliest of these journeys the landscape had a powerful influence upon him. 'I was born *again*, at three years old!' he wrote, which would put the date at 1822.² It was an aesthetic epiphany rather than a religious one that he called to mind, though the spiritual, the moral and the aesthetic were always closely associated in his thinking. On their visit to Keswick in 1824 John was taken by his nurse to Friar's Crag, a well-known viewpoint on Derwentwater, easily reached from the town. Here the five-year-old-boy, looking through the hollows in the mossy roots of the trees which crowned the crag, experienced a Wordsworthian moment of 'intense joy, mingled with awe' which would stay with him for the rest of his life.

Ruskin imitated his father's habit of keeping a journal of the family's tours. They were both relentless sightseers, taking note of all the houses, parks, ruins, castles, caves, lakes and mountains they encountered on their route, and rounding out their knowledge with reference books. Back at the family home at Herne Hill, south London, Ruskin amused himself by making his own guidebook to the Lake District. He was a hothouse child, coddled and overprotected, but also burdened with his parents' ambitions. John James foresaw a literary career; Margaret imagined a future archbishop.

During the Ruskins' trip of 1830 they visited Buttermere, where John was overawed by the crags at Honister. On the same trip the Ruskins called at Crosthwaite's Museum, which was still run by the heirs of its founder, and John was enthralled by its assorted exhibits. He would become a collector in his own right one day, with a particular enthusiasm for geological specimens. In adult life his mind came to resemble just such a cabinet of curiosities; he was hugely observant and endlessly absorbed in the details of the natural world. Although his fame rests mostly upon his writings on architecture and art – he was appointed the first Slade Professor of Fine Art at Oxford University in 1869 – he never lost his boyish enthusiasm for astronomy, geology and botany. The present-day Ruskin Museum in Coniston, with its mineral cases, memorabilia and local history displays, has something of this same magpie character.

The year 1830 was also the one in which Ruskin saw the first of his verses in print. Egged on by his father, he had sent his *Lines On Skiddaw and Derwent Water*, based upon his recollections of an earlier visit, to the *Spiritual Times* and they appeared in the February issue.

These early visits to the Lake District implanted a permanent affection in Ruskin for mountain scenery, an attachment which deepened when the family made their first trip to the Alps in 1833. Ruskin was a much greater enthusiast for Alpine scenery than Wordsworth ever had been, yet throughout his life it was the fells of Cumberland and Westmorland, where his love affair with mountains had begun, that remained the standard of comparison. The Matterhorn, he wrote in his autobiography, *Praeterita*, was 'too much of an Egyptian obelisk to please me (I trace continually the tacit reference in my Cumberland-built soul to moorish Skiddaw and far-sweeping Saddleback as the proper types of majestic form)'.[3] Though he loved to travel, he never courted danger, which put him off India for fear of tigers and Peru for fear of earthquakes, but also meant that he liked to contemplate his mountains from the security of the valley, rather than from some perilous ledge or thin ridge. He admitted that high altitudes were not very good for him and described himself as a 'stream-tracker' and 'cliff-hunter' who 'ranked mountains by the beauty of their glens than the height of their summits'.[4] Perhaps it was this that decided him, for, much as he loved Switzerland, this perpetual traveller made his final home in the 'English Alps'.

That home was Brantwood, overlooking the eastern shore of Coniston Water, which Ruskin purchased impulsively for £1,500 in August 1872, sight unseen, from the wood engraver, printer, social reformer and republican William James Linton. The following month Ruskin went to see what he had bought and was pleased with the view, though he thought the house dilapidated and dismal. In a letter he wrote: 'Here I have rocks, streams, fresh air, and, for the first time in my life, the rest of a purposed home.'[5] Ruskin's affection for Coniston dated from his childhood visits when the Ruskins had stayed at the Waterhead Hotel. On a visit in 1847 he had lamented the demolition of that building in favour of a bigger railway-style hotel 'with coffee room, smoking room and every other pestilent and devil-ish Yankeeism that money can buy or speculation plan . . .'.[6] Brantwood was little more than a cottage when Ruskin bought it and many alterations were required, the most significant of which was the lantern constructed in a corner of his bedroom, a little glazed space from which he could commune, across the lake, with the Old Man of Coniston.

In his heyday, Ruskin was a public lecturer who could entrance his audience. At a time when northern industrialists were indulging in civic boosterism, compet-ing with one another to endow city museums and art galleries, the great writer was often invited to give inaugural speeches. His hosts sometimes got more than they had bargained for, since Ruskin would use these occasions to lambast commercialism and competition, forces which he passionately believed were destroying society. He hated factories, not just for the smoke which billowed from their chimneys, but for the damage they did to traditions of craftsmanship. In this he was a direct influence upon the Arts and Crafts movement.

Ruskin was an admirer of Wordsworth's poetry and he championed Turner's art at a time when critics were comparing it unfavourably with the work of Claude, Poussin and Rosa. Later he became a supporter of the Pre-Raphaelites, and his vigorous prose and frank opinions won him a wide readership, particularly among the emerging middle classes for whom an appreciation of art provided an immediate social cachet. When he wrote about architecture, he took a Wordsworthian line, arguing the case for vernacular building in tune with its landscape. This led him to champion Gothic architecture over the Classical styles. He hated oppressive standardisation. The mason working on a medieval cathedral had not been constrained by ratios and proportions handed down by ancient rationalists, but had been free to express his love of God and his relationship to nature.[7]

Although many of his opinions were deeply conservative, he was profoundly disturbed by the consequences of unrestrained capitalism. While the Industrial Revolution had brought commercial prosperity, it had condemned the multitude of workers to lives of poverty, wretchedness and ugliness. Ruskin also worried about the effects of industry upon the natu-ral world. He described himself as 'Tory of the school of Homer' and as a 'communist, reddest of the red':[8] today we might call him a Green. He was certainly a radical in the sense that he thought society's problems went deep and needed to be rooted out, but it was a revolution of the spirit he hoped for, not one that would have workers fighting in the streets.

After 1860 Ruskin's social campaigning became more strenuous. He published his attacks on uncontrolled industrial development in the *Cornhill Magazine* and *Fraser's Magazine*, but the money-makers mobilised against him, prevailing upon the editors to deny him a platform. As he became increasingly isolated, he launched a quixotic, utopian scheme of his own devising, founding the Guild of St George at about the time he purchased Brantwood, and invoking the name of England's patron saint in the cause of spiritual, social and environmental regeneration. Putting the proceeds from the sale of his London home into this project, he imagined that he could lead this revival from his new Eden on the banks of a northern lake.

Considering that it once belonged to an apostle of beauty, Brantwood is an odd and ungainly house, in part because Ruskin, true to his principles, decided to buy a cottage and then enlarge it, rather than to build from scratch. This avoided the pitfalls of an alien classicism, but it presented difficulties of its own, particularly as Ruskin needed space to work and to house his artworks and sprawling collections. He did not buy Brantwood with the intention of being idle.

But the Ruskin who came to Brantwood was not a contented man. In his diaries he was already recording bouts of giddiness and languor. Without attempting to psychoanalyse him, it is safe to say that while his odd childhood laid the foundation for his eminent career, it did nothing for his emotional future. Rather like another well-known Victorian, Charles Dodgson, he related better to pre-pubescent girls than he did to mature women. This was particularly evident during his brief, unhappy marriage to Euphemia (Effie) Gray. As newly-weds they went to Venice, but rather than giving his attention to his wife he ignored her woefully and spent most of his time filling his sketchbooks with drawings of buildings. This was not the worst that Effie had to endure. On their wedding night Ruskin was unable to consummate the marriage. She later filed successfully for an annulment and married the painter John Everett Millais, Ruskin's protégé. The couple went on to have eight children. Ruskin later developed an impossible passion for Rose la Touche, the daughter of Irish gentry of Huguenot descent, who came to Ruskin's London home for drawing lessons. When they first met, Ruskin was nearly forty, Rose still only nine, a dream of wistful Pre-Raphaelite loveliness. Seven years later the middle-aged art critic proposed marriage, but her evangelist parents refused to allow the union. A letter from Effie Millais in which she drew attention to her former husband's coldness was enough to puncture Ruskin's fantasy. Everyone was damaged by this episode. Rose became anorexic in her twenties and died in a Dublin nursing home in 1875. In his grief Ruskin turned to spiritualism and started to imagine visits from his beloved. By 1877 he was exhibiting the first signs of the madness that would engulf his final years and turn his home at Brantwood into his asylum.

Ruskin did not live there alone. In the summer of 1873 his devoted cousin Joan Severn joined him there, along with her husband Arthur and their two young children, and in time a third storey was added to the house to accommodate the growing Severn family. There was an inward stream of guests, too, including Charles Darwin, the painters Holman Hunt and Edward Burne-Jones, the poet Coventry Patmore and the children's book illustrator Kate Greenaway. A frequent visitor was William Gershom Collingwood, one of Ruskin's pupils from Oxford, who in 1871 settled at Lanehead, about a mile from Brantwood, and became his mentor's secretary from 1881 onwards. Collingwood was a significant artist, writer and antiquary in his own right, with a particular interest in the Norse settlement of Cumbria.

The estate that went with the house was a mere sixteen acres when Ruskin bought it, but it grew, through additions, to reach 500 acres by the end of the century. Ruskin's land ranged from the open fell, through hillside woodlands to the water's edge. With a large staff of gardeners there was plenty of scope here for Ruskin to explore, in constructed form, his philosophical ideas about the relationship of human beings to the land. His mission for the Guild of St George was rooted in the ground, which was to be treated with care, but so improved that every acre gave of its best. Simultaneously modern and medieval, he imagined happy labourers living in simple but wholesome cottages, improving land through tillage and sending their children to agricultural schools to develop their skills. Donating large sums from the sale of his London house to the new brotherhood, he thought that Brantwood would become an exemplary project, copied throughout the country. Surrounded in his study by his vitrines and specimen cases, his rocks and fossils, his meticulous drawings of seeds and lichens, he planned the utter transmutation of England.

His favourite spot in the grounds at Brantwood, now known as the Professor's Garden, was based on the idea of a lowly crofter's plot, crammed, in cottage-garden style, with plants reputed to be beneficial to body and soul. Brantwood offered the cerebral Ruskin some physical release. He chopped his own wood, built paths, lent a hand in the gardens and went rowing on the lake.

Mrs Severn, who cared for Ruskin through his long illness, managed Brantwood for him and inherited the house upon his death, was an avid gardener and laid out many more walks and plantings. It can be difficult to see through these layers to imagine what the gardens were like in Ruskin's day, but they never had a fixed form. They were always a work in progress.

The people of Coniston village were proud of the illustrious figure who had chosen to become their neighbour. He involved himself in village life, setting up a little corps of gardeners among the boys of the village school. The girls from the school had the dubious privilege of visiting Brantwood, where Ruskin would tutor them himself in botany, literature and the Bible. Despite his predilection for young girls, this seems to have been innocent enough and driven by his zeal for education and natural history.

Ever the educator, Ruskin specified in his will that his collections at Brantwood should be open to the public for thirty consecutive days each year. Unfortunately the Severns, so attentive and dutiful during Ruskin's old age, decided not to honour this final wish; indeed, many of the contents were sent to auction. One of the keenest buyers, however, was John Whitehouse, founder in 1896 of the Birmingham Ruskin Society, who succeeded in purchasing the entire property in 1932. It is now looked after by a charity, the Brantwood Trust, and remains a place of pilgrimage for Ruskinians, although it has never attained the broad popular appeal of Dove Cottage.

At Brantwood Ruskin wrote with an urgency born of his social concerns. Central to his efforts were the letters supposedly addressed directly to working men under the title *Fors Clavigera*. For a deep thinker like Ruskin this title had associations of force, fortitude, destiny and seizing the moment, but Ruskin was never a popularist and certainly no rabble-rouser. Reading his high-blown and cryptic prose today it is easy to see why his *Fors* failed to move the masses. The same must be said for his various social experiments, such as the home factories set up at Keswick for metal working and linen weaving, which were never more than arts and crafts curiosities, not the growing tips of a social revolution, but if Ruskin failed in his direct efforts his ideas were later taken up by Christian Socialists and the founders of the British Labour Party.

Ruskin shared with Wordsworth a sacred view of landscape, in which some forms of intrusion were literally devilish. On a visit to the River Lune in 1875

Dawn Coniston (1873) by John Ruskin

he was horrified to find a new iron fence skewered into the riverbank. This was a scene once painted by his hero Turner, so the desecration was particularly piercing. Then he noticed two seats placed nearby by 'the improving mob' from Kirkby Lonsdale, their serpentine iron legs tipped with a pointed tail, which struck him as the perfect symbol for such aesthetic wickedness.

Ruskin felt as keenly as Wordsworth the encroachment of a world of commerce and industry which he detested. In the Preface to the second volume of *Modern Painters* he wrote:

> From my dining-room. I am happy in the view of the lower reach of Coniston Water, not because it is particularly beautiful, but because it is entirely pastoral and pure. Were a single point of chimney of the Barrow ironworks to show itself over the green ridge of the hill, I should never care to look at it more.[9]

The intervening topography made this rhetorical threat an idle one, though the mushrooming development at Barrow must have brought the Industrial Revolution uncomfortably close. In 1839 a youthful capitalist called Henry Schneider, whose family already had a financial interest in mineral exploitation, took a holiday in the Lake District, but arranged a detour to investigate the potential of the small iron-ore mines of the Furness peninsula. His company struck such rich deposits of haematite in the 1850s that Barrow, which had been nothing more than a sleepy fishing village, suddenly became the centre of an industrial frenzy with some of the hard-working, hard-drinking, hard-swearing characteristics of the Klondike. From 1857 Barrow was connected by railway to the west coast main line and the directors of the Furness Railway Company soon realised that it could be used for conveying holidaymakers as well as minerals. The Coniston Railway, originally built to transport copper from the local mines, was amalgamated with the Furness Railway in 1862. By 1868 there was another line connecting with Lakeside at the foot of Windermere, thus allowing the company to offer visitors the pleasure of a lake cruise on one of their own steamers. Schneider, meanwhile, who had done so much to get all this going, bought a grand house called Belsfield in Bowness. Whenever he had to attend to business in Barrow he would make his way down to his exclusive steam yacht *Esperance*, which would convey him to Lakeside, where the waiting train included his personal coach. His butler would follow the industrialist to the yacht at a respectful distance, carrying his breakfast on a silver tray.

Ruskin made his opinion of railways very clear in a pithy letter to the editor of the *Pall Mall Gazette*:

They are the loathsomest form of devilry now extant, animated and deliberate earthquakes, destructive of all wise social habit or possible natural beauty, carriages of damned souls on the edges of their own graves.[10]

He thought that fast travel was inimical to close observation, that it induced a sort of mental torpor and, worst of all, it destroyed the very scenery that the traveller ought to be observing. Nevertheless, Ruskin was prepared to sup with the devil or at least ride behind his engines. Since the Coniston line was already built, he used it, while fiercely opposing any further penetration of the Lake District by rails.

When he learned that Wordsworth's *bête noire*, the extension of the Windermere line to Ambleside and Rydal, was being reconsidered, he lent his support to the protest organised by Robert Somervell, owner of a shoe factory in Kendal. In the preface to a campaigning leaflet, Ruskin expressed a low opinion of 'the stupid herds of modern tourists' who 'let themselves be emptied, like coals from a sack, at Windermere and Keswick' and thought that:

> all that your railroad company can do for them is only to open taverns and skittle grounds around Grasmere, which will soon, then, be nothing but a pool of drainage, with a beach of broken gingerbeer bottles; and their minds will be no more improved by contemplating the scenery of such a lake than of Blackpool.[11]

Ruskin once suggested the creation of a series of museums, especially for the working classes and separate from those frequented by the upper classes.[12] Now he extended this institutionalisation of class into the viewing of scenery, echoing some of Wordsworth's elitist arguments:

> I have said I take no selfish interest in this resistance to the railroad. But I do take an unselfish one. It is precisely because I passionately wish to improve the minds of the populace, and because I am spending my own mind, strength and fortune, wholly on that object, that I don't want to let them see Helvellyn while they are drunk.[13]

The threat receded, only to be revived in 1886 by a new scheme to take a line right through the heart of the district to Borrowdale. In an outraged letter to the *Manchester Evening News*, Ruskin contemplated a dystopian vision in which Rydal Water and Grasmere had become open sewers, a refreshments room was opened on the summit of Helvellyn and the Vale of St John was laid out with tennis courts and billiard rooms.

When the railway proposal was scrutinised in the House of Commons, Mr Pember, the Queen's Counsel acting for the promoters, hoped that 'amateur reformers' societies and itinerant sentimentalists' would be excluded from giving evidence. 'I do not think,' he continued, 'we want professors of landscape of this kind to come and tell us *ex cathedra* what will be the consequence of making this line, nor any fanciful declaration after the manner of Mr Ruskin – especially his later manner – against the profanity of ordinary progress.'[14]

The elderly Ruskin did not give evidence, but many of the owners of estates likely to be affected by the line did. Captain Dunlop of Holehird spoke for them all when he said: 'Property in the district of Windermere Lake is all but worthless if the views of the lake and surrounding country are interfered with.'

A Study of Clouds over Mountains (undated) by John Ruskin

Lord Bradford, the owner of an estate at Applethwaite, said that the proposed line would pass within ninety yards of the house, in part on an embankment, and thought that the presence of the railway would deter the better class of summer visitors, a slip that was jumped on by Mr Pember who interpreted him as saying 'do not make it because it will allow so many people to enjoy the lakes'.[15]

On the other side of the argument, Colonel Rhodes, who had offered land in Ambleside for construction of the station, was asked whether the railway would be a great boon to visitors. He replied:

> There is not the slightest doubt about that, and tourists too. Visitors and tourists also, and masses of the pent-up towns in the manufacturing districts; from Bradford and Leeds and Halifax they come, and from Huddersfield they come, in large numbers; they arrive at Windermere Station and they cannot get to Ambleside – they wish to do so but they cannot get to it.[16]

Opponents of the bill attempted to make the proposers look as if they were driven wholly by commercial avarice. Proposers tried to make the opponents seem like smug, elitist and self-interested enemies of progress and the poor. Neither side had complete control of the moral high ground, and when the bill fell it was not because the amenity arguments had carried the day, but because the project was difficult and investors not forthcoming.

Many lovers of the Lake District will be thankful that the railway was never built, yet much of the opprobrium targeted on the railways is now routinely directed towards the motor car; indeed, the railway is now seen as the environmentally acceptable alternative to the motorway. As the popularity of the Settle–Carlisle line and North Yorks Moors Railway demonstrates, a historic line through a spectacular landscape can be a winning combination. It is impossible to say whether we might now be so positive about an Ambleside–Rydal–Keswick line, although the Lakeside–Haverthwaite railway, part of the old Furness Railway, seems to be well liked and uncontroversial, and there is no doubt about the popularity of the miniature railway in Eskdale.

For Ruskin the railways were just one manifestation of a more profound threat to the social and moral fabric of England. The serpents coiled in the cast-iron legs of the Kirkby Lonsdale seats were offspring of the dragon of capitalist greed which was devouring the nation, and which he, in his self-anointed role as St George, would have to wrestle with unto death.[17]

On 4 February 1884, at the London Institution, Ruskin gave one of his strangest but most powerful lectures. For years he had been studying the skies obsessively and he claimed to have identified a new phenomenon over England which he called the 'storm cloud' or 'plague wind'. His lecture was an odd mixture of meteorology, aesthetic analysis and apocalyptic prognostication. He quoted a diary entry made at Brantwood on 13 August 1879, in which he described 'a terrific and horrible thunderstorm' that woke him with its incessant rolling, 'like railway luggage trains, quite ghastly in its mockery of them'. The storm lasted over an hour before 'settling down into Manchester devil's darkness'. By the end of the lecture it was clear that Ruskin's subject was hardly meteorological at all, but metaphorical and spiritual. For all the apparent detail, he was not describing anything that could be verified empirically. The artist looked for auguries in the air and found them in the blanching of the sun and in the 'frightful ladder of light' that flashed above Wetherlam.

It would be comfortable to think that Ruskin was a prescient environmentalist, and that his 'storm cloud' was a harbinger of air pollution, global warming and climate change, but *The Storm Cloud of the Nineteenth Century* is too ranting, too apocalyptic and betrays too much of Ruskin's incipient paranoia. The storm clouds were already massing in his own psyche and sober reason would soon be lost for ever.

Entries from Ruskin's Brantwood diary indicate his unstable mood. He kept a running account of the weather, but it is difficult to separate the conditions around Coniston from the fluctuations within his psyche:

May 9 1876. Tuesday.
Yesterday one of the divinest days of intense and cloudless light and blue I ever saw, showing that all smoke and human disturbance of the air is comparatively powerless when the air itself is pure . . .

May 22 1876. Monday.
Rain at last but very quiet and soft – hardly felt here, dark on the Old Man. Since morning however the clouds have been natural in their old white wreath – now it is getting Manchestery.

In 1878 Ruskin was seized by the delusion that he was about to be taken by the devil and that the only way to confront him was to remove all his clothes and wait up for him naked. The illness lasted five weeks and by 1879 he was writing again in his diary, but his mood was now much darker:

September 5 1879. Friday.
All the Lancashire view lost in black smoke, and the outlines of Scawfell mass but seen, and no more – through the smoke of White Haven. Evidently no more a breath of pure air to be drawn in England.

The illness was progressive: in 1889 Ruskin retired permanently to Brantwood and wrote no more. Joan Severn cared for him until his death in 1900. For all his accomplishments, Ruskin did not lead a contented life and it is easy to see him as a tragic figure, flawed by his upbringing, thwarted in love, troubled in his soul and unable either to complete or to let go of the tasks he had taken upon himself. Brantwood is more welcoming nowadays, but it is hard to shake off the gloom of the sage's declining years. It still takes an effort to remind oneself that this was the home of one of the most influential men in Victorian Britain.

Overleaf: Kirk Fell and Great Gable from the shore of Wastwater

Kern Knotts Crack, Great Gable

13

'Soaped poles in bear gardens'

Rock-climbing Pioneers

Ruskin was an ardent admirer of the Swiss landscape, but his partic-ular enthusiasm was for the gentle rolling countryside around Lakes Geneva and Lucerne. He loved to look at mountains from afar, but found that when he was among them they restricted his liberty. 'Among the greater hills, one can't always go just where one chooses, – all around is the too far or the too steep, – one wants to get to this, and to climb that, and can't do either; – but in Jura one can go every way, and be happy everywhere.'[1] 'The real beauty of the Alps,' he once explained, 'is to be seen, and seen only, where all may see it, the child, the cripple, and the man of grey hairs.'[2] But among the hundreds of tourists who poured into Chamonix every year and were content with a distant view of the peaks, there was a tigerish group of Britons not satisfied by such uninvolved contemplation. To them the sublimity of the mountains was a provocation. They wanted to be among them, to climb them, to test themselves against them, to conquer them. An enthusiasm which germinated in the Alps would soon flourish among the crags, pinnacles and ghylls of the English Lake District.

It was a barrister, Alfred Wills,[3] who inaugurated what would become known as the 'Golden Age of Alpine Mountaineering' when he inter-rupted his honeymoon in 1854 to climb the Wetterhorn above Grindelwald. With railways dramatically cutting the travelling time, the 1850s saw an annual summer surge of middle-class mountaineers towards the Alps. In 1857 William Matthews, a Birmingham land agent and Alpine enthusiast, suggested to his climbing partner, the Reverend Fenton Hort, a Fellow of Trinity College, Cambridge, that they should form a club so that moun-taineers might gather to exchange information and swap experiences. On 22 December the Alpine Club came into being at an inaugural dinner at Astley's Hotel, Covent Garden. Initially there was a requirement that applicants for membership should have climbed to at least 13,000 feet, but this was later relaxed so that non-climbers with an interest in the region could join. Though the Alpine Club was less socially exclusive than other London clubs, the fees and the cost of the dinners nevertheless ensured that it was dominated by the upper middle classes. Of the 281 members in 1863, there were 57 barristers, 23 solicitors, 34 clergymen, 15 dons and 19 landed gentry.[4] There were no female members.

It was generally considered that the weather was unsuitable for winter climbing in Switzerland, so those enthusiasts who wanted to pursue their hobby off-season looked for mountains closer to home. As the snow-filled gullies of the Lake District bore some resemblance to the Alpine couloirs, this corner of north-west England became a popular training ground for members of the Alpine Club, but sometimes there was no snow, so the climbers scrambled on the rocks instead. At first the idea of climbing rocky crags just for their own sake was looked down upon by some as a sort of rock gymnastics, not in the true spirit of mountaineering, but others saw the potential for a parallel sport and by 1872 four distinct routes had already been found up Pillar Rock.[5] Scrambling on rocks evolved into rock-climbing and it became a summer activity in the Lake District.

The innocent enthusiasm of the Golden Age was destroyed by the disaster which overtook Edward Whymper's party on their descent from the Matterhorn in 1865. Three Englishmen and their Chamonix guide tumbled to their deaths. Only a broken rope saved Whymper and the two other guides from being dragged off the mountain with them. The press leapt upon the story, portraying young climbers as frivolous risk-takers, and Ruskin, who had only briefly been a member of the Alpine Club, joined in, calling for an end to all mountaineering. 'You have despised nature,' he scolded the Alpinists, 'that is to say, all the deep and sacred sensations of natural scenery. You have made racecourses of the cathedrals of the earth. The Alps, which your own poets used to love so reverently, you look upon as soaped poles in bear gardens, which you set yourselves to climb and slide down with shrieks of delight.'[6] Once the huffing and puffing had subsided, the tragedy on the Matterhorn did not put mountaineers off for long; indeed, the reality of the dangers made the activity only more attractive, and henceforth the *Alpine Journal* frequently carried obituaries.

But there has always been more to rock-climbing than youthful exuberance and bravado, and Coleridge was one of the first to relish the existential intensity of the activity. On his epic solo walk of 1802 he found himself in a very dangerous position during his inadvisable descent of Broad Stand, the band of rock which interrupts the apparent route from Scafell on to neighbouring Scafell Pike. Well-prepared walkers know that it is not a place for them, and make lengthy detours to avoid the difficulties. Coleridge came straight over the edge, slipping and slithering, jumping from ledge to ledge until the only way out was to go on. Towards the bottom of the crag, he reached what might be called the crux of his route:

> And now I had only two more to drop down – to return was impossible
> – but of these two the first was tremendous, it was twice my own height,
> and the Ledge at the bottom was exceedingly narrow, that if I drop
> down upon it I must of necessity have fallen backwards and of course
> killed myself. My limbs were all in a tremble. I lay upon my back to rest
> myself, and was beginning according to my custom to laugh at myself
> for a Madman, when the sight of the Crags above me on each side, and
> the imperious Clouds just over them, posting so luridly and so rapidly
> northward, overawed me. I lay in a state of almost prophetic Trance and
> Delight and blessed God aloud for the powers of Reason and Will, which
> remaining no Danger can overpower us![7]

Suitably composed, Coleridge found a way down, though he broke out in a rash from the effort of it all. At the bottom he found the carcass of a fallen sheep, which heightened his awareness of his lucky escape. It is sometimes said that he was the Lake District's first rock-climber, but he went down rather than up, and it is arguable that his uncontrolled and frankly reckless technique should not be dignified by the name of 'climbing'.

Though one can walk all day in the Lake District and never encounter the slightest danger, there is certainly an abundance of precipices to be skirted by the cautious. In Wordsworth's poem *The Brothers*, the poet used Pillar Rock as the setting for a tragedy. The seafarer's younger brother had slipped from the summit and had been smashed to pieces on the rocks below, leaving his crook rotting in a crack halfway down, but this gloomy tale did not deter a climber called John Atkinson, a local to the valley, from scaling this isolated tower in 1826, an ascent undertaken thirty years before the formation of the Alpine Club, which is regarded as the first recognisable rock climb in the Lake District. Sociologically speaking, this landmark climb seems to be an exception to the general rule that the history of leisure activities in the Lake District begins in the higher social strata and trickles downward. It is a reminder that history is skewed – the educated visitors had the ability and the inclination to write everything down.

In light of the sport's Alpine origins, it is not surprising that the pioneers of Lake District climbing were drawn at first to prominent rock features which had obvious tops to aim for. Three in particular stood out – Pillar Rock, the Scafell Pinnacle and Napes Needle on Great Gable. The latter will always be associated with Walter Parry Haskett Smith, the Old Etonian who first climbed it in 1886. The Alpinists and the Lake District cragsmen belonged to different, but overlapping circles. Haskett Smith was at home in both groups and has been dubbed the 'Father of British Rock-climbing' on the strength of his numerous first ascents of Lake District routes in the 1880s. When he first visited Wasdale Head in 1881 he had recently graduated in classics from Trinity College, Oxford, and was reading for an advanced degree in the humanities, so he divided his days between the study of Aristotle and Plato and the exploration of the surrounding crags and fells. Later he became a barrister, so in many respects he was a typical Alpine Club type, but his great contribution to the development of rock-climbing was the revolutionary idea that it was not necessary to get to the top of a mountain. Finding an interesting line up a crag was sport enough.

Napes Needle is a striking pinnacle detached from the face of the crag and its outline has become as emblematic in its own modest way as the silhouette of the Matterhorn. The Needle is not obvious from the valley, but Haskett Smith caught a glance of it on a misty day in the early 1880s, found it again on a visit in 1884, then in 1886, having said goodbye to his climbing companions in the morning, he climbed it solo (without partner or rope), 'feeling as small as a mouse climbing a milestone'.[8] He left his handkerchief on the top, anchored by a stone, to prove to others that he had done it.

Climbers who reached the top of Pillar Rock used to scratch their names on a slate, until someone took a tin box up there so that they could leave their calling cards. The first Lake District climbers were largely upper-middle-class, usually Oxbridge types, who brought the conversation of the Senior Common Room to the cracks and crevices of the rock faces. They invented nicknames for one another – the Professor, the Wanderer, the Bohemian – and played clever etymological games. They named one of the features on Pillar Rock 'Pisgah' after the mountain from which Moses saw the Promised Land, while those who climbed there regularly were dubbed

Napes Needle

the 'Pillarites'. They approached climbing with a studied nonchalance, as if performing an impossibly exposed manoeuvre over a yawning chasm was similar in kind to cracking a crossword clue.

But just as the early British explorers in the Alps would climb with local guides, so the Lake District visitors would often find climbing partners from the local community. There is a parallel with the 'gentlemen and players' arrangements of cricket, but in climbing the bonds must have been much closer, such was the degree of trust involved. One of the keenest of the local climbers was John Robinson of Lorton, near Cockermouth, a regular partner of Haskett Smith. He thought nothing of rising at 4.00 a.m. and walking to Wasdale Head to join a party of climbers. After a hard day's climbing he would walk back again.

The climbers chose the remotest and most austerely beautiful valley for their headquarters. Wasdale Head was centrally placed for their excursions, being within easy striking distance of Pillar Rock, Great Gable and Scafell, and with the completion of the coastal railway in 1857 it became somewhat easier to reach. When Harriet Martineau had visited the valley there was no inn, but she reported that two of the local families, the Tysons and the Ritsons, offered accommodation, cautioning her readers not to ask for or to accept alcohol from their hosts in case it landed them in trouble from the Excise men. Thomas and Annie Tyson of Row Farm kept a visitors' book from 1876 to 1886 which reveals much about the social backgrounds of those who came to climb. In March 1878 they were hosts to a 'readingless reading party' from Exeter College, Oxford, and the following month to visitors from Caius College, Cambridge. On 19 April, Captain Jonathan Duck of Belmont House, Liscard, Cheshire, 'arrived at Dame Tyson's in a state approaching knocked-upishness and forthwith revelled in clover'. Many of the entries are full of effusive praise for Mrs Tyson, several are in verse and one or two are in Greek.[9]

In 1857 Will Ritson, the huntsman to Wasdale Hall, added a wing to his farmhouse at Rowfoot, obtained a liquor licence and opened the Huntsman's Inn, which became a favourite first with literary visitors, including Wordsworth, De Quincey and John Wilson, then later with the rock-climbing set. It is now the Wasdale Head Inn. Ritson was a celebrated wit and raconteur who called himself the 'World's Greatest Liar' and loved to tell tall tales. Fond of hunting and walking, he was a rugged man who once wrestled Wilson, Cumberland-style, and won two times out of three, though he pronounced him 'a varra bad un to lick'. He claimed not to understand the attractions of rock-climbing, on one occasion asking a guest 'What's makkin' ye fellas fash yer'sens seea mich aboot climmin' t'crags? Isn't t'fells big eneugh for ye?', but he was the ideal host for the rumbustious climbing crowd.

Evenings in the inn could be very lively, as the Manchester artist Lehmann Oppenheimer described in his memoir *The Heart of Lakeland*. Fuelled by camaraderie and whisky the climbers would try to outdo one another in tests of strength and balance. Here Oppenheimer describes an attempt at the 'Billiard Room Traverse' by one of his companions:

> He takes off his coat and shoes, and placing his hands on the edge of the billiard table he walks backwards up the wall to within a yard of the ceiling. Then he moves along the table and wall simultaneously with hands and feet, avoiding the framed chromolithographs as well as he may. With an enormous stride he reaches from one wall to another at the corner of

the room, and is just saved from upsetting some half-emptied glasses of whisky on the mantelshelf by the terrified shouts of the owners.[10]

The long-suffering billiard table was abused in many ways. Another test was the circuit of the corner leg, or – if something more challenging was demanded – the middle leg. If the landlord was not in his office, a journey from the smoke room to the billiard room without touching the floor might be added.

Climbers saw themselves as a breed apart. Oppenheimer mocked the 'monotonous air of conventional respectability' that accompanied the non-climbing guests. He imagined a conversation between three aesthetically inclined tourists. 'What a splendidly buttressed pyramid the Gable is . . .', says one, 'and just look at those clouds blowing along between its peak and those sharp rocky teeth just beneath it.' That will be where the climbers are, his friend replies, 'they'll be getting drenched in the cloud and seeing nothing.' The third is damning: 'the anthropoid ape in man tends to disappear; but those fellows at the hotel won't let it die, they attempt to return to a stage that is past.'[11]

Oppenheimer was archly poking fun, knowing that the apes on the rocks included some of the best minds in the country, but if the climbers differentiated themselves from those they saw as mere tourists, they were seen by the local farming community as just plain 'daft'. Before Haskett Smith attempted a climb on Scafell Pinnacle, a shepherd gave the opinion 'Eh mon, nobbut a fleein' thing'll ever get up theer!' The idea that they were doing something for pleasure which most people thought was insane was a constant bond among the climbing fraternity. Revealingly, Oppenheimer recalls a day on Pillar Rock when their rest halfway up a gully was disturbed by the 'intrusion' of two farmers throwing planks off a cart to make a foot-bridge.[12] At times this intellectual and social elite could act as if the Lake District was their own private playground.

This attitude emerges very clearly from Oppenheimer's account of what in my days in the Boy Scouts would have been called a 'wide game'. The version he described was called 'Scouts and Outposts', and its military derivation is apparent, though it was introduced to Wasdale by some 'Cambridge men'.[13] The general idea was for a few scouts to attempt to penetrate a line of sentinels and reach an agreed target, such as the summit of a mountain. Scouts could sneak up and neutralise an outpost but it took two of the guards acting in concert to capture a scout. Oppenheimer revelled in the

Owen Glynne Jones

rowdiness of this activity, acknowledging that it was a kind of desecration, but his book was published six years before the outbreak of the Great War, which put an end to the manly sport of man-hunting

If Oppenheimer's views are representative, the rock-climbers were spiritually at odds with the Wordsworthians, seeking to challenge nature rather than to commune or become one with her. At a memorial service for Queen Victoria held in a church within sight of Fairfield, Oppenheimer was pleased to see 'that Lakeland is not yet given over to the tourist and those who depend on him – that the old life still goes on', but generally he found conventional religion oppressive and yearned for the next day, when he would 'go to a church of a different kind'. A life of quiet contemplation, reverence and renunciation was not what he yearned for. Perhaps he had read Nietzsche, because he hungered 'for the virility of great souls – body healthy, perfect; mind full of alertness and fire; sympathising with us weaker ones without praising or encouraging our weakness – their faculties ever eager for combat'.[14] He got his invitation to battle with the coming of war, serving as a lieutenant in the London Regiment, and was killed on the Somme, at the age of forty-eight, in 1916.

If there was an *Übermensch* among the Wasdale climbers it was O. G. Jones, a London physics teacher of Welsh descent, who was the most fiercely determined of climbers. He used to train for three months with dumb-bells to get ready for the Lake District. He liked to say that 'O. G.', which stood for 'Owen Glynne', actually stood for 'Only Genuine'. It must be said that in his wireframe spectacles and Norfolk tweeds he looked more the scholar than the hard man, but he had a muscular reputation and some of his colleagues thought him reckless. One such was the occultist Aleister Crowley, who climbed with Jones on Great Gable. The other members of the party were the local climber Robinson and a sixteen-stone Pole called Lewkowitch who was inexperienced and in descent had to be lowered slowly down Oblique Chimney on a tight rope. Crowley had difficulty in doing this and looked to Jones, the only man above him, for assistance, but saw that he was off balance and hampered by photographic equipment he had strapped to his back. Crowley thought this showed both irresponsibility and vanity: 'as nor Einstein or the Blessed Virgin Mary was there to suspend the law of gravitation, I have no idea how we got to the bottom undamaged'.[15]

The clash of personalities between two such strong-willed men is not surprising, and it came to a head when Jones accused Crowley of lying about his earlier climbs in Wales. Crowley, on the other hand, indicted Jones for being a showman who would rehearse his climbs on a top-rope before making a 'first ascent' in front of a crowd of admirers. Jones was killed on the west arête of the Dente Blanche in 1899, when a guide fell while attempting to scale a buttress, knocking him off the mountain, and there is nothing like an early death to cement a heroic reputation. Jones left an impressive tally of new routes in the Lake District on Dow Crag, Kern Knotts, Scafell and Pillar Rock, and wrote an engaging introduction to the sport, *Rock-Climbing in the English Lake District*, first published two years before the fatal accident. The tone is bright, clear and workmanlike, with touches of wry humour. 'Be it remembered that in crag climbing two heads are better than one,' he wrote, 'even if the second head is only used as a foothold' – the early climbers did indeed use one another's bodies to help them scale the rock.[16]

Jones had two close friends among the local climbers, the Abraham brothers, Ashley and George, from Keswick, where they ran a photographic studio. They met in 1896 and no doubt it was the Abrahams who encouraged Jones to record his climbs photographically. They were both outstanding cragsmen in their own right, but they heaved bulky cameras and tripods into the fells so that they could document the accomplishments of others. They left an extraordinary archive of climbing images, some of which reveal just how perilous these pioneering climbs must have been. In one image, which the brothers later titled 'How Not to Climb', George is shown leading their younger brother Sidney up a precipice on Blencathra. Neither climber is secured to the rock; if one had fallen, he could easily have taken his brother with him.

Photography added to the perils of rock-climbing, as is evident from this passage in Jones's book (which was illustrated throughout with Abraham Bros photographs):

> He (George) was in an awkward place and was much cramped in ensuring safety, but Ashley was dissatisfied and insisted upon him lifting the left leg. This gave him no foothold to speak of, but in the cause of photography he had been trained to manage without such ordinary aids. He grumbled a little at the inconvenience but obeyed, resolving that if he were living when the next slide was to be exposed he himself would be the manipulator and his brother the centre of the picture.[17]

The Abrahams' images, even after all this time, are curiously involving; it sometimes feels as if one is sharing the same rope. But when it came to rock-climbing guidebooks line drawings were much clearer and more matter-of-fact than dramatic photographs, and it was William Heaton Cooper who drew the pictures for the classic series produced in the 1930s.

George Abraham was a keen motorist as well as a climber, in the days when driving a car could still be considered a manly sport, and he wrote the first motoring guide to the Lakes. Although he did not approve of reckless speed, he liked the challenge of the high passes, describing them in detail and even using the climbers' jargon of 'pitches' when giving advice on how to get over them.[18] Motorcar and motorcycle hill-climbing trials became popular, but aroused opposition from those who saw the Lake District as a tranquil sanctuary.

For the climbing world there are histories written in terms of first ascents, noteworthy cragsmen and technical innovations. It was important that everyone should get their due, but they can make dense reading for the non-climber. In broad outline, climbing began in the gullies, where there was a comfortable sense of security, graduated to the narrower cracks and chimneys and finally, as all of these were conquered, was forced out on to the exposed ridges and faces. A. H. Griffin's memoir of his climbing life, *The Coniston Tigers*, returns repeatedly to the development of better clothing and equipment. In the 1930s there were no anoraks or waterproofs, so walkers and climbers still wore old tweeds and hoped for good weather. Taking a leaf from the Abraham brothers, Griffin and his companions took to wearing white pullovers because they showed up better in photographs. There were no nuts or slings or karabiners, and indeed protection was so poor that it was an unwritten rule that the leader must never fall, whereas today desperate things can be attempted in relative security, which accounts for the dramatic increase in standards. In fact, many of the climbs put up by the early pioneers are now considered very easy indeed.

The social profile of rock-climbing has also changed. The Fell and Rock Climbing Club of the English Lake District, which was formed in 1906 with Ashley Abraham as its first president, was far more democratic than the Alpine Club had ever been. Working-class members were welcomed from the outset, as were women climbers, who were even offered a reduced subscription. Women climbers had not been unknown in the pioneering days, but social restrictions and cumbersome clothing had prevented their full participation, and the men had tended to patronise and protect them; it was not until they formed their own association, the Pinnacle Club, in 1921 that they began to be taken seriously by the men.

The climbers completed the exploration and documentation of the Lake District begun by the Picturesque tourists. Though they avoided rock that was 'rotten' (i.e. dangerously loose), they clambered over all the rest. Their progress meant that even the most awesome and forbidding of crags became sites for recreation. As a keen motorist and climber, George Abraham wrote in 1913 that a road over Sty Head Pass was much needed. Had it ever been built, it would have made Wasdale Head much more accessible, which would have suited the pioneering climbers. There was, however, even in those early days of rowdy swagger, a recognition that it was the wider landscape that made climbing in the Lake District so satisfying. Although the first climbers might have seen the Lake District as a training ground or a playground, rather than a painting, a temple or 'God's second book', the Fell and Rock Climbing Club would soon turn into one of the champions of Lake District conservation.

*Overleaf:*Wasdale Screes

Wythburn (1802) (now Thirlmere reservoir) by William Green

14

Manchester's Thirst

The Lost Battle of Thirlmere

ORDSWORTH AND RUSKIN BOTH feared that the sixty or so miles which separated the Lake District from industrial Lancashire was not going to prove a sufficient barrier. Somehow the taint of the city was going to breach the mountain ramparts of their sanctuary. They were proved right, but not in the way they had imagined. The threat, when realised, came neither from diabolical engines nor the mysterious 'plague wind', but from the most prosaic and bureaucratic of sources – the City of Manchester's Waterworks Committee. Unsentimental and utilitarian, the Committee hoped to secure Thirlmere as a water-gathering ground. 'A lake's a very useless thing,' quipped *Punch*, 'unless its water is taken in pipes to towns.'[1]

The link between pure water and public health was not conclusively made until the middle of the nineteenth century, a discovery which put huge moral pressure upon local authorities in large towns and cities to supply their populations with clean water, but Manchester, with its thirsty textile industry and rising population, had already faced up to this need, employing the engineer John Frederic La Trobe Bateman to supervise the construction of a great chain of reservoirs in the Pennine valley of Longdendale.[2] Yet, even as this venture was nearing completion, Bateman was advising his employers that new sources would be needed to meet future demands. In 1852, the councillors of Glasgow had engaged him to devise a scheme to extract water from Loch Katrine; now their counterparts in Manchester began to look acquisitively at the waters and meres of the Lake District, which, though remote, were in some ways ideally suited to meet the city's needs. The long, narrow valleys, with their steep-sided glaciated profiles, were relatively easy to dam, while the igneous rocks of the area produced soft water which was potable without further treatment. Bateman's first suggestion was that water could be taken from Ullswater and Haweswater via a tunnel eight and a half miles long, 1,000 feet under Kirkstone Pass, at a rate of eighty million gallons a day (Longdendale only supplied 25.5 millions per day). It was enough to supply both Manchester and Liverpool and the cities contemplated a joint venture.

Councillors from Manchester, including John Harwood, who would later become chairman of the committee, came north on a fact-finding mission. After spending time at Ullswater, where they fretted about the number of expensive residential properties around the lake they might have to acquire, and convinced themselves that lead pollution from local mines might be a problem, they decided that they should inspect the watershed. Clad in city clothes, they got lost and wandered for hours over the summit of Helvellyn. Councillor Booth found the going so tough that he had to be put on the horse they had brought to carry their equipment, but later both horse and rider had to be rescued from a bog. After all this they tumbled exhausted into the Nag's Head at Wythburn at 10.00 p.m., where they had to wait a further three hours for transport to their Keswick hotel.

Liverpool then decided to go it alone and get its water from North Wales, so Bateman was asked to think again. On 22 June 1876 he put an alternative suggestion to the Manchester committee. Thirlmere, he concluded, would be a better option. It was fifty-six feet higher than Ullswater and this relative elevation meant that no pumping would be required.[3] Water could flow under gravity right into the throat of the conurbation. The tunnel that would be required under Dunmail Raise would be less than half the length of the Kirkstone proposal and could be built at a third of the depth. The whole scheme would be £170,000 cheaper and it could be built in five years rather than seven. The Bishop of Manchester saw the hand of providence in the placement of the lake. If it 'had been made by the Almighty expressly to supply the densely popu-lated district of Manchester with water,' he opined, 'it could not have been more exquisitely designed for the purpose'.[4]

The land around Thirlmere was held by farmers and there were none of the fancy villas that had worried the committee at Ullswater. Nevertheless, the purchase of the land did not go entirely smoothly. Sir Harry Vane, Lord of the Manor of Wythburn, haggled over the price and eventually got twice the original offer, while Countess Ossalinsky, the locally born widow of a Polish nobleman, took her battle for a fair price to the courts, and insisted that the corporation would have to buy all the sheep on her tenants' farms.[5]

Thirlmere Bridge, Looking North, Cumberland (c. 1845–53) by Thomas Allom, engraved by W. Le Petit, from *Lake Scenery*

The owner of the Leathes Water estate was the elderly Thomas Stanger Leathes, Lord of the Manor of Legburthwaite, who was implacably opposed to the whole project and would not even allow Manchester's representatives to go over his land. Fortunately for the Manchester councillors, they only had to wait until 1877 for the old man to die, whereupon his son George, who had lived much of his life in Australia, had no hesitation in selling. A curious consequence of this purchase was that Alderman John Grave, chair of the Waterworks Committee, became Lord of the Manor and was obliged to keep a stallion, a bull and a boar for the use of his tenants.

Before it became a reservoir the lake went by three different names, each with variations in the spelling. Thirlmere or Thirlemere was also known as Wythburn, Wytheburn or Withburn Water, sharing its name with the hamlet at its southern end, and to some it was Leathes Water, taking its name from the family who built Dale Head Hall. Or else it was two lakes, one called Leathes Water and the other called Wythburn Water. Though Thirlmere was never as celebrated as Derwentwater, Ullswater or Windermere, the early tourists did not just pass it by. West may not have ringed it with viewing stations, but he did write of it in admiring prose:

A thousand huge rocks hang on Helvellyn's brow, which have been once
in motion and are now seemingly prepared to start anew. Many have
already reached the lake, and are at rest. The road sweeps through them,
along the naked margins of the lake. The opposite shore is beautified with
a variety of crown-topped rocks, some rent, some wooded, others not,
rising immediately from or hanging towards the water; and all set off with
a background of verdant mountains, rising in the noblest pastoral style.
Its singular beauty is its being almost intersected by two peninsulas, that
are joined by a bridge, which serves for an easy communication among
the shepherds that dwell on the opposite banks.[6]

This mattered little to the Mancunians, who were convinced that human
needs trumped aesthetics. Stealthily the Corporation began to buy up land
in the catchment, hoping to avoid paying the inflated prices that might ensue
once their intentions were known. Then, in 1878, a private bill was introduced into Parliament. The Waterworks Committee expected opposition,
but mostly from landowners in the vicinity of the proposed reservoir or
the pipeline, so they must have been surprised by the hornets that suddenly
poured out of the nest. Resistance coalesced around the rapidly formed
Thirlmere Defence Association.[7] Among the more vocal Lake District

Thirlmere (1888)

residents were Robert Crewdson, who lived in Wordsworth's old house at Rydal Mount, John Harward, a Grasmere landowner, and the shoe manufacturer Robert Somervell. An angry letter from Ruskin, who had not yet collapsed mentally, was printed in *The Times* of 20 October 1877, accusing Manchester of 'plotting to steal the waters of Thirlmere and the clouds of Helvellyn'. Protesters from further afield included Thomas Carlyle, a host of Oxford and Cambridge dons and the social reformer Octavia Hill, who brought in the Open Spaces Society. Harvey Goodwin, Bishop of Carlisle, wrote to *The Times* to say that 'a time might come when instead of a trip to the Lakes we should hear of a trip to the tanks or month at the reservoirs'.[8] While the Defence Association contained many who were implacably opposed to the project on aesthetic grounds, it also included local landowners who could be bought off, once opposition had forced up the price of land. The opposition was not wholehearted and it was not mobilised in time.

The man who would later become the staunchest of the Lake District's defenders, Hardwicke Rawnsley, found himself in an agonising moral dilemma. He believed that the Lake District was one of God's finest creations, that walking the fells brought people closer to heaven and that Manchester's proposals were a desecration, but he had also worked with the poor in Oxford, London and Bristol and he knew how much good pure, clean fell water might do in Manchester.

With prominent and articulate champions, the case against the reservoir was, however, taken up widely in the press. In January 1878 the *Gentleman's Magazine* thundered:

> May Cottonopolis be sent nearer home for its water supply and not interfere with the public pleasure in things on which it has never set any value; the solemnity of solitude, the unruffled aspect of nature, the glories of mountain, the peacefulness of the mere.[9]

Even though the protesters fought with gentle weapons – emotive arguments, sonnets and angry letters to a batch of editors – they made the future of a Lakeland valley into an issue of national concern. It was a turning point. Prior to this time, the aesthetics of landscape had largely been the province of private landowners with sufficient funds to spend on 'improvement'. Now, at the close of the nineteenth century, they had become a matter for everyone. People who lived hundreds of miles away from the Lake District felt that they had a share in the ownership, not of the land itself, but of views over that land.

When battle was joined in the House of Commons, Isaac Fletcher, MP for Cockermouth and a supporter of the Manchester scheme, tried to turn the argument around to portray the Lake District's villa builders as the true vandals. At the bill's second reading, on 12 February 1878, he even attempted to represent Manchester Corporation as conservationists:

> The effect of this Bill will be to reclaim 11,000 or 12,000 acres of the most beautiful part of Cumberland from the incursions of those aesthetic gentlemen who come down surveying the district and building Gothic villas upon the shores of this beautiful Lake. The Corporation of Manchester have no intention of selling any portion of the area for building purposes; and, in fact, so far from Thirlmere being spoiled, I look upon it as a great public improvement, and as a brand plucked from the burning.[10]

He was elegantly countered by Stafford Howard, MP for East Cumberland, who began by saying that when he had first heard of Manchester's plans he had not thought them unreasonable, but now saw the need for a full public inquiry into the whole question of how such manufacturing towns were to obtain their water.

There was, of course, much technical argument about the validity of Manchester's projections of demand, with opponents arguing that the Corporation was asking for too much, so that it could make a profit from supplying nearby towns, but beneath all this there was a visceral clash of values. William Foster, MP for Bradford and an opponent of the scheme, spoke in Parliament against shouts of 'No, No!' from his antagonists. The lake was, he asserted, 'one of the most beautiful objects in England'. Though the Corporation of Manchester said it was not going to spoil it, Foster was sure that the water level would fluctuate by about fifty feet and that 'instead of a very beautiful Lake, you will have a great pond, with a constant exposure of mud or ugly shingle'.[11]

The House decided that the bill should go before a specially constituted Select Committee, so that the wider issues of water supply could be examined. Although the bill's opponents often had to accept the utilitarian ground for the debate, they tried to topple arguments about the advantages of fresh water by using counter-arguments about the benefits to city dwellers of access to unspoilt countryside, but Manchester's need for water, and the impossibility of getting it from anywhere other than a

lake, were impossible to gainsay. The aptly named chairman of the Select
Committee, Lyon Playfair, said that they had looked at the whole question
impartially, but 'they had to deal with a general meteorological fact, for the
great south-western winds swept over the Atlantic and evaporated a large
quantity of water on the way, while the high mountains of Westmorland
and Cumberland acted as condensers, so that the water was poured over the
district in which those mountains were situated'.[12] The Committee reported
in favour of the dam and the bill was given Royal Assent on 23 May 1879,
though an economic downturn delayed the start of construction for another
six years.

Temporary camps were set up to accommodate the influx of navvies
brought in for the works. Huts were erected not only at sites around
Thirlmere but also on White Moss Common near Grasmere, beloved by the
Wordsworths and their friends, and on bleak and windy Dunmail Raise. In
fairness to the Manchester engineers, the massive dam, faced with millstone
grit and sandstone and filled with huge granite boulders, has never been a
dominant feature in the valley, but the scheme also involved the construction of new roads and the straightening of the main road on the eastern
side. Water was extracted from the lake via a straining well and there is also
a valve house controlling the flow into St John's Beck. Both structures were
finished off in faux-medieval style, and it was easy to read their castellations as intimidatingly defensive, particularly when the Corporation barred
access to the shores of the lake with threatening signs.

The reservoir began slowly to fill, though it would take twelve years to
reach capacity. The promontories which had so pleased West and Martineau
were early casualties but in time both Armboth House and the hamlet at
Wythburn known as 'The City' vanished beneath the waters.

One of the most poignant moments during construction was the dyna-
miting by the engineers of the Poet's Rock, trysting place of the six friends,
William, John and Dorothy Wordsworth, Coleridge, and Mary and Sara
Hutchinson. When Rawnsley realised that the boulder where they had
carved their names was to be blown up, he got permission to move it, but
the masons he engaged found the task beyond them. Once it had been shattered, Rawnsley and his wife gathered up the pieces and built them into
a memorial cairn. In 1984, following two nearby landslips and with the
prospect of tree-felling in the vicinity, it was arranged that the fragments
should be taken and embedded in the rock face immediately behind the new
Wordsworth museum at Grasmere.

To inaugurate the reservoir, Manchester decided to have two ceremonies, one at the straining well, where the valves would be opened, and another the following day in Albert Square, Manchester, to greet the arriving water and watch it play in a fountain erected for the purpose. Thus, on 12 October 1894, Sir John Harwood addressed a small crowd on the banks of Thirlmere. He challenged those who had objected to the dam with his rhetoric:

> Well, have you seen in your journey around the lake any semblance to a mill dam? Is there anything hideous in the handsome embankment we have formed?
>
> Is there one of you who thinks that jaded men and women, who seek restoration to health and strength in the quiet contemplation of the unspeakable beauties of nature, will be deterred from seeking all they need in this sequestered region because we have applied this watershed to the purposes of civilisation? No. A thousand times no.[13]

One might have expected Rawnsley, having switched sides midway on the principle of the reservoir, to have kept discreetly out of the proceedings, but it was not his nature. Instead he introduced the Thirlmere ceremony with a prayer – 'Let this river of God flow through the far off city to cleanse and purify; to help and heal' – and at the celebration lunch which followed he made an ingratiating speech in which he praised the far-sightedness of Harwood and his colleagues. In Manchester, understandably, the Thirlmere scheme was greeted as an unalloyed engineering triumph. 'Of course the inhabitants of that district did not desire to see their country disfigured,' said the Lord Mayor at the opening ceremony, but sentiment 'ought to have given way in the face of the necessity of conferring upon a large and crowded population the inestimable boon of a good supply of water'.[14] The irony is that Manchester's citizens also drank their fill of Lake District scenery; their civic art galleries overflowed with it.

Apologists for the Thirlmere scheme made the sorts of spurious claims that are often trotted out at public inquiries nowadays. Far from impairing the beauties of the Cumbrian landscape, their works would somehow enhance them. A new carriage road would make the best views of the lake more accessible. By purchasing the whole drainage ground of the lake the Corporation would, paradoxically, preserve Thirlmere from the depredations of tourism and commerce. The reality was very different.

Thirlmere, from Hell How (1892)

Thirlmere, general view (1929)

The water from Thirlmere was pure enough to send to Manchester taps without any treatment, but to ensure that this remained the case the Corporation kept people away from the reservoir. Access was denied by municipal-looking signs and railings. It could have been even worse; without opposition from the TDA and the Commons Society, Manchester could well have fenced off the whole catchment.[15]

Meanwhile, the sparkling becks that fed the lake were redirected through concrete channels, while the hillsides around the reservoir, which the engineers said must be stabilised, were planted with close-set ranks of conifers. A secondary aim was to make money from the timber. The predicted fluctuations in water level produced an ugly rim around the reservoir, devoid of vegetation, as the objectors had predicted. W. G. Collingwood expressed the feelings of many when he wrote of Thirlmere:

The old charm of its shores has quite vanished, and the sites of its legends
are hopelessly altered, so that the walk along either side is a mere sorrow
to anyone who cared for it before; the sham castles are an outrage, and
the formality of the roads, beloved of car-drivers and cyclists, deforms the
hillsides like a scar on a face.[16]

Locally this was the dominant opinion and it lasted for generations. I
can remember my father's muttered imprecations, whenever our family
excursions in the 1960s passed alongside Thirlmere, about Manchester
Corporation and the lake that they had ruined. But there were those in the
early days, including George Abraham, who were hugely impressed by the
scheme. As a motorist he was thrilled by the levelness of the new road. He
thought that the conversion of Thirlmere had been done so thoughtfully
and artistically that 'few would recognise the fact unless they knew the lake
previously in its double form of Leathes Water and Wythburn Water'. In an
age scarcely troubled by environmental concerns, he could enthuse about
'man's conquest over Nature', and the engineers were heroes:

Huge cuttings have been blasted through the solid rock, and the granite
walls reverberate with the hum of the modern chariot, where only a few
years before no wheeled thing but a wheelbarrow could travel happily.
The motorist soon realises what wonderful and hitherto unknown views
this new road provides.[17]

That driving has its own aesthetic and that views can be appreciated through
a windscreen are matters frequently overlooked in knee-jerk antagonism
towards cars, but Abraham's novel vistas must mostly have been lost as the
conifers got up. It was the ill-considered planting that caused the deepest
and longest-lasting resentment. Instead of the improved views promised,
Thirlmere was soon surrounded by the conifers that Wordsworth thought
so out of place in Lakeland, as if someone in authority was so ashamed of
the mess that had been made of this lake that it had to be hidden. It was not
until 1985, when Susan Johnson of Ravenglass, daughter of the Reverend H. H.
Symonds, a doughty campaigner against afforestation in the 1930s, took
the North West Water Authority to court, that matters began to improve.
In front of the Keswick magistrates, Johnson pulled the rug from beneath
the feet of the opposing legal team by going back to the original Thirlmere
Act of 1879 which stated that the authority had to pay 'reasonable regard

to the beauty of the scenery in general' and, more specifically, that the lake shore should be planted with native trees such as oak, ash, birch and alder. Since that time, and in line with changes in forestry practice elsewhere, aesthetics and recreational opportunities stand alongside more commercial issues. Only in 1989 –110 years after Manchester got its Act of Parliament – was a water treatment facility built and public access to the water's edge restored. Thirlmere is a lot more open and attractive than it was in my youth, although the ugly draw-down rim seems likely to remain for as long as Mancunians drink water.

The large-scale planting at Thirlmere foreshadowed further forests at Bassenthwaite and Ennerdale, while the battle over the reservoir was only the first of several similar tussles. Manchester was able to appropriate Haweswater with much less opposition. Although the valley opens to the east, it is a cul-de-sac, not much visited except by walkers wanting to climb the towering High Street range. Construction works began in 1929 but extraction did not begin until 1941. In the process of raising the water level by twenty-nine metres, the village of Mardale was flooded, including four farms, the local school, a seventeenth-century church and the Dun Bull Inn, where shepherds used to meet. Though Haweswater is not shrouded by coniferous forests, it does have the characteristically ugly shoreline, and when the waters are very low the doomed village reappears to admonish those who condemned it to a watery grave.

By the 1960s the demand for water had not abated, but society's attitudes towards landscape and environment had shifted significantly. When Manchester revivified its old ambition to extract water from Ullswater it had a fight on its hands. Amenity organisations such as the Friends of the Lake District had become much more organised. While thousands signed petitions, prominent journalists attacked the scheme. The *Daily Telegraph* columnist Peter Simple declared that he was ready to sit down on the banks of Ullswater, with the great shades of Wordsworth, Coleridge, Ruskin and Arnold at his side, if that was what it would take to see Manchester off. Lord Lonsdale spent six weeks in London tirelessly lobbying his Tory friends and colleagues against the bill. Opposition in the House of Lords was spearheaded by Lord Birkett of Ulverston, a Cumbrian-born lawyer who had served as a judge at the Nuremberg trials. His eloquent plea was that Ullswater should not suffer the same fate as Thirlmere and Haweswater, 'both lovely lakes which have now been murdered'.[18] On 8 February 1962 the offending clauses were struck out of the Manchester Corporation Act by 70 votes to 36, but the strain was too much for the ailing and exhausted Birkett, who died two days later. In 1965 Manchester tried again, this time seeking a Statutory Order to permit extraction at Gale Bay. It had to submit to a public inquiry in Kendal which lasted nineteen days, at which a large number of amenity bodies, including the Council for the Protection of Rural England and the National Trust, gave evidence. Although Manchester got its permission, it was hedged by stringent conditions. Most significantly, the amount of water that could be taken would be controlled by a weir, so that the beauty of the shoreline would be protected. Rather than building a boastful castellated dam, Manchester built the most discreet of pumping stations. There is virtually nothing to show that Ullswater is a reservoir.

The next serious struggle came in 1978 when the North West Water Authority, seeking increased supplies for West Cumbria in general and the nuclear plant at Windscale in particular, applied for permission to take supplies from Ennerdale Water. While the opposition was still rallying, British Nuclear Fuels Limited announced their own plan to extract water from Wastwater. Local politicians were divided, but a host of amenity groups, representing anglers, ramblers and rock-climbers, as well as farmers, naturalists and environmentalists, came out strongly against both projects. The public inquiry which followed took fifty-seven days, during which the most touching evidence was given by April Roberts, aged eleven, of Ennerdale Bridge Primary School, who said that she and her schoolfriends thought of Ennerdale Water as their own lake: 'we live by it, walk there and play there'.[19]

A more seasoned advocate, Christopher Horden, the dark-suited lawyer putting the Lake District Special Planning Board's case, made the philosophically interesting claim that the value of the Lake District was intrinsic and did not depend upon the number of people who saw it. Then he made a direct comparison with a 'great picture or statue'. If the Lakes were to be preserved, they had to be protected from careless handling. 'If it be right that any place in England should remain inviolate,' he pressed, 'surely Wastwater is one of them.'[20] For all the difficulties that swarm around the notion of treating living landscape as a museum or gallery piece, the Inspector in essence agreed, reporting to the then Secretary of State, Michael Heseltine, that both schemes were unacceptable on environmental grounds. The Ennerdale project would have involved substantial remodelling of the northerly shore, 'completely out of keeping with such a scene', while in the Wastwater case he shared the objectors' fears about the possible draw-down rim. The clinching argument was that the projects were not even necessary. Enough water could be found for Windscale by taking it by pipe from the River Derwent. The Secretary of State rejected the Ennerdale Water and Wastwater proposals in a letter dated 22 December 1981. The following day the *Guardian* ran a headline which read 'Heseltine Decision Delights the Lake District'.[21] With the subsequent loss of heavy industry in the north of England, the accompanying decline in population and the decommissioning of Windscale, the threat to the lakes of Lakeland seems at last to have receded, but if climate change occurs as quickly as many scientists fear it will, water could become a precious commodity and the pressure to tap the Lake District might return.

Overleaf: Head of Borrowdale

Yachts on Windermere (1869)

15

A Sort of National Property

Hardwicke Rawnsley and the Formation of the National Trust

A T THE END OF his *Guide through the District of the Lakes*, Wordsworth hoped that he would be 'joined by persons of pure taste throughout the island' when he deemed that the English Lake District was 'a sort of national property, in which every man has a right and interest who has an eye to perceive and a heart to enjoy'.[1] This is stirring stuff and sounds democratic until we remember the poet's distaste for those excursionists who did not share his aesthetic sensibilities. Nevertheless, that phrase – 'a sort of national property' – caught the imagination of those who cherished the Lake District. Wordsworth has been adopted as the patron saint of conservation.

It might seem odd to link Wordsworth with the National Trust and to the National Park. Wordsworth died in 1850, after all, while the Trust was not formed until 1895, and the National Park had to wait until 1951. But Wordsworth created the climate of opinion which made both of these advances possible, with Ruskin providing the crucial link to later generations of conservationists.

The Lake District has had some stalwart champions over the years, but none more remarkable than the Reverend Hardwicke Rawnsley – 'Hardie' to his friends. He was not born until the year after Wordsworth's death, and, like so many of the Lake District's most passionate advocates, he was an off-comer. Indeed, his family came from the lowlands of Lincolnshire, though he grew up in Shiplake-on-Thames, in the rectory opposite the church where his father had officiated in the wedding of Alfred Tennyson and Emily Sellwood. Tennyson, who succeeded Wordsworth as Poet Laureate, was a distant relation and family friend. Poetry would become one of Rawnsley's passions; he could knock out a half-decent sonnet for any occasion.

Rawnsley got his first taste of mountains when the headmaster of

Uppingham School in Rutland, Edward Thring, invited his young pupil to join his family for their holidays in the Lake District. Then, as an undergraduate at Balliol, Rawnsley met Ruskin at a college breakfast, and quickly became a disciple. Ruskin put him in touch with Octavia Hill, the prominent housing reformer, and Rawnsley, who came from a line of Anglican clerics, was soon working in a London hostel for the destitute.

The work must have been particularly demanding, since the usually energetic Rawnsley succumbed to a nervous breakdown within months. Hill suggested a period of convalescence at Croft, on the shores of Windermere, where he would be looked after by her friends, the Fletcher family. He could also visit Thring in Grasmere and his cousin at Wray Castle. The cure was successful, and Rawnsley rejoined the fray, this time as a missionary to one of the poorer parts of Bristol. He ran a boisterous Temperance Club for a group of disruptive youths, organising football matches and taking them on countryside walks, but not everyone in the parish appreciated his efforts and he was dismissed. It might have been the end of his career, but his Lake District cousin came to the rescue, offering him the living at St Margaret's church at Wray. This small and sleepy rural parish perhaps seemed a backward step to an ambitious young man, but it laid the foundation for a life of unceasing activity. Rawnsley was ordained at Carlisle Cathedral in 1877 and a month later, in the middle of one of the coldest winters the Lakes had ever known, he married Edith Fletcher, the daughter of his former hosts at Croft.

Compared to Bristol, or even to the tourist bustle on the eastern shore of Windermere, life at Wray was slow indeed, but Rawnsley soon found causes into which he could pour his almost bottomless energy. For one thing there was the plight of the agricultural poor, since the Lake District had not escaped the effects of a general agricultural downturn caused by cheap imports. Hardie saw education as the key to fighting unemployment and the drift of rural workers toward the cities, and the wood-carving classes which he and Edith organised for winter evenings were just the first of many similar initiatives over the course of his career.

But what would soon become Rawnsley's overwhelming passion was the future of the Lake District landscape. He arrived at the Low Wray vicarage in time to be caught up in the campaign against the extension of the railway from Windermere to Keswick. Then, as we have seen, he was faced with a moral dilemma over Manchester's plans for Thirlmere, eventually plumping for the utility of the reservoir over the aesthetics of the landscape.

When it came to the plans of a syndicate of quarry owners for a mineral line to carry slate down from Honister, however, Rawnsley found his true voice. In a letter to *The Standard*, published in February 1883, he wrote:

> Are the proprietors who work a certain slate quarry up in Honister to be allowed to damage irretrievably the health, rest and pleasure of their fellow countrymen who come there for needed quiet and rest, in order that they – the owners – may put a few more shillings a truckload into their private pockets? . . . Let the slate train once roar along the western side of Derwentwater, let it once cross the lovely vale of Newlands, and Keswick as the resort of weary men in search of rest will cease to be.[2]

As arguments over the Braithwaite and Buttermere Railway Bill continued, both inside and outside Parliament, another line was proposed to carry iron ore out of Ennerdale. Rawnsley threw himself into organising the opposition to both schemes. Soon there was a Borrowdale and Derwentwater Defence Fund, and, as at Thirlmere, what might have remained a local tussle became a matter of national significance, with large sections of the press weighing in against the quarrymen. Ruskin wrote to Rawnsley to offer his support, but he had grown unduly pessimistic: 'you may always put my name without asking leave to any petition against the railways. But

Bowness Ferry Boat (1896)

it's all no use. You will soon have a Cook's tourist railway up Scawfell and another up Helvellyn and another up Skiddaw, and then a connecting line all round.'[3] The wording suggests that he was more worried about day trippers than loads of slate or iron, but in any case he misjudged the tide of events. Rawnsley won both of his battles and after 1887 no further railway plans were put forward in the Lake District.

The sturdy country vicar with the bright eyes and the bristling moustaches had been transformed into the 'Defender of the Lakes', a figure of some national importance. In 1883 he moved to St Kentigern's, Crosthwaite, Keswick's parish church, on the invitation of Bishop Goodwin of Carlisle, who said 'the post which I offer you is as near heaven as anything can be'.[4] Rawnsley was made an honorary Canon of Carlisle Cathedral in 1893. Although he loved to travel, he never seriously considered living outside the Lakes, even turning down the opportunity to become Bishop of Madagascar in 1898, and, while he became a local grandee, he never lost the common touch and was often seen at sheep-dog trials, sheep-shearings and shepherds' meets. Like Ruskin, he recognised that the preservation of a landscape was impossible unless the ways of life associated with it could be sustained. In 1899 Rawnsley and his son Noel were involved in the formation of the Herdwick Sheep Breeders' Association, a group that is still active today.[5]

One of Rawnsley's parishioners called him 'the most active volcano in Europe',[6] an epithet which conveys both his energy and his volatility. It was not just threats to the landscape that irked him: he could get just as worked up about the closure of footpaths, cruelty to animals, drunkenness, white-bleached bread, lurid novels and saucy seaside postcards. His irascible streak did not always win him friends; even his own church gardener once called him 'a peppery old swine'.[7] Although he often set himself up in opposition to things that annoyed him, he was active in positive causes, too, pressing for public libraries, public health measures and better schools.

If the Thirlmere episode and subsequent battles had shown anything, it was the value of being prepared. Fighting each threat that came along on an *ad hoc* basis was not the way to proceed. Hardie was never confident that the inhabitants of the Lake District, left to their own devices, would not opt for short-term gain, so he made his pitch to the wider intellectual elite who had taken the Lake District into their hearts, choosing the annual meeting of the Wordsworth Society in College Hall, Westminster, to launch his appeal. He called for a permanent Lake District Defence Society, which was to be a watchdog, with the protection of picturesque beauty as its main concern: it fights on today, in transmogrified form, as the Friends of the Lake District. The Defence Society soon had six hundred members, including such worthies as Ruskin, William Morris, Octavia Hill, the artists Edward Burne-Jones and Sir Frederick Leighton, the Manchester-based architect Alfred Waterhouse, the Duke of Westminster and Benjamin Jowett, the Master of Balliol. The poetic provenance of the Society was marked by the membership of Robert Browning, Matthew Arnold and Alfred Lord Tennyson. The creation of this society recognised that the Lake District was a landscape of national significance, but only 10 per cent of the membership were residents of the Lake counties. More than a quarter lived in London and the Home Counties, with a further quarter from Lancashire, mostly Mancunians. The *Cumberland Pacquet* dismissed them as 'a handful of enthusiasts' who were determined to shut out the inhabitants from the benefits of modern travel,[8] while the *Whitehaven News* thought that Rawnsley's recruits were 'cheap aesthetes' who were interfering with the livelihoods of local people.[9] It is a familiar complaint, which has not lost its edge. An inescapable consequence of becoming 'a national property' was that decisions would not be left entirely to the indigenous community. There was now a wider community which believed it had a stake and a say in the future of the Lake District.

Even among the great and the good there were dissenters. The biologist Thomas Huxley was invited to join, but, as he wrote to his son, he feared that the society would be dominated by the 'irrational fanatics amongst its members'. He could not see much harm in roads or railways:

> Only the other day I walked the whole length of Bassenthwaite from Keswick and back, and I cannot say that the little line of rails which runs along the lake, now coming into view and now disappearing, interfered with my keen enjoyment of the beauty of the lake any more than the macadamised road did. And if it had not been for that railway I should not have been able to make Keswick my headquarters, and I should have lost my day's delight. People's sense of beauty should be more robust.[10]

Another organisation appeared alongside the Defence Society. The English Lake District Association drew a good deal of its support from the hoteliers of Bowness and Windermere, and devoted much of its energy to advertising the virtues of the Lakes as holiday destination, although it also campaigned for better footpaths, cleaner lakes and better signposting. The

Association sought to make the Lake District more appealing to visitors and in the process did things which were anathema to the purists of Rawnsley's stamp, such as placing iron seats at beauty spots. To any Ruskinian, the Association was compromised by its commercial concerns, whereas there was a radical edge to the Defence Society's membership, for whom notions of property and ownership were not sacrosanct. It opposed new roads over the mountain passes that could have wrecked their character, and overhead telegraph wires that could have done the same to the valleys, and it remained active right up until the First World War. Ironically, when Rawnsley retired in 1916 shortly after Edith's death, he moved into Allan Bank, the Grasmere house that Wordsworth had once lived in – and once condemned as ugly. Rawnsley remarried, but died in 1920. His widow Eleanor was instrumental in forming the Lake District Safeguarding Society, another conservation-minded body, but different from its predecessors in that it was composed of representative landowners from the various valleys.

Rawnsley's successful opposition to the railway schemes had brought him into collaboration with his old friend Octavia Hill and with Robert Hunter, a battling solicitor who had won many victories for the Commons Preservation Society, an organisation founded in 1865 (which makes it Britain's oldest conservation body). It championed public access to open spaces against domineering landlords by unearthing and reaffirming neglected common rights, which made them more likely to be acquired for public recreation. Common land was particularly vulnerable to proposals from railway companies and housing developers, so it is easy to see how Rawnsley and Hunter found common cause. While Rawnsley and his allies had been fighting railways in Borrowdale, Hunter had been striving to preserve Epping Forest for public recreation.

Hill had met Ruskin while she was running a charitable toy workshop for Ragged School girls, from the back of London's Fitzroy Square. She trained with him as an artist, but social work remained her vocation, and in 1864, with a loan from Ruskin, she bought three properties and began her career as a housing reformer. Like Ruskin, she was a depressive who found solace in the countryside, and she had been introduced to the pleasures of fellwalking in the 1860s by her friend Mary Harris, who had a house in the Lake District.[11] She joined the Commons Preservation Society in 1875, having earlier enlisted Hunter's support in a failed attempt to preserve fields at Swiss Cottage in London.

Later there was a cooling, then a rift, between Hill and Ruskin. Having turned herself into an exemplary landlord, Hill was prepared to work with capitalism, while Ruskin was averse to it. Hill sought to redeem London, but Ruskin had retreated to Brantwood and thought that all big cities were doomed. She thought he was 'a visionary whose teaching could not always be taken literally'.[12] Yet Ruskin's influence permeated many of the overlapping causes of the day. The Kyrle Society, for instance, named after a Scottish philanthropist, strove to improve the quality of life for the urban poor by tackling the ugliness of their surroundings. The idea came from Octavia's sister Miranda, who first suggested a more evocative title for the organisation – the 'Society for the Diffusion of Beauty'.[13]

The very Ruskinian idea that a property might be entirely removed from the marketplace in order to ensure its protection was first mooted in 1875 when the descendants of the diarist John Evelyn wished to donate his house in Deptford to the Metropolitan Board of Works, but could not find a legal way of doing so. Hunter thought a joint stock company could be formed, but Hill suggested a 'trust' would be better, as this would emphasise its benevolent character. The idea stewed for more than a decade, until in 1893 several properties in the Lake District came up for sale and Rawnsley started to ring bells of alarm.

Hunter, Hill and Rawnsley called a meeting at the offices of the Commons Preservation Society on 16 November. One of those in attendance, Hugh Lupus Grosvenor, first Duke of Westminster, a keen supporter of the Kyrle Society, was invited to become first president of the proposed body, the National Trust for Places of Historic Interest or Natural Beauty – which we now know as the National Trust. This was a shrewd move, since a great landowner could encourage those who might bequeath land and money to the Trust. Rawnsley became the organisation's Honorary Secretary, a position he would keep until his death. 'Mark my words, Miss Hill,' said the duke when they were discussing plans for the new organisation, 'this is going to be a very big thing.'[14]

We often associate the National Trust with country houses and perhaps think of it as a right-of-centre organisation with close links to the aristocracy and the countryside lobby, yet its founders were essentially left-of-centre liberals who hoped to provide the urban poor with 'sitting rooms' in the countryside. With close links to the Commons Preservation Society, they were even anti-landlord, to the extent that they believed in free access to

Woman crossing the stepping stones at Ambleside (1888)

land. Just how progressive they were is shown by Hunter's suggestion that the Trust should seek powers to force the sale of threatened lands and that the public purse should provide the funds.[15] Nevertheless, they were shrewd enough to court wealth and influence from the outset.

The shift towards the acquisition of country houses and estates, which would dominate the middle decades of the twentieth century, was a response to changes in death duties and inheritance tax which forced many landowners to put their properties on the market. Critics have caricatured the Trust as 'a vast system of outdoor relief for decayed gentlefolk',[16] but this was never the intention of its founders and in its early decades it was much more concerned with conserving land than with taking over buildings. Just as Ruskin compounded political views from the left and right of the political spectrum, so too has the National Trust, over the decades, seemed at times progressive, at others reactionary. Its vision of England, as represented by the folksy goods on sale in its many gift shops, is the nostalgic reverie of an England of contented agricultural workers and thriving cottage industries, not far removed from the dreams of the Guild of St George (of which Rawnsley was once a member).

Many prominent members of the Lake District Defence Society, such as Sir Frederick Leighton and Alfred Waterhouse, served alongside Rawnsley on the provisional council of the National Trust. Thomas Huxley must have changed his view of the 'fanatics' because he too joined the council. The Trust was, in a sense, a Lake District institution before it became a national one, yet its first property was in Wales. Fannie Talbot, a friend of both Ruskin and Rawnsley, donated Dinas Oleu, acres of clifftop land above Cardigan Bay, in the hope that she could save it from 'asphalt paths and cast iron seats of serpentine design',[17] a Ruskinian sentiment through and through.

At first there were no acquisitions in the Lakes, although Rawnsley persuaded the Trust to raise objections to the replacement of old bridges at Portinscale and Grange-in-Borrowdale, the erection of telegraph poles on White Moss Common, an electric tramline between Bowness and Ambleside, a proposed sewage works at Windermere and the use of the lake by seaplanes. In 1900 he raised subscriptions to place a memorial to Ruskin on Friar's Crag in the form of a rough-hewn slab of Borrowdale slate, carved and inscribed with Ruskin's own words, to a design by his secretary, W. G. Collingwood. The memorial was vested in the National Trust, so the tiny plot on which it stood was technically the Trust's first land in the Lake District.

When the 106 acres[18] of Brandlehow Park, on the shores of Derwentwater, beneath Cat Bells, were placed on the market in 1900, Rawnsley galvanised another successful appeal, raising the purchase price within five months. Though there were some large donations, the Trust gave much publicity to the smaller sums contributed by the less well off. 'I am a working man,' wrote one donor, 'and cannot afford more than 2s., but I once saw Derwentwater and can never forget it. I will do what I can to get my mates to help.'[19]

For an organisation with a streak of radicalism, the Trust was remarkably successful in attracting support from the very highest echelons. Princess Louise, Queen Victoria's fourth daughter, attended the opening ceremony at Brandlehow in 1902 and in the same year became the Trust's President, a position she kept until her death in 1939. A watercolourist and sculptor of some talent, she had been brought into the Trust by Octavia Hill, whose housing work she also supported. Octavia later described the event to her mother in a letter:

It was very successful, very simple, real and unconventional. The place was looking lovely. I never saw light more beautiful, it was not what people call fine, but it was *very* beautiful and did not rain. The wind was high and tore the tent to ribbons when it was being put up, but I think it really did better because the simple little red dais was out under the free sky, with the great lake lying below, and the golden fern clad slopes of Catbells above. It was funny and primitive and the nice North country folk were quite near and saw and heard all. The Princess was most friendly and kind and really did show an interest in the National Trust work.[20]

Securing lakeside land became a particular objective of the Trust, though it was a difficult one, since this was the most desirable and thus most expensive property in the District. Four years later it was able to acquire 750 acres of the most culturally resonant land in England, Gowbarrow Park beside Ullswater, where the daffodils had once danced for Wordsworth. This purchase also included Aira Force, one of the most celebrated waterfalls, and its rocky fairyland of a valley. The appeal leaflet made an audacious suggestion: 'Why not nationalise the English Lake District?'[21] The means were also found to purchase Manesty Park near Brandlehow, a property which had already been divided up into building plots. Another appeal secured Grange Fell and land in Borrowdale, including the Bowder Stone. Princess Louise put in £100 and dedicated Grange Fell as a memorial to her brother, Edward VII. An Act of Parliament in 1907 gave the National Trust the power to declare land inalienable, thus safeguarding it in perpetuity for public benefit.

The years just before the First World War were good ones for the Trust. It bought lake shore land on Ullswater, just north of Stybarrow Crag, and secured both Castlerigg Stone Circle near Keswick and the Roman fort at Borran's Field near Ambleside, along with Queen Adelaide's Hill above the upper reaches of Windermere. After the war, three considerable gifts were presented to the Trust as memorials to those who had died in the conflict. Lord Leconfield gave Scafell Pike, Sir William and Lady Hamer, whose son had been killed in action, made a gift of Castle Crag in Borrowdale, and the Fell and Rock Climbing Club purchased and donated an impressive cluster of summits: Great Gable, Green Gable, Kirk Fell, Great End, Brandreth, Grey Knotts, Base Brown, Seathwaite Fell, Glaramara, Allen Crags, Broad Crag and Lingmell.

In 1920, the year Rawnsley died, the Trust held over 1,387 acres in the Lake District, and the gifts and subscriptions kept coming. The canon's friends and admirers got together an appeal to buy land around Derwentwater as a tribute to him; thus the Trust gained Lord's Island, some land in Great

Wood and – most fittingly – the Friar's Crag promontory, where, twenty years earlier, at Rawnsley's instigation, the Ruskin memorial had been sited. In 1925 Gordon Wordsworth, the poet's grandson, and A. C. Benson gifted the remainder of Scafell, and in 1929 the Cambridge historian Dr George Macaulay Trevelyan donated 410 acres in Langdale, including the Dungeon Ghyll Hotel. By 1944 the Trust owned 17,000 acres, and after the war its holding grew to 122,000 acres, a quarter of what would eventually become the National Park.

The formation of the National Trust is a success story and its achievements in landscape conservation have been exemplary, but even in its early, leftish days, it was tainted by class snobbery. Quite deliberately, pragmatically perhaps, its founders had ensured that its governing council would be packed with MPs, nominees from the old universities, aristocrats and Old Etonians. An exception was Thomas Burt, a Northumberland miner who became MP for Morpeth in 1874. A keen walker, he had been captivated by reading Ruskin's *Unto This Last* and he was elected to the National Trust's council, but only served for two years.[22] More generally the Trust took on an Establishment character which would only deepen in the next century. When Brandlehow Woods were opened, the Trust's Annual Report could not refrain from a schoolmasterly warning: 'It is for the people who visit it to prove that they can be trusted to use it in the right way and that they can themselves be the most jealous guardians of the order and beauty of their own possession.'[23] The Trust never sought to be popularist or democratic and the tension between access and preservation was always resolved in favour of the latter. 'Only extremists would ask for much more access than there is today,' wrote Bruce Thompson, the Trust's land agent, in 1945. He also devoted several pages to grumbling about litter louts and 'comers and goers' who left gates open, or rolled boulders down the fellsides.[24] Birthwaite people, no doubt. But the irony is that Thompson's family had owned the Ferry Hotel in Bowness for generations and he was married to Mary Rigg, whose family were proprietors of the celebrated Windermere Hotel.[25] The Trust's top man in the Lake District owed quite a debt to the tourists, the railway and the coach trade.

Overleaf: Townend, Troutbeck

'Mrs Tabitha Twitchet at Hill Top',
from *The Tale of Tom Kitten* by Beatrix Potter

16

Visions of Childhood

Beatrix Potter and Arthur Ransome

T HOUGH THE WEATHER ON the mountain tops can be extreme and the fellsides dangerous, it is more often the homely and reassuring vision of the Lake District that prevails. The neatly walled fields and the cheering fireside eternally trump the bleak hillside and the shattered crag. Nowhere is this more evident than in the field of children's literature, where the Lake District is represented by the work of two popular writers, Beatrix Potter and Arthur Ransome.

At first sight, these two seem different in every way. She was the timid child of rather stuffy Victorian parents and liked to play with animals; he was the adventurous son of a history professor and loved to mess about in boats. She became a sheep farmer; he was a globe-trotting correspondent. She wrote books in which the world is full of perils and safety is found in hearth and home; he wrote books featuring children free from adult supervision, who were at liberty to become self-sufficient explorers. But they also had a great deal in common. Both came from secure middle-class backgrounds and both created fantasy worlds based upon their childhood experiences of the Lake District, though Potter's was peopled with talking animals and Ransome's with precocious, imaginative children.

Both wrote books that were, in some sense, instructive, though their lessons were quite different. If Potter's characters transgress the rules or stray too far from home, like Timmie Willie in *The Tale of Johnny Town-Mouse*, they find themselves in trouble – better to stay with the known and the understood. Ransome's heroes and heroines, on the other hand, live on the boundary between reality and imagination and their creator urges them on into adventures.

*

Beatrix Potter was born on 28 July 1866, at 2 Bolton Gardens, South Kensington. Her father, Rupert Potter, was a barrister, but in 1884 he inherited the fortune made by Beatrix's grandfather, Edmund Potter, who had been a calico printer in Glossop, Derbyshire. Rupert had the leisure and means to move in artistic and intellectual circles, and his pioneering amateur photography was admired, particularly by Millais. His wife Helen, on the other hand, was a more straightforward snob who aspired to move up in genteel London society. The Potters' North Country and Nonconformist origins were a hindrance in the capital, yet Beatrix, who found London bourgeois life stultifying, took pride in them. One of Beatrix's great-grandfathers on her father's side, Abraham Crompton, had been the owner of Holme Ground, a farm in the Tilberthwaite Fells above Coniston.

Like Ruskin, another cosseted and lonely child, Beatrix found holidays a blessed escape, and fortunately the well-heeled Potters took them frequently. In spring they would usually go to the West Country, but in summer her father would rent a large country house in Scotland or the north of England. For most of Beatrix's childhood their destination was Dalguise House, on the banks of the River Tay near Dunkeld. It was a landscape which stoked her romantic imagination, and the stark entry in her secret diary for Monday 10 July 1882 – 'Papa took Wray Castle' – suggests that she might have been unhappy with the switch, at least initially. On Friday the 21st she recorded their arrival, noting rather tartly that the house had been built by Mr Dawson, a doctor, in 1845, with his wife's money: 'She was a Liverpool lady. Her father Robert Preston made gin; that was where the money came from.'[1] Plenty of the latter was needed, for it is said that Dawson stopped keeping accounts once the figure had exceeded £60,000, and the architect, a Mr Lightfoot, reputedly drank himself to death before the house was finished. The term 'pile' could have been coined for Wray Castle, for this full-blown medieval daydream, with its faux arrow slits and top-heavy castellated battlements, makes even the most glaring of Arcadian villas seem bashful.

It is difficult to imagine Beatrix, who in later life showed a strong preference for cottages, liking such a house, but she was soon won over by the landscape and the local people. She admired the ornamental grounds at Wray, where there was a mulberry bush planted by Wordsworth, and took gentle walks across the fields to cosy Hawkshead. She also went on a Windermere cruise (down the lake on the steamer *Teal* and back on the *Swan*). In October, when the coaches and steamers had stopped running, she walked to Elterwater and celebrated Harvest Festival the next day in the church at Wray.

For more than twenty years, on and off, the Potters would holiday in the Lake District. They divided their visits between Windermere and Derwentwater. They twice rented Holehird, near Troutbeck Bridge (now the base of the Lakeland Horticultural Society), and often stayed at Lakefield (now Ees Wyke), a large Georgian house above Esthwaite Water built originally for a Lancashire mill owner. At Derwentwater they took Fawe Park in 1903 and leased Lingholm, another house on the western shore of the lake, no fewer than nine times.

The Dr Dawson who built Wray Castle left it to his nephew, Edward Preston Rawnsley, who invited his cousin Hardwicke to take the vacant living of St Margaret's church in 1875. Thus it was that, when the Potters arrived for their very first Lake District holiday, they immediately fell in with the charismatic young vicar, whose interest in art, natural history and local traditions at once appealed to Beatrix and her father. They met him again while holidaying at Lingholm, following his move to the parish of Crosthwaite. The prolific versifier turned out a collection of *Moral Rhymes for the Young* in 1897, and it was his mentoring, at least in part, that prompted Beatrix to think she might have the makings of a children's writer and illustrator. Over the years Beatrix had often written illustrated letters to the children of her former governess, Annie Moore. It was Annie who suggested that some of these stories might be turned into books, but Beatrix's first attempt met some of the stumbling blocks often encountered by new authors. After rejections from six publishers she decided to pay for an edition of five hundred copies to be printed. The book was to be called *The Tale of Peter Rabbit*. Rawnsley, meanwhile, had interceded on her behalf with Frederick Warne & Co., but had translated the story into his own moralising verse. Potter's biographer Linda Lear suggests that it might have been the awfulness of Hardie's rhyming version which persuaded the Warne editors to reconsider Beatrix's manuscript. When the book was published by them in October 1902 it was a runaway success, selling 28,000 copies before the end of the year.

In Potter's tales, as in many fairy stories, the veneer of civilisation is shown to be thin. Bunnies may wear blue jackets and ducks stroll out in shawls and poke bonnets, a hedgehog can be a washerwoman and have a kitchen with an iron range, but red-in-tooth-and-claw nature is never far away. Tom Kitten narrowly escapes being baked in a pudding by a couple of

'Owl Island', from *The Tale of Squirrel Nutkin* by Beatrix Potter

malevolent rats, the shopkeepers Ginger and Pickles often think of eating their customers, and Tommy Brock the badger abuses Mr Bouncer's hospitality by abducting his grandchildren to put them in a pie. The stories can be gruesome and remarkably unsentimental. Some critics have seen in them the stirrings of a feminist environmentalism, inviting readers to engage on equal terms with wild creatures. It is difficult to imagine a pet-loving girl writing them, much easier to think of them coming from a down-to-earth countrywoman. The paradox is that when Beatrix became that country-woman, she lost interest in writing tales for children.

The story of Beatrix's ill-fated love for Norman Warne, her editor and youngest son of Frederick Warne, was at the heart of the 2006 movie *Miss Potter*, which was largely filmed in the Lake District and on the Isle of Man. Though the script contained some historical inaccuracies, the central tragedy was true to the facts: despite opposition from her snobbish parents, Beatrix, who was already thirty-nine years old and had seem destined to enter middle age as a spinster, accepted a marriage proposal from Norman in July 1905. The Potters departed for their annual summer holiday (this time to Wales) and Beatrix never saw her fiancé alive again. He took to his bed on 29 July and died on 20 August, succumbing swiftly to lymphatic leukaemia.

By the time of Norman's death, Warne had published five of Beatrix's stories, including *The Tale of Squirrel Nutkin* (1903), the first to be expressly located in the Lake District. It was conceived during a family holiday at Lingholm in 1901 and Owl Island, the destination for the squirrels' little flotilla of twig rafts, is based upon St Herbert's Island on Derwentwater. Norman and Beatrix had planned to buy a small farm in the English Lakes. Hill Top Farm at Near Sawrey had been on the market since spring. Now, with the clarity and determination that grief can bring, Beatrix pressed ahead with the purchase, supplementing her royalties with a small legacy. Though the rest of her dreams had been shattered, she was determined to secure this fragment. Her parents had tried to efface their northern origins, so this purchase was an intentional act of defiance. Family duties meant that she would have to live most of the year in London, but she had established herself, in a small way, as a Lancashire landowner.

In the film version of her life, Beatrix is rescued from her grief and loneliness when she is reunited with William Heelis, a friend from childhood holidays. She did indeed become Mrs Heelis, but there was no such reunion. She first met William, a Hawkshead solicitor, when buying a neighbouring farm in Near Sawrey. In 1909 he carried out the conveyancing for Castle Farm (often called Castle Cottage) and it was this property, rather than Hill Top, that became the Heelises' home when Rupert Potter died in 1914 and Beatrix finally felt free to relocate permanently to the Lake District. Her elderly mother, donning widow's weeds, bought Lindeth Howe near Bowness the following year, but she did not lose her high and mighty airs, retaining her coach and her liveried coachman.

Beatrix's increasing attachment to place is revealed through her books. Some of the earlier tales are set in the northern Lake District she knew through holiday visits. *The Tale of Benjamin Bunny* (1904), for example, was developed while she was staying at Fawe Park, though the background landscapes seem generic. *The Tale of Mrs. Tiggy-Winkle* (1905) is expressly set in the Newlands valley and was dedicated to Lucie Carr, daughter of the local vicar. The background views are more specific and in the story the washerwoman-hedgehog takes in the coats of the lambs of Skeghyl, Gatesgarth and Little-town, recognising them by their sheep marks. Seven of the tales, however, are set around Hill Top, Sawrey or Hawkshead. The drive and porch of Hill Top are identifiable in the opening illustration of *The Tale of Tom Kitten* (1907) and there are interior scenes based upon the staircase and bedrooms. The iron range, cupboards and closets of the farmhouse feature in *The Tale of Samuel Whiskers* (published in 1908, but written in 1906). The village shop in *The Tale of Ginger and Pickles* (1909) was based upon the one in Sawrey, while the 'town' in *The Tale of Johnny Town-Mouse* (1918) was the bustling metropolis of Hawkshead.

Beatrix's metamorphosis into Mrs Heelis, the North Country farmer, was accompanied by a change of wardrobe. She had never cared much for fashion. Now she chose to wear wooden-soled clogs, a hard-wearing grey suit of Herdwick wool and a brown felt hat, an outfit which belied her wealth and social standing, but she shared the financial acumen of her manufacturing forebears. Once, in her journal, at a time when she was contemplating an emotionally forlorn future, she had written about the comfort and independence that money might bring.[2] She was one of the first children's authors to recognise the merchandising potential of her stories. She patented a Peter Rabbit doll in 1903, only a year after publication of the book, and this was followed by a jigsaw puzzle, nursery wallpaper and a board game. She called these 'side-shows' but they became the basis of an industry.

Beatrix still needed her royalties and profits to support her farming ventures, but even in 1911 she had begun to be fatigued by the publishing treadmill. When Warne responded coolly to her idea for an updated version of Aesop's fables, she replied, '. . . you don't suppose I shall be able to continue these d . . . . d little books when I'm dead and buried!! I am utterly tired of doing them, and my eyes are wearing out.'[3] In her heyday as an author, which lasted until 1909, her output was generally two *Tales* per year, but as her involvement in farming grew so the writing dwindled. She managed a book a year from 1910 to 1913, but during the First World War her production became sporadic. Her last story was *The Tale of Little Pig Robinson*, published in 1930 and set not in the Lake District, but at the Devon seaside. When her father died in 1913 she inherited £35,000 (equivalent to around £1.8 million today) and a very much larger sum came when her mother passed away in 1932.

Mrs Heelis, as we must now think of her, used some of her wealth to acquire more Lake District land. At first the purchases were small, as she added to her holdings around Hill Top whenever the opportunity arose, then in 1923 she purchased Troutbeck Park Farm, a property of 2,000 acres,

Beatrix Potter

thus becoming the owner of a large flock of Herdwick sheep. In 1930, to her great satisfaction, she was able to buy the Monk Coniston Estate, which included the land once owned by her great-grandfather. The estate, which belonged to James Garth Marshall, covered 4,000 acres between Little Langdale and Coniston. It included Tarn Hows, one of the Lake District's most celebrated beauty spots, created, ironically enough, not by nature but by a dam built by Marshall, the son of a Leeds industrialist. Heelis immediately sold half the land at cost price to the National Trust, intending to gift the remainder to the organisation in her will.

When it came to establishing her credentials as a Lake District farmer, Beatrix laboured against some substantial prejudices. Though she might have seen herself as someone with local roots, to the established farming community she was an off-comer. She was distanced from her neighbours by class, wealth and upbringing, but most offputting of all she was a woman, dabbling, as they saw it, in a man's world. It says much for her strength of character, thickness of skin and managerial abilities that she was not daunted by any of this. It helped that her husband was a well-respected local man with an amiable disposition and a love of country sports. Lear documents Mrs Heelis's man-management in some detail. Not only was she a good judge of character, generally able to pick the right people to become farm managers or shepherds, but she had the wisdom to delegate responsibility where appropriate. A key appointment was Tom Storey, who became her shepherd at Troutbeck Park and later her farm manager at Hill Top. It seems that even in 1927 it was hard to make Herdwicks pay. Tom told Mrs Heelis that cross-bred sheep would provide more profitable meat and wool, but she had by this time developed an attachment to the breed and was keen to compete in the local agricultural shows. Her Hill Top sheep were identifiable by a newly registered 'smit' mark on their fleeces, the letter 'H' for Heelis.[4]

It was not long before Mrs Heelis and her shepherds began to win prizes. In 1929 she won at Keswick, Cockermouth, Ennerdale and Eskdale, and she carried off top honours at Ennerdale and Keswick again the following year. As the silverware began to accumulate, so her reputation grew. A lifetime of drawing animals had given her a particularly good eye for the form and qualities of farm animals and in 1935 she was named president of the Keswick Agricultural Show. Two years later the organisers of the show at Lowick invited her to be one of the judges for the Herdwick sheep and the collie dogs. She was seventy-one when this honour arrived, but the ultimate accolade came in 1944 when she was voted president-elect of the Herdwick Sheep Breeders' Association. In April of that year the abstemious septuagenarian was even called upon to chair the monthly meeting of this august male-dominated body in a local pub.[5]

Socially and politically Mrs Heelis, it is fair to say, was a natural conservative, though, as with Ruskin and the later Wordsworth, her conservatism had a greenish cast. That these three should have so much in common does make one wonder whether there is something inherent in mountain scenery which produces conservatism – though Ransome and Martineau were not affected. It is easy to see how radicalism prospers in cities, which is where change is most evident both for good and ill. In the countryside change appears slower and, as cultural geographers are fond of pointing out, the landscape itself can be a sort of veil which, in its apparent stability, hides genuine social tensions and conflicts of interest. Mountains are natural barriers and can easily be construed as bulwarks against unwelcome social and economic realities.

As Lear tells us, Beatrix was a 'believer in breed',[6] and she thought in such terms not just about farm stock, but also about people. She attributed her own robust and outspoken independence to her Crompton ancestors. Nature was given precedence over nurture. It is not a creed which aligns with socially progressive thinking and some of Mrs Heelis's attitudes were Victorian, though they were leavened by her Unitarian upbringing. When considering the 'lower orders' she seems to have had no qualms about distinguishing between the deserving and the undeserving. Often it was the misuse of drink which decided the issue, a recurrent theme in her journal. A long entry for 16 August 1885 mentions the news that five Keswick men and one from Penrith had gone to the Lodore Hotel to drink, and drowned on the way back when their boat was upset in the course of a fight. 'They belonged to the lowest set in town, and will not be missed,' Beatrix wrote, 'but unfortunately the catastrophe has had no effect on the survivors, they were fighting in Keswick within an hour.'[7] Although she could be crusty, she liked to gossip and seems to have got on well with her country neighbours, but in a letter to her sister-in-law, written in March 1918, she disparaged 'wretched shirkers & unsound youths & odious self conscious girl workers.' Incongruously for an author who had made a good deal of money from children's stories and rabbit dolls, she thought modern youngsters were too pampered with toys and books. The Girl Guides, however, had her blessing and they were allowed to camp in her fields.

Beatrix could support education for women, but found suffragettes alarming. Throughout her life she valued permanence and had a horror of revolution. In her journal entries for 1883 she worried about dynamite-hurling Irishmen, street disturbances and the implications of electoral reform. She could feel pity for the poor and the unemployed, but was hostile to agitators and reformers. Beatrix expressed a little of her own distaste for cities in *The Tale of Johnny Town-Mouse*, and, having escaped from the city, she was not always happy when elements of the urban population intruded into her new world. She could tolerate hillwalkers, who did not do much harm once they were on the peaks and ridges (which were not, in any case, her favourite terrain), but she grumbled if they left gates open when they returned to the valley. Socialists and trade unions were beyond the pale and with the coming of the Second World War she developed an uncharitable fear that swarms of refugees from Barrow were going to be billeted in the Lake District. 'No one would grudge them asylum in a raid,' she wrote, 'but the dockers' families are rough, mostly Irish Catholics.'[8]

If her politics could be reactionary, her attitude towards progress was more discriminating. As a farmer, she was happy to embrace scientific methods and she was no Luddite; she used the train and the Heelises had two cars, though Beatrix never learnt to drive. On the other hand, she resisted electric lighting in her farmhouses, preferring candles or gaslight. Surprisingly perhaps, she wrote in her journal for 9 September 1895: 'There are some beautiful exposures of rock along the new road between Skelwith and Elterwater, a road whose newness may enrage sentimentalists but strikes me as a good thing well done.'[9]

But some manifestations of progress were simply out of place, she believed, and the development which aroused her greatest ire was the construction in 1911 of an aeroplane 'factory' at Cockshott Point, on the eastern shore of Windermere. In fact, it was a large hangar housing a couple of hydroplanes and painted green to minimise its scenic impact, or so its owner Mr E. W. Wakefield claimed. 'There is a beastly fly-swimming spluttering aeroplane careering up & down over Windermere; it makes a noise like 10 million bluebottles,' Beatrix wrote in a letter,[10] and she joined forces with Hardwicke Rawnsley to swat the irritation. It was a hazard to boat users, she argued, and upset livestock transported on the ferry. Well-tried tactics of protest were employed: a campaign of letters to *Country Life* and *The Times* was coupled with a petition. When she wrote to her friends in the world of publishing to enlist their support, she signed herself 'Beatrix Potter'. When writing to members of the local community she appealed to them as 'H. B. Potter, *farmer*'. Wakefield, meanwhile, justified his activities in a letter to *Flight* magazine (an appeal to believers), invoking military need and claiming that Windermere was 'an ideal place for experimental purposes', while arguing that 'almost everyone who has seen [the plane] flying agrees that it adds to the great natural beauty, like a fine bird, between water and sky in changing lights'.[11] However, the protesters forced the government to hold a public inquiry and before the end of 1912 the aeroplanes had gone, though during the Second World War a flying-boat factory would be established further north at White Cross Bay.

Like Wordsworth, Heelis believed that the Lake District was a unique and fragile landscape that could be easily harmed. As her views on conservation developed, she became determined to do what she could to preserve the countryside to which she had become so attached. As one of Rawnsley's earliest recruits, her father had become the National Trust's first life member. When Beatrix purchased Troutbeck Park, she was already considering plans to bequeath the farm to the Trust. In 1926 she put fifty autographed drawings up for sale in an American magazine to raise money for the Trust's Windermere Fund, which ultimately succeeded in purchasing Cockshott Point to preserve it not just from a buzzing aerodrome, but also from more conventional forms of urban sprawl. Her purchase of Monk Coniston was motivated not merely by personal sentiment, but by a real concern that if she did not intervene the estate would be parcelled out for bungalows and holiday homes.

Mrs Heelis's dealings with the National Trust, especially its local representatives, were not always harmonious. In particular she had a prickly relationship with Bruce Thompson, who became land agent for the Trust's northern district in 1936, by which time Beatrix had reached her seventies. Though Thompson was a well-educated Windermere man and had known Canon Rawnsley personally, Heelis did not take to him, and she sometimes took her grumbles to his superiors in London. According to Lear, she feared that he might be an inept dilettante, who could undo all her work at Monk Coniston, where she had worked as the Trust's voluntary land agent before his appointment. Her anxieties seem to have been misplaced, and Thompson was too diplomatic to mention any of their disagreements when later writing his own account of the National Trust's activities in the Lake District. He could hardly have done otherwise, because when Beatrix died in Castle Cottage in 1943 she left her entire property of over 4,000 acres to the Trust, which was, as Thompson put it in his land agent's prose, 'the most munificent devise' the charity had received in its fifty years of existence.[12]

With her connections to Rawnsley and the National Trust, it is easy to place Mrs Heelis within the tradition of conservative-minded landscape preservation initiated by Wordsworth and continued by Ruskin. Her contemporary, Arthur Ransome, is much harder to place, because he was not a social conservative and he did not involve himself in efforts to halt landscape change. His books seem to advocate a very active involvement with the landscape, untainted by our contemporary anxieties over 'Health and Safety'.

The parents of Ransome's child heroes demonstrate an extraordinary equanimity in the face of their offspring's playful exploits: 'We are going home at the end of the week. It would be a pity if two or three of you were drowned first.' In his youth Wordsworth had much in common with Ransome's characters, running wild on Lowther land 'like a savage', stealing boats on Grasmere, and there is an innocence about this phase of

Arthur Ransome

Wordsworth's life, just as there is in the world that Ransome created. It is a world of play and the reader knows that no real harm is going to come to any of these children.

Ransome wrote of his father that he 'was a fisherman who was Professor of History in his spare time'.[13] Cyril Ransome held an academic chair at Yorkshire College, which became Leeds University, and the family lived in well-heeled Headingley, but each summer they would go to stay at the Swainsons' farm at High Nibthwaite on Coniston Water, where the professor could fish for trout on the lake. Cyril had been born on the shores of Morecambe Bay, within sight of the hills, and held himself an exile in Leeds. To make amends for his eldest son being born in a city, he carried the infant Arthur to the summit of Coniston Old Man. In his autobiography Arthur recalled a ritual, begun on his childhood holidays:

Without letting the others know what I was doing, I had to dip my hand in the water, as a greeting to the beloved lake or as a proof to myself that I had indeed come home. In later years, even as an old man, I have laughed at myself, resolved not to do it, and every time have done it again.[14]

Cyril, who had at one time rowed for his Oxford college, schooled Arthur in the use of the oars, but Arthur's first experiences on water were in 'a heavy farm-boat with oars that worked on pins instead of in rowlocks (so that a fisherman could drop them instantly if a pike or a char took his trailed spinner)'.[15] He would owe many of his greatest pleasures, including his passion for angling, his love of boats and his deep connection with the southern Lake District, to his father, but Cyril often had such high expectations of his son that Arthur was frequently oppressed by feelings of inadequacy.

Arthur, who was born in 1884, grew into an energetic and adventurous boy. On holiday he loved to fish for minnows and perch on the lake, and he wore out his knickerbockers sliding on a smooth, steep rock amid the bracken and sheep-cropped grass on the slopes above the farm, whereupon they were duly darned by Mrs Swainson. Sometimes Cyril would row the whole family across to Peel Island for a picnic. On one occasion, in August 1896, the Ransomes arranged to rendezvous there with the Collingwood family. Cyril Ransome and W. G. Collingwood were already acquainted through their work. Collingwood had undertaken archaeological excavations on the island and discovered the remains of a Viking settlement. He had also written a fictitious account of the life of a Norse settler called Thorstein (the old name for Coniston Water was Thurston's Mere) which he had sent to Ransome. Christina Hardyment, who has tracked down many of the events and locations which influenced Arthur when writing his children's novels, suggests that this encounter planted the imaginative seed for the confrontation between the Walker and Blackett children in *Swallows and Amazons*.[16]

The following year at Nibthwaite, on his way back from fishing for seatrout in the dark, Cyril tripped over an old grindstone, and damaged a bone in his leg. Thinking it no more than a sprain he ignored it, but the injury developed into a form of tuberculosis and his leg had to be amputated at the foot, then at the knee and finally at the thigh, but nothing could save him. This immense emotional blow also meant the end, for a while, of Arthur's Lake District holidays. He was sent to Rugby School, then went to study science at his father's university, but left without completing his degree to find a job in publishing.

In 1903 Ransome was given a week's holiday by his employer, the Unicorn Press, and caught the night-train to Coniston. It was on the first day of this vacation, as he lay on a flat rock in the middle of the gushing Copper Mines Beck, dreaming a young man's dream of becoming a poet, that by chance he met up again with Collingwood, who was returning from a sketching expedition on the slopes of the Old Man. It was a fortunate meeting because Collingwood, who was already in his fifties, became a surrogate father to Ransome, inviting him to spend time with his family at Lanehead and encouraging his literary ambitions. Ransome always thought of him as a Norse storyteller or bard and nicknamed him 'The Skald'. In the easy-going Collingwoods Arthur found a supportive second family. He learnt to sail with the Collingwood children, Barbara, Dora, Ursula and Robin, in their dinghy *Swallow* and in a larger boat, *Jamrach*, which they borrowed from neighbours at Tent Lodge. The Collingwoods were a talented family of writers, artists and thinkers – Robin would one day hold a chair in philosophy at Oxford – and under their gentle tutelage Arthur began to apprehend that his vocation was to write for children.

In 1908 Ransome fell in love with Ivy Constance Walker and they married the following year but the union was never to be a happy one. In 1913, partly to escape the frictions at home, he left for St Petersburg, intending to collect Russian folk tales for a book. For the next few years his life story reads like the plot of a John Buchan novel. He became a correspondent for the *Daily News* throughout the First World War, and then found that he had a ringside seat at the Russian Revolution. Indeed, he was so close to the Bolshevik leaders that he beat Lenin at chess and fell for Trotsky's personal assistant, a hearty Russian girl called Evgenia Shelepina.

While in Russia, Ransome often felt homesick for the Lake District. In a letter to his mother, dated 1 May 1917, he wrote:

> Your two pictures of Coniston hang on the wall beside a bit of Peel Island and an ikon of Saint Nicholas. They give me great pleasure every day. I do so often wonder whether I shall be back with you all again and thinking about better things than correspondence. Joyce [his sister] and I MUST some day do a book just as full of lake country as ever it can. Hestbank [sic] and the sands and the whole lovely place.[17]

In 1919, fearing for Evgenia's life if she were to be captured by the White Russians, he successfully brought her out of Russia, putting himself in great personal peril. He avoided being shot by the Reds by mentioning his acquaintance with Lenin, and only escaped the same fate at the hands of his White captors because the unit's commanding officer turned out to be a former chess opponent. All of this excitement took its toll on Ransome's health, but by 1925 he had returned to England, found a new job with the *Manchester Guardian*, divorced Ivy, married Evgenia (Genia) and settled down to a much less nerve-racking life at Low Ludderburn, a low-beamed, thick-walled cottage overlooking the Winster valley, east of Windermere.

It was in this house that he began the series of books which would make his reputation. In 1928 Dora Altounyan, née Collingwood, brought her husband Ernest and their five children back from Syria to stay in a farm close to her old home at Lanehead. Ernest was a half-Irish, half-Armenian doctor, educated in England, who helped his father to run a hospital in Aleppo. On this holiday Arthur gave sailing lessons to the Altounyan children – Taqui, Susie, Mavis (known as Titty), Roger and Brigit. In return they presented him with a pair of red Turkish slippers. This explains the dedication at the front of *Swallows and Amazons*, first published in 1930: 'To the Six for whom it was written, in exchange for a pair of slippers.' Although in later years Arthur would play down the connection, his involvement with this family clearly breathed life into his book. Ransome chose names for three of the fictional Walker children – Susan, Titty and Roger – which were plainly based on those of the Altounyans.

Five of the twelve books, *Swallows and Amazons* (1930), *Swallowdale* (1931), *Winter Holiday* (1933), *Pigeon Post* (1936) and *The Picts and the Martyrs* (1943) are set in Ransome's fictionalised version of the Lake District. Others are set in the Caribbean, on the Norfolk Broads, the Essex coast, the North Sea, the China Sea and in the Hebrides.

The unnamed lake which is introduced in *Swallows and Amazons* is an amalgam of Windermere and Coniston Water. It has been suggested that the map shown on the endpapers of *Swallows and Amazons* resembles the view of Windermere that can be obtained from the well-known viewpoint of Gummer's How. Ransome explained that no real island on Windermere had such a good harbour as Peel Island on Coniston Water, so he borrowed it and fused it with Blake Holme to create the fictional Wild Cat Island.[18] Lanehead, the Collingwood family home, was the model for Beckfoot, the home of Peggy and Nancy Blackett (the Amazons). Belle Isle on Windermere, where Mr English built his extraordinary circular house, became the Swallows' Long Island, and Silver Holme became Cormorant Island. The mountain of

Kanchenjunga, which the children climb in *Swallowdale*, is in reality Coniston Old Man, while Captain Flint's houseboat was largely based upon the steam launch *Gondola* operated by the Furness Railway Company on Coniston Water. In his childhood Arthur became friendly with the captain, who often let him steer. Happily, *Gondola*, now owned by the National Trust and restored by workers from the Barrow shipyard, is once more cruising the lake.

Ransome's Lake District is never prettified and it materialises as a real place inhabited by real people with real jobs, such as farmers, shepherds and the charcoal-burners who feature in *Swallowdale*. Ransome had learnt about the importance of charcoal-burning in the economic life of the southern Lake District from Collingwood and in his bohemian days he had made friends with some of the charcoal-burners, who used to sweeten clay pipes for him in their fires. Ransome's books encourage an active and involved appreciation of a peopled landscape, not a high-brow Picturesque detachment. Like Wordsworth he was interested in those on the fringes of society, seeking out gypsies, for example, so that he might hear their folk tales. Though he

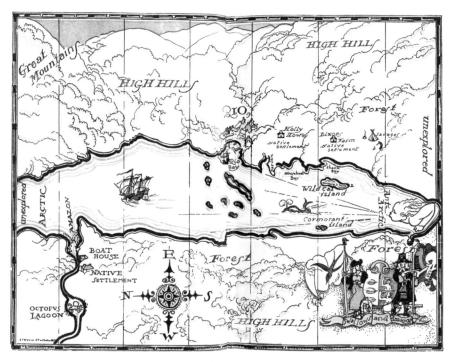

Map from the endpapers of *Swallows and Amazons* by Arthur Ransome

was evidently a man of his age, one who was devoted to England and fearful of Prussianism, he was a liberal by nature, a subversive by temperament and a man of the left who seems to have been happily free of prejudices.

The Ransomes were very happy at Low Ludderburn, although Genia was never fully reconciled to the raininess of the north-western climate. Arthur had a chronic ulcer which seemed to improve when he was nearer to the sea. As they got older, the inconveniences of the house, which had an earth closet and no running water, began to trouble them more and more, so in 1935 they sold up and went to live at Pin Mill on the River Orwell in Suffolk. When the war came they felt too near to the front line in Suffolk and decided to retreat to the Lakes, but this time Genia insisted upon a place with electricity and water. They found The Heald, a modern, stone-built house with half a mile of lake frontage on Coniston Water and better views, so Arthur wrote, than those from Brantwood. It even had central heating.

Unfortunately, Genia never took to The Heald and Arthur's health deteriorated. His doctor banned him from sailing and fellwalking and even put restrictions on the sort of fishing he might do: he defied his doctors and devised a way of trolling for char from a sailing boat. In 1945 the Ransomes decided to move to London and stuck it for three years before moving back to the Lake District, this time to Lowick Hall, near Nibthwaite. By 1950 they were back in London again, but the pull of the Lakes remained too strong. They rented houses in Haverthwaite and finally bought one called Hill Top, but by 1960 Arthur was in decline. He died in a Manchester hospital on 3 June 1967, and was buried in the churchyard at Rusland, where, in 1975, Evgenia was laid beside him.

Ransome has some ardent fans. The Arthur Ransome Society (TARS) was formed in 1990, and groups of admirers get together in many parts of the globe to do Ransomish things, such as sailing traditional boats, exploring caves or talking like a pirate all day for charity. Ransome's children's books are all still in print, though fashions have turned against books which feature privileged English children whose parents can afford to take them on long holidays and provide them with boats. It is not difficult to imagine that if Ransome were writing today he would do things differently, expanding his cast of characters both socially and racially. The surprise is that the original books, the first of which was written almost eighty years ago, still hold their appeal, despite huge changes in society.

Overleaf: High Pike, with a view towards Morecambe Bay

Wainwright at work, late 1980s

17

Ramblers

Rights of Way and Alfred Wainwright

THE BEST-KNOWN NAME IN Lake District walking is the late Alfred Wainwright. Indeed, just as Wordsworth is given too much credit for making the area popular, so is Wainwright credited – and sometimes blamed – for opening up the fells to the common man, when in fact that process had been underway for decades before Wainwright's first bus trip from the smoke-blackened streets of Blackburn to Windermere in 1930.

This history is beginning to catch up with my own life, because my parents had been fellwalkers for years before the publication of Book One of Wainwright's *Pictorial Guide to the Lakeland Fells* in 1955 – which, incidentally, was the year I was born. In fact, if it were not for the well-established tradition of working-class walking, I might not be here at all. Much of my parents' courtship took place on the fells. Who is to say? Without the Barrow & District Rambling Club, they might never have married and I would not be here to write this book.

It must be twenty-five years since I last walked with the Barrow Ramblers, but they still seem to be going strong. Every Sunday a coachload of walkers sets out for the hills, splitting, as they have done for decades, into three groups: an elite 'A' party which knocks off the summits at breathtaking speed and is not daunted by tricky scrambling over rock; a 'B' party which gets to a few summits but at a more leisurely pace; and a 'C' party which stays below the 1,000-foot contour on much easier terrain. Just about the only thing that has changed is the equipment. Nowadays everyone will be clad in breathable waterproof fabrics, with bright, ergonomically designed backpacks. My parents carried ex-army rucksacks and wore old gas capes when it rained. Anoraks were still a novelty. Shipyard workers banged nails into their work boots to give them a better grip.

I was still at junior school when my father and great-uncle initiated me as a fellwalker. They took me up Helm Crag, a modest height, but an inspiring one for a young boy. I was captivated by the view of the valley from high up, and the way that every time we stopped for a breather the cars and houses seemed to have dwindled. The imposing summit rocks were a tremendous reward for the effort of the climb. Many more walks followed: with the family, with the Boy Scouts, with the Ramblers and with the grammar school. Poorly equipped schoolboys, we teetered along Striding Edge in a gale, hoping that the wind would not get under our yellow cycling capes and lift us off. We met wild ponies in the mists of High Street. We waded through February snowdrifts on Scafell, while the wind whipped particles of ice against our bare cheeks. We were startled, in true Alpine fashion, by a Brocken spectre on Crinkle Crags. We met an American school party whose leader said, 'Boy, your mountains ain't big, but they sure are rugged.'

No one quoted Wordsworth and no one, except perhaps a schoolmaster or two, had even heard of Ruskin. Nevertheless, we were all the heirs to a great tradition with its roots in the Romantic wanderings of Wordsworth and Coleridge – and Rousseau, too, though he never set foot on Haystacks or

Barrow ramblers (*c.* 1970) by J. H. Thompson

Helvellyn. Working-class lads, we had this much at least in common with Leslie Stephen, the mountaineering philosopher who was president of the Alpine Club from 1865 to 1868. In 1878, having abandoned his riskier pursuits in middle age, he inaugurated the Sunday Tramps, a London group which made lengthy forays into the countryside of Kent and Surrey. Their tongue-in-cheek title belied the social stature of the membership, which was drawn from the intellectual top drawer and included many academics, explorers, politicians, writers, physicians and lawyers. Stephen's long routes, which were contrived to start and finish at railway stations, frequently involved trespass over private land, but the Tramps were not short of legal advice and had a ready formula for dealing with awkward gamekeepers. Chanting in unison, they would give notice that they did not claim any right of way, then they would present the perplexed warden with a shilling by way of amends. They knew that the signs which said 'Trespassers will be Prosecuted' were technically wrong – trespass was a tort, not a crime.[1]

Though I might feel some affinity with this distinguished group, my fell-walking roots are much more modest and provincial. They tap into the great Nonconformist rambling tradition of northern England, which derived its ethos from the environmentalism and proto-socialism of Ruskin. 'There is no wealth but life,' Ruskin had written in *Unto This Last*, his radical critique of political economy. The wealth of a nation should be gauged, not by the accumulation of capital or possessions, but by the number of noble and happy human beings it nourished, both in body and in spirit. It was in this vein that the Reverend Thomas Arthur Leonard, a Congregationalist minister from the struggling mill town of Colne in Lancashire, decided that he should take some of his younger male parishioners walking in the Lake District. The countryside could provide not only an antidote to the oppressive conditions of the industrial city, but also a spiritual alternative to the brash and tawdry commercialism of Blackpool.

In June 1891 thirty of Leonard's charges spent four days based at Ambleside, for the modest sum of twenty-one shillings per person. The experiment was such a success that the clergyman soon broadened his scope. Women were invited along and by 1893 the numbers taking one of the minister's holidays had grown to 268 and his organisation had a name, the Co-operative Holiday Association. He left the church and the CHA, which was soon running its own guesthouses in places of scenic beauty, became his mission. Meanwhile, the ubiquitous Hardwicke Rawnsley became one of the trustees. While the free-thinking Sunday Tramps had relished the idea of walking on the Sabbath, it was an obstacle for the Reverend Leonard, who stepped around it by including morning prayers in the guesthouse routine. Convivial but teetotal activities were organised for the evenings in a house-party atmosphere, which often included edifying lectures on scientific or literary subjects. The formula might seem austere in our more individualistic times, but it was hugely successful. So many women wanted to take CHA holidays that steps had to be taken 'not to allow the proportion of females to exceed two thirds of the entire party'.[2] So many couples first met on walking holidays that it became an in-joke that the initials CHA stood for 'Catch a Husband Association'.

By 1911 the CHA had 14,000 members, but the Reverend Leonard grew worried that the holidays offered were becoming a tad too comfortable and out of reach of the poorer people he had always tried to help. Other committee members thought the future lay in providing better accommodation, so there was a rift, with Leonard resigning as secretary and going off to form the Holiday Fellowship in an attempt to rekindle the original spirit, but this was not an acrimonious split; indeed, the CHA did much to support the new organisation. The HF still runs two guesthouses in the Lake District, one at Monk Coniston, the other in Pocklington's old house at Derwent Bank.[3]

Though the CHA and the HF were mostly working-class organisations, they lacked the hard political edge of some of the early rambling groups. Prominent among these were the Sheffield Clarion Ramblers, established in 1900 as the first 'Sunday workers' rambling club in the North of England' by the socialist G. B. H. Ward. It took its name from the left-wing newspaper the *Clarion*, which was edited from Manchester by Robert Blatchford. The attitude of the Clarion Ramblers to the landowners and gamekeepers who sought to keep them off the moors can easily be gauged from the lyrics of *The Trespasser's Song*, penned by Ward and sung to the tune of *The Lincolnshire Poacher*. 'There is no keeper in the Peak whom I could not lose, And if he watch'd me for a week, I'd tread the moor I choose,' runs one of the verses, which is followed by the chorus 'Oh 'tis our delight, be it storm or bright, to wander anywhere'.[4] The struggle for access to uplands in the Peak District and the Pennines reached a famous climax in the Mass Trespass of 1932, when ramblers from Manchester, led by an unemployed motor mechanic called Benny Rothman, organised an illegal walk on the plateau of Kinder Scout in Derbyshire. 'Ours is a grouse against grouse,' said Rothman, 'we are willing no longer to be deprived of the beauties of the country for the convenience of the landowners.'[5] The outcome was a pyrrhic victory for the owners. A thousand or so well-drilled ramblers, some singing the 'Red Flag', rallied on the moors and scuffled with the keepers sent to stop them, but six of their leaders were arrested and put on trial. Rothman was sentenced to four months' imprisonment for incitement to cause a riotous assembly. So

Kinder Scout trespassers (1932)

harsh were the sentences that public opinion swung behind the ramblers and the moral case for access to the countryside was considerably advanced.

What little grouse moorland there is in the Lake District is confined to the margins, so the area was hardly in the front line of this conflict, but there had been some earlier battles over rights of way. In 1887 Mrs Spencer-Bell, the owner of Fawe Park on Derwentwater, decided to close the footpath which ran from Nichol End to the foot of Cat Bells, which had once been a packhorse route. This was a red rag to Rawnsley, who revived the Keswick and District Footpath Preservation Association to contest the issue. Angry Keswickians marched on Fawe Park and pushed aside the tree trunks and brambles with which Mrs Spencer-Bell's gardeners had tried to barricade the path. On the same day, these rambling shock troops set off up Latrigg, the little fell which the townsfolk had long treasured as a viewpoint. Here the landowner, a Mr Spedding, had piled a heap of ironwork, timber and barbed wire, before coating this monstrous assemblage with tar. A first attempt to get through failed, but the Footpath Preservation Association declared that it was a test case and that the whole future of public access to mountains was at stake. Accordingly, on the first day of October 1887, two thousand protesters, including twelve hefty men with pickaxes and crowbars, assembled at the foot of Latrigg and, singing 'Rule, Britannia!', they swept away all obstructions on their route to the summit. They were led by Henry Jenkinson, a guidebook writer and secretary to the Footpath Society, and Samuel Plimsoll, the campaigning MP, whose association with the Lake District went back to childhood years in Penrith. The Reverend Cuthbert Southey, the poet's grandson, was one among the many who testified that they had never known any restriction of access on Latrigg. The court's decision was a fudge, because the public's right of access to the summit was maintained, but not by way of the contested path; nevertheless, it was a signal victory for the access lobby.

Fellwalkers are not saints. It is not always easy to keep to the allotted path when coming off a hill in mist, and, if faced with a choice between clambering over a dry-stone wall or laboriously backtracking to get back on route, only the virtuous would opt for the latter, but even the frankly confrontational Clarion Ramblers had a countryside code which cautioned members not to leave gates open or to defile the landscape with orange peel.[6] Many of the working-class walkers who came to the Lakes had been schooled in Wordsworthian or Ruskinian values through their association with rambling clubs or the youth hostel movement. For the most part the relationship between the farming community and the ramblers was amicable. The walkers were well-mannered and tried to do no harm. The farmers had a long-standing tradition of hospitality and could make a little money from providing teas for weary parties, or letting rooms for bed and breakfast.

The Youth Hostel Association was formed in 1930 in response to a surge of interest in hiking holidays. It was influenced by the German Youth Movement (only later hijacked by the National Socialists), in particular the Romantic cult of the *Wandervogel*, a migratory bird of passage. Germany had 2,320 youth hostels by 1932, Britain a meagre 73, but the organisation would grow rapidly.[7] Though tastes have become more luxurious, the Lake District still has twenty-six hostels, which range from the relative comfort of Grasmere's Butharlyp Howe to the Spartan simplicity of Black Sail, a former shepherd's bothy at the head of Ennerdale, which can only be reached on foot.

In the economically depressed 1930s, long before the advent of cheap flights to sun-and-sand destinations, rambling offered an affordable escape from the humdrum and a degree of unchaperoned licence, though any moral panic was averted by the thought that a vigorous day's walking did not leave much energy for love-making – and the sexes were rigorously segregated in youth hostel dorms. Though the inter-war years are often described as rambling's heyday, the impact they made upon the Lake District must have been slight, or so it would seem from the memoirs of the late A. Harry Griffin, who for over fifty years wrote 'Country Diary' articles for the *Guardian*. Recollecting a lifetime among mountains, he wrote:

> The Lake District was a much quieter, far less crowded place in the late 1920s, when I started climbing. Outside holiday times it was almost a secluded paradise. What wonderful spacious days they were: carefree, youthful days on uncrowded crags, long, long before even the threat of war. There were few motor cars, the much narrower roads being almost deserted at times, and no caravan sites, car parks, public conveniences or litter bins that I can remember. Grassy, uneroded tracks, hardly noticeable in places, wound gently over the fells; farmers drove to market on Saturday mornings in two-wheeled horse-drawn gigs; and four-in-hands were still going over the passes.[8]

There were no climbing huts or youth hostels in the Lake District in the 1920s. Griffin recalled that the first to be opened was the Robertson Lamb hut in Langdale in 1930. Though rambling clubs were certainly visiting the area by this time, Griffin was not aware of many 'hikers'; indeed, the word was not even in circulation.

I was pleased to read in *The Coniston Tigers* that Griffin was taken up his first Lake District hill by masters from my Alma Mater, though they had probably all retired years before I donned the blue and gold blazer of Barrow Grammar School. Incredibly, this was the costume Griffin and his chums wore on their ascent of Stickle Pike, complete with caps, satchels and very draughty short trousers.

'Don't, whatever you do, drink from the streams; this will spoil your wind,' Griffin's geography master had cautioned him.[9] 'Keep your hats on; you mustn't lose body heat,' our biology teacher told us, four decades later, which was probably better advice. The standard kit of the Middle School Rambling Club, circa 1970, had progressed to anoraks, long, thick trousers and boots with vibram soles, though I remember a concerned member of staff turbaning a scarf around the head of one boy whose ears were purpling with cold as we struggled through thigh-deep snowdrifts.

There were a few among us who knew something about the illustrious mountaineer-journalist and old boy, and kept an eye out for his craggy profile (pipe clamped between teeth) while out on the fells – but our watchfulness was never rewarded. But we had more chance of spotting Griffin than we ever did of glimpsing the elusive Wainwright, who by this stage had completed his famous series of guidebooks and was already a cult figure among fellwalkers. At home, we had a row of his little books, neat in their colour-coded jackets, on a shelf in the glass-fronted bookcase. 'They're not just guidebooks,' said my father, 'they're works of art.' It was an opinion that would be widely held one day, but at the time Wainwright's books were for connoisseurs, the fellwalking *cognoscenti* who knew their crags from their knotts and their pikes from their dodds. If Gilpin wrote the best Lake District guidebook of the eighteenth century and Wordsworth the best in the nineteenth, then Wainwright took the laurels in the twentieth.

Griffin might have preferred his Lake District to be empty, but he was essentially a gregarious, clubbable sort who enjoyed climbing with a small band of comrades. Wainwright, on the other hand, was a solitary who shunned company on the fells. He avoided youth hostels and would have hated walking with a rambling club, even in the 'A' party. The overarching irony of Wainwright's life is that this most private, reticent and at times downright misanthropic of men should have written the books which opened up the fells to so many new walkers. His books might have been love letters to the Lake District – his own phrase – but he was keen to share his passion with others, even if it meant that undisclosed routes had to be revealed.

Wainwright may have been shy and socially maladroit, but, as Hunter Davies's 1995 biography revealed, he had a healthy opinion of his own abilities as a writer and illustrator, even in the days when he was working as an accountant in the Borough Treasurer's Office in Blackburn. The model for the guidebooks was his unpublished account of a two-week solo walking holiday taken in the Pennines in 1938. A.W. (as he preferred to be known) even went so far as to work up a flyer for this mock publication and wrote an imaginary publisher's report in which he compared the author's flair for natural description with that of J. B. Priestley and his feelings for mountains with those of Wordsworth. A part of him craved recognition for his talents and this must explain why, in later life, he not only wrote a memoir, but also agreed to take part in television programmes. The reclusive author became an unlikely celebrity.

The key moment in A.W.'s life occurred in 1933, when this son of a Lancashire stonemason visited the Lake District for the first time. Beyond Preston the mill chimneys were left behind and the young traveller got his first-ever glimpse of Morecambe Bay. Indeed, it was the first time he had ever seen the sea. The bus passed along the main street of Kendal and into what he would later describe as 'a colourful fairyland', so different was the Cumbrian landscape from anything he had ever known. Wainwright's epiphany took place at Orrest Head when he first saw Windermere, a

moment which bears comparison with Ruskin's response to the view of
Derwentwater from Friar's Crag. This is how Wainwright remembered it:

> I saw mountain ranges, one after another, the nearer starkly etched,
> those beyond fading into the blue distance. Rich woodlands, emerald
> pastures and the shimmering waters of the lake below added to a pageant
> of loveliness, a glorious panorama that held me enthralled. I had seen
> landscapes of rural beauty pictured in the local art gallery, but here was
> no painted canvas; this was real. This was truth. God was in his heaven
> that day and I a humble worshipper.[10]

The Wordsworthian flavour of this passage is striking, but A.W.'s origins
and upbringing show the weakness of the poet's argument that townsfolk
had to be gradually prepared to appreciate the qualities of a mountainous
landscape. Wainwright had been brought up in a poverty-stricken mill
town where most people's idea of a holiday was the annual pilgrimage to
Blackpool. His family lived in a two-bedroom terraced house with stone-
flagged floors, no garden, no bathroom and a privy in the backyard. If he
had any preparation for the Cumbrian hills it was the solitary walks he
took around Lancashire exploring the roads and lanes that linked the many
industrial communities. Even as a boy, with a pocketful of jam sandwiches
and no money for tram fares, he would seek out the wilder parts of the
county, those spaces coloured brown on his map to indicate an elevation of
more than 1,000 feet. All of this came from within. He needed no tutoring
and had no one to guide or accompany him on his explorations.

On this first visit he was accompanied by his 'more prosaic' cousin, who
fell asleep on the grass, but A.W. could not get enough of the scene. The
Langdale Pikes seemed to beckon to him and they looked friendly and exciting. The experience transformed him:

> I felt I was some other person. This was not me. I wasn't entitled to such
> a privilege. I was an alien here. I didn't belong. If only I could, sometime!
> If only I could! Those few hours on Orrest Head changed my life.[11]

A few days later A.W. and his cousin ventured on to the narrow ridge that
is Striding Edge. Wainwright often reminded his readers that the mountains were their friends and not to be feared, but he always had a healthy
respect for their more challenging features. The cousins crept along the

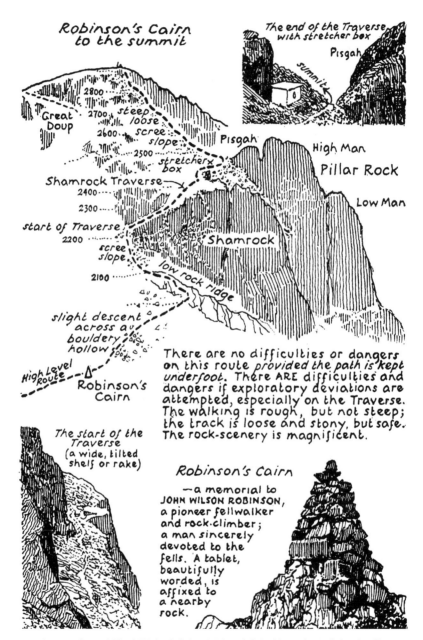

Robinson's Cairn
to the summit

The end of the Traverse,
with stretcher box
Pisgah
summit

2800
Great
Doup
2700 steep
loose
2600 scree
slope
2500 Pisgah
stretcher
box
Shamrock Traverse
2400
High Man
Pillar Rock
Low Man
2300
start of Traverse
2200
scree
slope
2100
low rock ridge
Shamrock
slight descent
across a
bouldery
hollow
High Level
Route
Robinson's
Cairn

There are no difficulties or dangers
on this route *provided the path is kept
underfoot.* There ARE difficulties and
dangers if exploratory deviations are
attempted, especially on the Traverse.
The walking is rough, but not steep;
the track is loose and stony, but safe.
The rock-scenery is magnificent.

The start of the
Traverse
(a wide, tilted
shelf or rake)

Robinson's Cairn

—a memorial to
JOHN WILSON ROBINSON,
a pioneer fellwalker
and rock-climber;
a man sincerely
devoted to the
fells. A tablet,
beautifully
worded, is
affixed to
a nearby
rock.

A page from Alfred Wainright's *A Pictorial Guide to the Lakeland Fells,*
Book Seven: *The Western Fells* (1966)

spine 'in agonies of apprehension' until they came to a memorial to someone who had fallen to his death, which did nothing to ease their anxieties. The swirling mist, Wainwright remarked, had mercifully hidden the precipitous drops to either side. Even though the rain washed down for the rest of the day and the cousins arrived back in Keswick in sodden clothes, the experience did nothing to dent A.W.'s ardour.

A large part of the joy of this first holiday was the freedom. In complete contrast to the reception received by the Kinder Scout trespassers, Wainwright and his cousin were free to wander anywhere they liked above the intake walls of the farms. There were no 'keep-out' signs, no policemen or keepers with shotguns. The locals they met were generally solicitous and friendly. Wainwright felt, as had Wordsworth before him, that something of the serenity of the hills must have permeated their lives. He moved to the Lake District as soon as he could, taking a cut in salary in order to follow his dream. By his own account the work for which he will be remembered began in 1952 and it was a project to fill his leisure time, once he had built and planted his garden. Walking was A.W.'s first love, but he adored studying maps and liked to draw. Now he saw a way of uniting all of these pleasures. He would produce a set of seven guidebooks, covering all the fells of Lakeland. He thought it would take him about thirteen years, but he smacked his lips at the prospect. His innovative maps usually combine a plan view of the valley bottom with an elevation of the fellside, disregarding cartographer's conventions, despite which they work brilliantly. Unlike the landscape painters of the eighteenth century he did not bother with easels or sketchbooks; indeed, one might even say that he cheated. He took photographs then produced the pen and ink drawings in the comfort of his home. But when it came to the text he shunned standard typesetting and wrote the whole by hand, taking great pains to get both margins absolutely straight and never to break a word with a hyphen.

The Wainwright revealed in Davies's biography, first published four years after the walker's death, was a much more complex character than his devoted followers could have expected. There was much that confirmed the legend – A.W.'s love of maps, his use of public transport, his penchant for fish and chips, his disdain for special clothing, his hatred of school parties on the fells, his curmudgeonly side, his dry humour – but for most of his admirers (I include myself) it was the first we had heard about his rocky first marriage and his secret affair in late middle age with Betty McNally, who would eventually become the second Mrs Wainwright. The strait-laced Borough Treasurer of Kendal was shown to have had a passionate and romantic nature all along.

Davies spotted that in Book Six of the *Pictorial Guide* (The North Western Fells) A.W. wrote of Cat Bells with almost the ardour of a lover. The fell had 'a bold "come hither" look . . . no suitor ever returns disappointed'.[12] It seemed a plausible surmise that Wainwright had been channelling his libidinous energies into his walking, so I scanned the other books for similar passages (academics do this sort of thing) but I was disappointed. Some mountains are described as 'shapely' or 'attractive' but most have been given conventionally masculine attributes. They tower or dominate or 'assert their superiority'. They are rugged or forbidding. Great Gable, though, is a mountain for metrosexuals, 'strong yet not sturdy, masculine yet graceful'.[13]

The improbable television star has posthumously crossed another unanticipated threshold. His guidebooks have become objects of scholarly study. A recent paper co-written by the philosopher Emily Brady and geographer Clare Palmer analysed A.W.'s aesthetic attitudes. If Gilpin saw the Lake District as a collection of paintings just waiting for the brush, Wainwright saw the same landscape as a collection of routes to be taken. His outlook owed much to the Picturesque and the Sublime. The combination of roughness or rockiness with height appealed to him, and he was dismissive of cultivated rural lowland – that was just something to be got through quickly on the way to the fells. But his appreciation of the land was intimately connected with the act of walking, which is why he liked fine ridges and interesting rocky features, was bored by smooth, grassy summits and abhorred places that were soft, boggy and wet. He also distinguished between good or tidy walkers, who kept to the paths and disturbed nothing, and bad walkers, who were noisy and clumsy and increased erosion by not respecting the gentle zigzags of the well-trodden way. As Brady and Palmer put it: 'walking carefully, quietly and without leaving a trace, manifested for Wainwright a kind of life-virtue; and failing to do so, a life-vice'.[14]

Wainwright's dedication to fellwalking and his life-long immersion in the Lakeland landscape turned him into an expert. We usually think of farmers as the 'insiders' who know the land, but Wainwright, an off-comer, came to know the whole of the Lake District more intimately than anyone else and this gives his books an authority that will last for generations.

On a few occasions Wainwright and Griffin, who both lived in Kendal, went out on the fells together. They were contrasting characters. Wainwright, by his own admission, was no rock-climber, while Griffin, who kept climbing until he was seventy-eight, was taken aback to discover that his companion could not use a compass and would make lengthy detours to avoid clambering over dry-stone walls. The two remained on good terms, although Griffin blamed Wainwright in

'Blencathra from Clough Head' by Alfred Wainwright, from *A Pictorial Guide
to the Lakeland Fells*, Book One: *The Eastern Fells* (1955)

print for taking away some of the adventure of mountaineering by 'almost leading people by the hand up the fells' and also for causing the erosion of the more
popular paths, albeit indirectly.[15] Changing demographics and improved roads
might have had more to do with it. Wainwright could be cavalier about rights
of way, but should he be faulted for sharing his enthusiasm with a wider public?
He gave people a pinch of the courage necessary for exploration and encouraged
his readers to investigate many of the less familiar tops and to attempt unaccus-
tomed routes. Even his detractors had to admit that he was a remarkable man.
'I'm very honoured to have known him fairly well,' wrote Griffin, before adding,
'Perhaps he was some sort of genius, who knows?'[16]

Overleaf: View from the Fairfield Horseshoe, with a patch of sunlight

Harrison Stickle in winter by J. H. Thompson

18

For All the People

The Creation of the National Park

O NE SUNDAY IN JUNE 1946, Nella Last, the middle-aged woman from Barrow whose wartime diary would, decades later, be turned into the successful TV drama *Housewife, 49*, recorded an outing to Bowness and Ambleside. She had never seen so many visitors, even before the war, but she harboured none of the resentment once voiced by Wordsworth and Ruskin. 'South Lancashire crowds don't behave "tripperish" in the Lakes as they do at Blackpool,' she wrote. 'The quiet dignity of the hills and lakes seems to welcome and impress them. There never seem loud raucous voices raised in song. Perhaps, though, that type don't come. It may be that they who come have a love of calm serenity.' 'My deep love of the Lakes,' she continued, 'never makes me want to shut out trippers . . . come and share it. Hold up your arms to the everlasting hills and draw their peace and beauty and healing calm into your tired minds.'[1]

Nella's husband's grandfather had been brought up on a lonely sheep farm and could not read until he was eighteen. In her fair-minded and level-headed way, she was concerned that the benefits of progress should reach the dales and this put her at odds with her uncle, 'a rabid "Friends of the Lakes"' man. 'He would put a wall round if he could, so high that no one could see over. I would be very stern with people who wanted to build jerry houses, make wide motor roads, build factories or works, or run a railway through, but I don't understand or agree with him in other ways. People who are shut in ugly soulless towns need our lakes and fells.' Nor would she 'tear down ugly pylons as he and his friends would',[2] if it meant that farmers had to live like medieval peasants without access to modern amenities. She worried that she was being inconsistent; in fact, she was stoutly grappling with competing and incommensurable virtues. It is the very stuff of politics, planning and landscape management, and it can be agonising.

Wordsworth, as we have seen, wanted the Lake District to be protected as 'a sort of national property' but equally he did not want it turned over to an untutored, insensitive rabble. What he really wanted was to preserve it for people who felt the same way about it as he did, and here lies a problem. If this history has shown anything, it is that there have been many ways of seeing and valuing the Lake District. The very earliest travellers projected their fears on to it, so that mountains were 'horrid' and Borrowdale was given 'jaws'. Then came a set that would have turned the area into an Arcadian fantasy, dotting it with Classical temples, mansions and follies. The Romantics wanted nature to be left alone – it was to be learnt from, rather than improved – but while poets and artists communed, others were treating the District as a giant playground, an outdoor gymnasium, even a testing ground for fast aeroplanes and speedboats. Working-class fellwalkers, meanwhile, regarded it as a liberation. And while all these various conceptions collided, Cumbrian hill farmers still had to tend to their walls and to their sheep.

In 1887 Ruskin supported a proposal made in the *Lancaster Observer* that 'the whole Lake District should be bought by the nation for itself',[3] but a long history of cultivation and centuries of documented ownership made it difficult to establish national parks in England. The situation was different in the United States, where the land in question was regarded as 'wilderness' (cultural landscapes of the Native Americans were often seen this way). The concept of a national park is thus very different in the United States and in Britain. In the States it will be an area where no one lives. In Britain it will be a place where whole communities exist and most of the land has been managed for centuries. The British model involves an inherent tension between the social and economic interests of the resident population and the imperative to conserve the landscape for the benefit of the whole nation.

As we have seen, many of the Lake District's staunchest defenders have come from outside the area. It is no surprise, therefore, to find that the same is true of those who campaigned for the National Park. One indicator of this is the correspondence column of the *Manchester Guardian*, where we can follow debates about the future of the Lake District from the last decade of the nineteenth century through to the creation of the park sixty years later. The newspaper, which had been founded in 1821 by Nonconformist businessmen, had developed a more radical edge under the editorship of C. P. Scott and was supportive of many progressive causes. Reflecting the concerns of its reader-ship, who were more likely to be visitors to the Lake District than residents, the newspaper's coverage of conservationist issues was thorough.

On 9 March 1889 the newspaper carried a letter from 'A Lake Visitor' under the heading 'More Vandalism in the Lake District' in which the writer complained about a quarrying proposal on Loughrigg Terrace, putting it into the context of recent railway initiatives. The letter concluded by suggesting that the only way to save the Lake District 'for the full enjoyment of the people' was to put it under the protection of Parliamentary Commissioners, so that no harm could be done to it 'without the consent of the national assembly'.[4] The Lake District's defenders often wrote to the editor expressing dismay about some new development. In 1900 it was the prospect of an electric tramway between Windermere and Ambleside which upset 'A.E.B.', who wrote: 'Why, I would ask, should a body of London capitalists and a Windermere firm of electricians be allowed to spoil a national possession?'[5] The indifference and 'worse than indifference' of the local inhabitants was a frequent theme. A member of the Lake District Defence Society wrote in 1889 that 'every victory that the Defence Society has won for the tourist public has been won in spite of and against the clamour of the residents'.[6]

In 1908 Oppenheimer's privileged rock-climbers considered the whole debate with supercilious amusement. 'Nay, when I become a millionaire I'll buy up the whole of the Lake District for the nation,' said the Tall Man, '. . . and then we'll have a Trust to see that there are no more railways or sordid industries.' 'And the paths shall be made straight,' replied his companion the Bohemian, cynically, 'and finger-posts plentifully supplied that we may all walk therein. No, I'll not put my confidence in Trusts, nor my trust in would-be benefactors.'[7] Oppenheimer and his friends knew that the Lake District would change and that, as it became more popular, so it would become more managed. 'If only,' lamented the Tall Man, 'Lakeland could be left for each of us exactly as he first knew it.'[8]

The most serious threats to the aesthetics of the Lake District have never come from tourists. They have come from industry, from local government or from the state, and of these it has been the state which has caused the greatest anxiety. Though conservationists in the mould of Nella Last's uncle can come across as pettifogging meddlers, there is no doubt that the whole delightful character of the Lake District could have been destroyed had the Forestry Commission been allowed to have a free hand after the First World War. Someone had to take them on.

Wordsworth might have railed against private plantations of larches, but any aesthetic detriment from these had long been overshadowed by the large-scale afforestation associated with Manchester's Thirlmere scheme. Then, in 1919, an Act of Parliament established the Forestry Commission, which, largely for strategic reasons, was charged with improving timber supplies. It is generally a mistake to create powerful organisations with singular purposes, because all other considerations, in this case woolly things like beauty and amenity, can be shouldered out of the way. Here was a threat which made Thirlmere look like a skirmish. Straight trunks were favoured for pit props and telegraph poles, and, since there was nothing in the Commissioners' mandate that called upon them to consider beauty, they saw the Lake District as a suitable planting ground and phalanxes of softwoods began to invade the scenic fellsides. The foresters went about it with a ruthless, military efficiency and were answerable to no cabinet minister. By the end of September 1933 the Commission had planted one and a quarter million larches and over five million spruce in Ennerdale and on the Thornthwaite Estate near Keswick.[9] On more exposed ground sombre Norway spruce and Sitka spruce were their favoured species. Wainwright would later write of Thornthwaite Forest that 'there is no objection to the public use of the forest roads (on foot) but (a) the gloom of the plantations, (b) the silence, (c) the lack of views, and (d) the close confinement between evergreens, are more than most people can stand'.[10]

The Forestry Commission's early plantations were easy to hate, so when, in 1934, the Commissioners acquired 7,000 acres of land in upper Eskdale and Dunnerdale, opposition swiftly coalesced around the figure of the Reverend Henry Herbert Symonds, a champion who might have been cut from the same ecclesiastical cloth as Canon Rawnsley. Symonds had been Head of Classics at Rugby School before becoming headmaster of the city-maintained Liverpool Institute in 1924. He was an outdoor enthusiast and had written a popular (pre-Wainwright) guidebook, *Walking in the Lake District* (1933). He believed as passionately as had Rawnsley in the sanctity of the Lake District's open fells and in 1934 he approached members of the old Lake District Safeguarding Society, including the elderly Gordon Wordsworth, to suggest the formation of a new society, the Friends of the Lake District.

In 1935, when the Forestry Commission went public with its plans to afforest a third of the land it had purchased, the tested mechanisms of protest were swiftly engaged. The best-selling novelist Horace Walpole, who owned a house on the slopes of Cat Bells, wrote to *The Times* declaring that to plant Eskdale 'with larch and spruce is to ruin it once and forever'.[11] A petition was organised which quickly garnered 13,000 signatures, of which some 2,500 were those of people residing either in the county of Cumberland or some other part of the Lake District. The names included those of eight bishops, the lords-lieutenant and high sheriffs of Cumberland, Westmorland and Lancashire, the editors of the *Cumberland Herald*, *Westmorland Gazette* and *Whitehaven News*, the lord mayors of Newcastle and Liverpool, the vice-chancellors of the universities of Oxford, Manchester, Birmingham and Liverpool, and a former British ambassador to the United States. Nowadays we could anticipate the presence of some headline-grabbing television presenters, rock musicians or soap stars, but in those less popularist times the notable signatories included the conductor Sir Adrian Boult, the economist John Maynard Keynes, the zoologist Julian Huxley, the author and alpinist Geoffrey Winthrop Young, the first president of the Fell and Rock Climbing Club, Ashley Abraham, and the philosopher R. G. (Robin) Collingwood.

Faced by such a legion of illustrious opponents, one might have expected the Commissioners' resolve to crumble, but they were chaired by a forceful and tenacious man, Sir Roy Robinson, an Australian-born former Rhodes Scholar and the principal architect of the Forestry Commission, who was not going to be pushed around. The petition had been presented in mid-October 1935. The Commissioners waited for two months before responding in *The Times*, when, in Symonds's words, 'nothing was conceded, not a pine needle, not a stone'.[12] When the petition was six months old and still no agreement had been reached, the petitioners sent a distinguished delegation to the Commissioners. It was headed by the Archbishop of York and included the Windermere-born composer Sir Arthur Somervell (son of the founder of K Shoes), Norman Birkett KC and the administrator and social reformer Sir William Beveridge. Also present was the architect and rambler John Dower, who was married to Lady Pauline Trevelyan of Wallington Hall in Northumberland. He would play an important role in ensuing events. They asked that an area of 390 square miles in the core of the Lake District should be protected from further state forestry. When the Commission issued its White Paper on 26 August 1936, it conceded 'approximately 300 square miles'. This was something, but it fell far short of the 520 square miles the Council for the Preservation of Rural England had requested the previous year, or the 700 square miles that Symonds believed to be the true extent of the Lake District.

Symonds was so frustrated by the protracted negotiations and the parsimony of the Commissioners that he published his own response to the White Paper. *Afforestation in the Lake District* is a masterpiece of polemical writing and it boils with righteous anger, barely disguised. Having recently completed his fellwalking guide, Symonds knew the ground far better than the

Commissioners and he was able to run rings around their arguments. He made their claim that forestry did not restrict access to the open fells look foolish by showing just how the fencing at Ennerdale had constrained walkers:

> The wire-netting has an effective height of about three feet six inches: you can straddle it, at a squeeze and quite unofficially, where the previous routes into and out of the plantation run against the fence. At the point where it runs under, and to either side of, the famous Pillar Rock, which is one of the best-known places in the British Isles for rock-climbing, it is particularly unfortunate that the wire netting is barbed on the top: possibly the many tailors in Savile Row, who are neighbours of the Commissioners' head office there, are shareholders in the concern, and have arranged for a reliable trade in patching up torn breeches.[13]

Like Oppenheimer's climbers, Symonds hated and dreaded the effects of bureaucracy in the landscape, which were inimical to a sense of freedom:

> Like all others who love and know the district, I abominate the regimentation and cross-gartering of tracks, and hanker for the old-fashioned, skimble-skamble, bandy-legged divergencies which took us as the spirit moved or the slope invited: I lack the proper mentality to enjoy some enlarged and interminable Southport Flower Show, with all visitors kindly requested to keep on the proper pathways: for that is the distant semblance or attenuated wraith of the national playground which men pray for.[14]

He pooh-poohed the Commissioners' argument that, since coniferous trees were not out of place in the Alps, they were suitable for planting in the Lake District, observing, as had Wordsworth, the significant difference in scale between the two landscapes. Forestry on such a large scale would also damage sheep-farming, Symonds argued, since the holdings the Commission sought to buy were precisely those dale-head farms that were essential to the maintenance of the Herdwick breed and the way of life associated with it: 'if human values have for you a value that is absolute, you will not willingly see a proud people regimented out of existence by the invasive conifer and the indifference of administrative persons'.[15]

The result of all this pressure was an uneasy compromise. A map was agreed which protected 300 square miles of central Lakeland within a thick black line. Within this demarcation there would be no more state forestry, but there were shaded areas to the south and west of the boundary, including Eskdale, Dunnerdale and High Furness, where the Commission would still seek to acquire land. The ideal for the Lake District, Symonds argued, was a national park, not a national forest, and legally confirmed access to the fells had to be included. The cause of the National Park had gained momentum, but the Second World War would stop it in its tracks.

The ferocity of the opposition to forestry in the 1930s had its effect, in the longer term, upon the foresters. It came to be recognised that forestry should not just serve narrowly defined goals of production, but could also meet needs for amenity, employment, recreation and wildlife conservation.

Although a committee had been formed in 1929 to investigate the feasibility of setting up national parks,[16] the economic downturn two years later put the idea on to the back burner, where it simmered away through the Depression and the Second World War. Hiking, as we have seen, had become enormously popular during the 1930s, particularly among the working classes and the unemployed, and special trains to the Lake District were often run from industrial centres such as Manchester. In 1936 a number of organisations promoting outdoor recreation, including the Ramblers' Association, the Youth Hostels' Association and the Council for the Preservation of Rural England, got together to form the Standing Committee on National Parks, which then lobbied government for legislation. This was a remarkable consensus, considering that the Ramblers had tended to view the Preservationists as reactionary and conservative. In the meantime, the Access to Mountains Bill was passed in 1939. This was the culmination of a campaign that had begun fifty-five years earlier when James Bryce failed to get such a measure through Parliament, but the 1939 act was flawed. It compromised walkers' rights by making trespass a criminal offence in some circumstances and it was later repealed.

The enthusiasm for the National Park was not universal. In 1939 the Herdwick Sheep Breeders' Association, fearing that state control might jeopardise their interests as farm owners and landowners, passed a resolution opposing establishment of the National Park in the Lake District. According to a report in the *Manchester Guardian*, their president, Mr W. Butler of Broughton-in-Furness, thought that the whole idea had been dreamt up by summer holidaymakers who never saw the District for the rest of the year. People already had every access to the mountains, provided they shut the gates and kept their dogs under control. He did not see what more they could want.[17]

After the war, however, the national mood much favoured the creation of the parks. Sir Norman Birkett summed up it up in a pamphlet, *National Parks and the Countryside*, where he wrote:

> It is at least inevitable that after so much suffering so nobly borne it should be felt that some compensation might be found for so large a calamity, that something nobler should emerge for those who had endured so much, that there should be in the somewhat wistful phrase – a better world.[18]

A report on national parks was produced in 1945 as part of the new Labour government's post-war reconstruction. Its author, John Dower, understood that improved access was essential if the goals of landscape and nature conservation were to be supported by the public. Dower defined a national park as:

> an extensive area of beautiful and relatively wild country in which, for the nation's benefit and by appropriate national decision and action, (a) the characteristic landscape beauty is strictly preserved; (b) access and facilities for public open air enjoyment are amply provided, (c) wildlife and buildings and places of architectural and historic interest are suitably protected, while (d) established farming areas are effectively maintained.[19]

The next step was to set up a committee under Sir Arthur Hobhouse, chairman of the County Councils' Association, to consider the practicalities. In 1949 the long-cherished dream became reality with the passage of the National Parks and Access to the Countryside Act, though it was two more years before the Lake District finally became a national park. Lewis Silkin, a member of the Ramblers' Association and Minister of Town and Country Planning at the time, said it was 'the most exciting Act of the post-war Parliament'.[20]

It must be said that local opinion did not count for much in any of this. In the post-war period the expert knew best. Countryside planning was 'top-down' and largely driven by landed interests and notions of landscape quality derived from the high culture of artists and poets. In the Lake District opposition to the National Park was soon expressed in the formation of the Society of Dalesfolk in 1949. The *Manchester Guardian* sent a reporter to a rowdy but good-humoured meeting in Grasmere, where another activist vicar, the Reverend E. E. Oliver of Staveley, argued that while the National Park could be a good thing, it could turn into an instrument of persecution and deprive local people of their livelihoods.

The empty factory at Calgarth, where Short Sunderland flying boats had been built during the war, was the most knobbly bone of contention. With its large hangar, big enough to construct three aircraft, it was hardly an ornament to the landscape and the government had given a pledge to Symonds that it would go. Oliver thought this was 'disgusting', but Symonds, who attended the meeting, said that while the Friends were all for maintaining efficient agriculture and restoring traditional rural industries, they could see no place for factories on any considerable scale.[21]

The goals of economic development and landscape conservation often seem to conflict. Echoes of the Calgarth argument can be found on a present-day website, 'People in the Park', whose author, Paul Renouf, an Ambleside resident, argues cogently that while present policies have successfully protected the landscape and encouraged tourism, they have done little for local communities.[22] Aside from farming, tourism is the main industry, but it is a sector which offers mostly low job satisfaction, poor pay and unsocial hours. There is not much in the area to retain talented and ambitious youngsters, while the preserved landscape remains a magnet for affluent retired people who see the Lake District as 'an antidote to everything they dislike about the modern world' and join amenity societies to make sure it never changes. At the same time, the inward migration of the affluent has pushed up property prices, making it difficult for local first-time buyers.

Supporters of the national park cause have also had their grievances. The Hobhouse Committee had recommended that £50 million of public money should be set aside to purchase open country if necessary, but this was not forthcoming. Lack of adequate funding to meet the costs of conservation and recreation became a chronic grievance. Similarly, Hobhouse had suggested that the new authorities should have complete control over planning decisions in their parks, but intense lobbying from the Ministry of Agriculture and the Forestry Commission ensured that farming and forestry kept many of their privileges.[23]

Farmers, of course, remain the essential inhabitants of a British-style national park. It is they who, through their time-honoured practices, maintain the landscape in the form that visitors have come to love. Farmers may have absorbed some Picturesque values, but they have their own aesthetics, rooted in the productivity and health of the land. After the war, like farmers throughout the country, hill farmers were encouraged to intensify production. The system of 'headage' payments (part of the Common Agricultural Policy of the European Union) encouraged overgrazing of the fells, which damaged heaths and bogs, leading to a loss of bio-diversity. Too many sheep meant too much trampling and led to the compaction of soils. The land-scape's ability to act as a giant sponge was also compromised, contributing to flooding problems downstream.

The policy shifted in 2003, away from production incentives towards payments linked to environmental goals. Subsidy regimes are so complicated and change so swift that only a foolhardy author (and one who did not mind boring his readers) would attempt to describe them in detail. Farmers have had to become adept at form-filling to survive and there are even organisa-tions dedicated to helping them make sense of all the paperwork. Add this burden to the harshness of the life and the limited financial returns, and it is easy to see why young people are leaving the hill farms. If current trends continue, farms will get larger by amalgamation and land will be taken out of production. Re-wilding might become more commonplace, and it is at least arguable that some of the main attractions of the area to walkers, ease of access and the openness of the views, might be compromised by greater tree cover. There would certainly be a lot more bracken.

So while major threats such as reservoir projects or insensitive forestry initi-atives seem to have retreated, there are still powerful socio-economic forces at work, many of which operate at a global scale. Cheap imports force down food prices, making life close to impossible for the hill farmer, who has only been kept going at all through government subsidies. A subsidy regime which recognises the farmer's role as steward of the land makes far more sense than one which promotes overstocking in the name of production. An impending 'oil crunch' could, however, drastically increase the price of imports and transform the expectations of indigenous producers for the better. As the broadcaster Brian Redhead, who was president of the Council for National Parks in the 1980s, succinctly put it: 'It is important that farmers farm, and do not feel they are simply glorified Park keepers.'[24] Another way of expressing this would be to say that farmers do not want to be the curators of an extensive museum of farming.

We might wonder, too, whether Dower's vision of an inclusive National Park, truly open to all-comers, has ever been realised. Although working-class walkers and even trippers (of the right sort) came to feel at home there, for some groups the Lake District is apparently just too white and middle-class. The photographer Ingrid Pollard, who was born in Guyana in 1953, came to public attention in 1987 with her series 'Pastoral Interlude' in which she photographed black people, including herself, in rural settings. In one image she sits with her back to a barbed-wire fence. The caption para-phrases Wordsworth: 'I thought I liked the Lake District where I wandered lonely as a Black face in a sea of white. A visit to the countryside is always accompanied by a feeling of unease, dread . . .'[25] There is an echo here of the language of the original tourists, encountering sublime landscapes for the first time, but her fear is born of isolation and a feeling of not belonging.

For all that it has been represented as an Arcadia and site of rural innocence, the Lake District has some troubling associations with the slave trade. Whitehaven was involved in the triangular trade, and Storrs Hall on Windermere, now a luxury hotel, was bought and extended by John Bolton, the son of an Ulverston apothecary, who became a Liverpool merchant and made enough money from dealing in slaves, rum and cotton to buy the hall and extend it. He held a lavish Pocklington-style regatta on Windermere in 1825 which was attended by Wordsworth and Sir Walter Scott. The Cumbrian connection to slavery might not be obvious, but it is inescapable – we should remember the link every time we taste that local delicacy rum butter. Pollard's images pose awkward questions for everyone who loves the Lake District, but particularly for those with a say in its planning, management and promotion, but perhaps her experiences were not typical. The journalist Maya Jaggi, writing in the *Guardian* in 2008, fondly remembered her childhood holidays with her family on Windermere. The ingredients of her ideal holiday were fixed by a day messing about in a rowing boat, followed by a masterclass in boning trout from her aunt, the TV cook Madhur Jaffrey. Maya's parents often borrowed a friend's cottage at Ulpha, near Coniston Water, and she grew up with *Swallows and Amazons*. 'For my displaced, cash-strapped parents,' she wrote, 'the Lake District may have been a landscape in which to recreate for us aspects of their own childhoods. My father, whose family lost land in Punjab during Partition, would roll up his trousers and wade gamely into the becks, much to my adolescent embarrassment, while packed lunches on the fells could conceivably stand in for the lavish picnics at Himalayan hill stations that were a mythic part of my mother's Old Delhi family.'[26]

Though the elites who first found qualities to cherish in the Lake District wanted to hang on to them and, to a greater or lesser extent, to keep them to themselves, the history of the area has been one of a gradual opening up to mass enjoyment, and no one who cares about social justice can see this as anything but a good thing. When change is sudden, such as the transformation of Birthwaite into Windermere, it causes a panic, but many of the changes that the visitors brought were small and gradual – a path diversion here, a lay-by there – and people are more able to accept landscape change if

Grasmere campsite in the 1960s

it is incremental. As we saw in Wordsworth and Ruskin's objections to the railways, transport has long been one of the most disputed issues in the Lake District. The big car parks created to serve honeypot destinations such as Grasmere and Hawkshead were controversial – and Wordsworth, we can be sure, would have hated them – but considering the numbers of visitors who arrive by car, for most of the year the District is remarkably uncongested. Numerous ways of making transport more environmentally sustainable are being considered, from water buses on the principal lakes, to cycle routes and park-and-ride schemes. More controversially, some form of road pricing could be introduced. Ironically, given the historical roots of landscape conservation, it is not inconceivable that light railways might form part of the solution. The Ravenglass and Eskdale Railway (or 'L'aal Ratty') provides a precedent. Originally built to carry haematite ore from Boot down to the main line, it has also carried passengers since 1876, and in its present narrow-gauge form it ranks as one of the area's best-loved attractions.

Change is the key issue for the National Park, but the notion of 'preservation' should yield to that of 'conservation'. The former suggests that change can and must be prevented; the second recognises, not only that some changes are desirable, but that many are likely to happen anyway, despite attempts to arrest them. The best we can do is to manage change in terms of speed, scale and appropriateness. There is surely a danger that the too smotheringly conserved landscape will end up seeming sterile. Consider how many of the eccentric villas and follies, such as Claife Station, Belle Isle or Wray Castle, which now add interest to the Lake District, would never have been given permission had strict conservation policies been in place. Even if our goal is to conserve heritage, there needs to be room for the creation of new heritage.

And living landscapes cannot be set in aspic. When the national parks were set up, habits of deference were strongly ingrained. It is hard to dismiss the criticism that the views of local people were easily overridden, and we might wonder what sort of landscape would have ensued if they had been given most of the say. We live in a different era now, one in which the buzzwords have become 'inclusivity', 'participation' and 'empowerment', and the European Landscape Convention, signed by the United Kingdom in 2006, supports a much more democratic, citizen-led approach to decision-making. Indeed, so far has the pendulum swung that planners working for the National Park Authority believe that residents might already be suffering from 'consultation fatigue'.

On many issues the National Park Authority, the National Trust and the Friends of the Lake District see eye to eye. The Friends have offices almost adjacent to the Park Authority on a Kendal business park. Whether this is a holy or an unholy alliance depends upon your point of view, but these organisations may not be as hidebound by Wordsworthian conservation values as they once seemed. The Friends certainly put landscape conservation ahead of economic concerns when responding to development proposals – that is what the organisation was created to do – but even here there is a recognition among the officers and the more thoughtful of the membership that if the local farming community is prevented from making a comfortable living, the very basis of the landscape and heritage they strive to conserve will crumble. National Park Authority officers accept this, too. Keeping farmers farming requires an openness to the diversification of their businesses. Allowing farmers to convert a barn into a bunkhouse or to build a couple of suitably designed chalets might mean the difference between a life lived on the margins and a financially secure future.

Planning for change can be difficult enough in settled times, but Lake District officers recently met to discuss the pressing problem of rain. The hamlet of Seathwaite, deep within Borrowdale, is reputedly the wettest place in England, but mere quantity is not the present concern: the planners are more worried about a predicted change in weather patterns, linked to global warming. Hotter summers with less rainfall are predicted, but for the rest of the year intense bursts of heavy rainfall are likely. Park managers are already worried that this weather pattern is likely to worsen the footpath erosion which already disfigures many popular mountains.[27] Tarns are silting up with eroded material and some could disappear. Hotter temperatures could cause grass to die back and make farming even more marginal, while also increasing soil compaction, run-off and the possibility of flash flooding in settlements downstream. Once more the familiar scenery of the National Park falls under the sway of greater forces from a wider world and, for all the effort that has gone into defending the existing landscape, change is a certainty. Is it too radical to suggest that one can love a place deeply but still be willing to let it evolve?

New problems prompt new solutions, but these are not always welcomed. Advertising images often use the bright white wind turbine to signify a pure green future, but in practice communities often revolt against them. A plan to construct twenty-seven turbines at Whinash, north of Kendal but outside the present boundary of the National Park, was turned down in 2006 after a six-week public inquiry. The objectors, who included all the local councils, the Friends of the Lake District, the Tourist Board, the National Park Authority and many local people, including such resident celebrities as the

Lambrigg Windfarm, near Kendal

climber Chris Bonington and the broadcasters Eric Robson and Melvyn Bragg, believed that the scheme would inflict visual and cultural harm on 'an icon of upland beauty and tranquillity'.[28] A victory for local democracy and landscape conservation, worth celebrating perhaps, but a spokesperson for Friends of the Earth lamented that the project had been the victim of a vocal NIMBY campaign, and thought the decision set a dismal precedent if the government was serious about tackling climate change. Again it seems that it was the scale and the suddenness of the proposed change that caused the mischief and one wonders if a more local, community-based approach to this technology might run into less opposition. The irony of this particular dispute was that both camps could call themselves environmentalists.

To whom does the Lake District belong? Is it the people who live there, or the nation as a whole? Our democratic principles might incline us towards the inhabitants, but how long does it take to become a local? Does this deny a voice to those who live elsewhere but feel a powerful connection to the place? Or is trusting the natives a dangerous policy, as Rawnsley seems to have thought? As a landscape architect, it pleases me that there are places in Britain where the conservation of high-quality landscape is the prevailing objective of public policy, but should we not be seeking quality everywhere, rather than just in 'beauty reserves'? If we considered landscape quality in our quotidian landscapes, perhaps we would not need designations like 'National Park' or 'Area of Outstanding Natural Beauty'. This is certainly the thrust of the European Landscape Convention, which applies to the 'whole territory' of the signatories and thus concerns 'not just remarkable landscapes but also ordinary everyday landscapes and blighted areas'.[29] But, of course, this approach only works if we are confident that our best, or most treasured, landscapes are safe from thoughtless harm. Once again, the precedents are not reassuring. So for the time being, at least, until we really learn to value our connections to land and landscape, vigilance must still remain the watchword. At the same time, we should be careful that those whose values or aesthetics diverge from the present consensus (trippers, motorists, Manchester mechanics, power-boaters, admirers of echoing cannon and perhaps sometimes even farmers) are not derided and pushed out of the conversation.

An inclusive view of the Lake District has to recognise that it belongs to everyone, both to its residents and to the whole nation, in all its social, racial and economic diversity. Policy has to be balanced between local and national interests. Indeed, there is a strong argument that the Lakes belong not just to England or Britain, but to the world. In 1986 and 1989 the Lake District was put forward for inscription by the United Nations as a World Heritage Site. This would amount to recognition that the Lake District has outstanding value for the whole of humanity.

However, both these bids were based on the idea that the Lake District was an outstanding *natural* landscape, like Yosemite or Yellowstone, and thus they failed. At the time UNESCO did not have a category for *cultural landscapes,* which, of course, is how the Lake District should be considered. Indeed, so embarrassed were the assessors by their own conclusions that they called for the rules to be rethought. Previously the listings had been either cultural (including buildings such as the Tower of London or whole city centres such as those of Luxembourg or Prague) or natural (such as the Giant's Causeway or the Everglades). Since 2005, candidate sites have had to meet at least one of ten criteria, and the Lake District would seem to fulfil at least three of these, in that it is an outstanding example of a traditional land use (sheep-farming) which is representative of a distinctive and to some degree vulnerable culture; it is tangibly associated with living traditions, ideas, beliefs and artistic and literary works of 'outstanding universal significance'; and it contains areas of 'exceptional natural beauty and aesthetic importance'.

The Lake District is currently on the United Kingdom's 'tentative list' but since each country is limited to one nomination per year, it might have to wait a little longer yet – and, since committees make strange decisions, there is no guarantee of success. Yet the case made by the bid's supporters appears to be strong. It is one which stresses the District's part in the emergence of the Picturesque movement, its central role in the emergence of the Romantic sensibility and its importance in the development of landscape conservation, ecological thinking and the National Park Movement. The bid's supporters stress that inscription will not bring more limitations on the way that Cumbrians can lead their lives, though it might provide the area's custodians with more clout when asking central government for funds. It would be ironic, to say the least, if the Lake District should fail to be recognised by UNESCO, when it has played such a prominent and integral part in the very philosophy that underpins the conservation of landscape heritage. If the bid is successful, the Lake District will take its place among such company as the Grand Canyon (inscribed in 1979), the Great Barrier Reef (1981) and the Great Wall of China (1987). This is surely where this strikingly scenic, historically significant and culturally unique landscape must belong.

The Thompson family car (*c.* 1960) by J. H. Thompson

Overleaf: Castlerigg Stone Circle

Barrow House Cascade

Notes

Introduction

1. Hutchinson, W., *An Excursion to the Lakes in Westmoreland and Cumberland; with a Tour through Part of the Northern Counties, in the Years 1773 and 1774*, printed for J. Wilkie and W. Charnley (1776): 65–6.
2. Ibid.: 66–7.
3. Ibid.
4. Ousby, I., *The Englishman's England: Taste, Travel and the Rise of Tourism* (Cambridge: Cambridge University Press, 1990): 152.
5. Interview with Steve Ratcliffe, Lake District National Park Authority.
6. Statistics are a minefield. This figure is taken from the website of the Cumbria Tourist Board, http://www.cumbriatourism.org/about/, accessed 17/10/2007, and is based on figures for 2006.
7. Wordsworth, W., *Wordsworth's Guide to the Lakes*, 5th edition (London: Henry Frowde, 1906 [1835]): 22.
8. Ibid.
9. Gambles, R., *The Story of the Lakeland Dales* (Chichester: Phillimore, 1997): 6.
10. The Hobhouse Report of 1947 (Report of the National Parks Committee to Parliament Cmd 7121).
11. Nicholson, N., *Greater Lakeland* (London: Robert Hale, 1996 [1969]): 230.
12. http://www.spartacus.schoolnet.co.uk/ITmanchester.htm. Accessed 10/02/2009.
13. Prentice, A., *Historical Sketches and Personal Recollections of Manchester: Intended to Illustrate the Progress of Public Opinion from 1792 to 1832* (London: Routledge, reprinted 1970 [2nd edition 1851]): 289.

1 The English Alps: From Defoe's 'horrid mountains' to a Revolution in Taste

1. Pat Rogers's introduction to the 1989 edition of Defoe, D., *A Tour Through the Whole Island of Great Britain*, ed. Pat Rogers (Exeter: Webb & Bower, 1989).
2. Defoe, *A Tour Through the Whole Island of Great Britain*: 195–6.
3. Howell, J., *Instructions for Forraine Travell*, ed. Edward Arber (London: English Reprints, 1869 [1642]): 25.
4. William Camden, *Britannia*, transl. Philemon Holland (London, 1610). The full text can be viewed at http://www.philological.bham.ac.uk/cambrit/

5. Fiennes, C., *The Illustrated Journeys of Celia Fiennes 1685–c. 1715*, ed. Christopher Morris (London: Macdonald & Co., and Exeter: Webb & Bower, 1982): 166.

6. Ibid.: 169.

7. Ibid.: 168.

8. Wordsworth, W., *The Prelude*, Book IV, lines 333–41.

9. Quoted in Black, J., *The British Abroad: The Grand Tour in the Eighteenth Century* (Stroud: Sutton Publishing, 1992): 34.

10. Addison, J., *Remarks on Several Parts of Italy, Etc. in the Years 1701, 1702, 1703* (Dublin, 1703): 261.

11. Gray, T., Letter to his mother from Lyons, 13 October 1739, *Correspondence of Thomas Gray*, ed. Paget Toynbee and Leonard Whibley, vol. I (Oxford: Oxford University Press, 1935), Letter 71.

12. Gray, T., Letter to Mr West from Turin, 16 November, 1739, Ibid., Letter 74.

13. Dalton, J., *A Descriptive Poem addressed to Two Young Ladies at their Return from Viewing the Mines near Whitehaven* (Keswick, 1755).

14. Brown, J., *Description of the Lake and Vale of Keswick* (Newcastle, 1767). The most significant passage is reproduced in *The Lake District: An Anthology*, compiled by Norman Nicholson (Harmondsworth: Penguin, 1978): 92–3.

15. Avison, C., quoted in William Gilpin, *Observations, Relative Chiefly to Picturesque Beauty*, vol. I (London: R. Blamire, 1786): 183.

16. Carnie, J. M., *At Lakeland's Heart* (Windermere: Parrock Press, 2002): 133.

17. Brown, *Description of the Lake and Vale of Keswick*.

2 Pathfinders: From Thomas Gray to William Gilpin

1. Gray, T., Letter to Richard West, 16 November 1739, *Correspondence of Thomas Gray*.

2. Gray, 'Journal in the Lakes', reproduced in *The Lake District: An Anthology*: 251.

3. Ibid.: 252.

4. Edmund Burke's *A Philosophical Enquiry into the Origin of our Ideas of the Sublime and Beautiful* had been published in 1757. Burke tried to explain our liking for two very different categories of landscape in terms of our 'leading passions', which were linked with procreation and survival – or, as Woody Allen might put it, with sex and death. He wrote from an entirely masculine point of view, equating beauty with what he regarded as feminine virtues, such as smallness, smoothness and delicacy. To appreciate beauty in an unsullied form one had to subtract any feelings of lust or desire. Similarly, feelings of sublimity arose when one was in the presence of something powerful, frightening or awe-inspiring, yet in a position to contemplate it from a place of safety. 'When danger or pain press too nearly,' he wrote, 'they are incapable of giving any delight, and are simply terrible; but at certain distances, and with certain modifications, they may be, and they are delightful, as we every day experience.'

5. Southey, R., *Letters from England* (Gloucester: Alan Sutton, 1984 [1807]): 242.

6. Collingwood, W. G., *The Lake Counties*, 2nd edition (London: Frederick Warne & Co., 1932): 65–6.

7. The remark is quoted in Boswell's *The Life of Samuel Johnson LL.D.* The detractor was the Reverend Dr Percy, who was an heir of the ancient Northumberland family. Percy thought Pennant had written disrespectfully and inaccurately about the duke's estate at Alnwick.

8. From 'Pennant's Second Tour in Scotland', in Pinkerton, J. (ed.), *A General Collection of the Best and Most Interesting Voyages and Travels in the World* (London:

Longman, Hurst, Rees & Orme, 1809): 198.

9. Ibid.: 198.

10. Young, A., *A Six Months' Tour Through the North of England*, vol. II (London, 1770): 221.

11. West, T., *A Guide to the Lakes of Cumberland, Westmorland and Lancashire*, 11th edition (Kendal: W. Pennington, 1821 [1778]): 2.

12. Ibid.: 41.

13. Wilberforce, W., *Journey to the Lake District from Cambridge, 1779*, ed. C. E. Wrangham (Stocksfield: Oriel Press, 1983).

14. Nicholson, N., *The Lakers: Adventures of the First Tourists* (London: Robert Hale, 1955): 41.

15. West, *A Guide to the Lakes of Cumberland, Westmorland and Lancashire*: 9.

16. Walpole, H., *A History of the Modern Taste in Gardening* (New York: Ursus Press, 1995 [1782]): 43.

17. Gilpin, W., *An Essay on Prints* [1768], 4th edition (1792): xii.

18. Solnit, R., *Wanderlust: A History of Walking* (London: Verso, 2001): 95.

19. Austen, J., *Northanger Abbey* (Cambridge: Cambridge University Press, 2006): 113

20. Austen, J., *Pride and Prejudice* (Cambridge: Cambridge University Press, 2006): 174–75.

21. Combe, W., *Tour of Doctor Syntax in Search of the Picturesque* (London: T. F. Bell, 1865 [1809–11]): 17.

22. Ibid.: 125.

3 'Settled Contentment': The Lake District of Wordsworth's Youth

1. Carlyle, A., *Autobiography of the Rev. Dr Alexander Carlyle; containing memorials of the men and events of his time* (Edinburgh: Blackwood, 1861).

2. Wordsworth, W., *Wordsworth's Guide to the Lakes*, 5th edition (London: Henry Frowde, 1906 [1835]): 68.

3. Scott, S. H., *A Westmorland Village* (London: Archibald Constable & Co., 1904): 261.

4. Carnie, *At Lakeland's Heart*: 53.

5. Young, *A Six Months' Tour through the North of England*, vol. II.

6. Rollinson, W., *A History of Man in the Lake District* (London: J. M. Dent & Sons, 1967): 98.

7. Nicholson, *The Lakers*: 68–9.

8. Wordsworth, D., *The Grasmere and Alfoxden Journals*, ed. Pamela Woof (Oxford: Oxford University Press, 2002): 9.

9. Young, *A Six Months' Tour Through the North of England*: 376

10. Burkett, M. E., and Sloss, J. D. G., *William Green of Ambleside: A Lake District Artist (1760–1823)* (Kendal: Abbot Hall, 1984): 82.

11. Gell, W., *A Tour in the Lakes, 1797*, ed. W. Rollinson (Otley: Smith Settle, 2000): 10.

12. Quoted in Woof, R., 'The Matter of Fact Paradise', in *The Lake District: A Sort of National Property*, papers presented to a symposium held at the Victoria & Albert Museum, (1984): 14.

4 Showmen: 'King Pocky' and 'Admiral' Crosthwaite

1. Gell, *A Tour in the Lakes*): 22.

2. Ibid.: 26.

3. Hankinson, A., *The Regatta Men* (Milnthorpe: Cicerone Press, 1988): 13.

4. *Cumberland Pacquet*, 10 September 1782.

5. Peter Crosthwaite's Memorandum book. Entry for 18 March 1799. Keswick Museum.

6. Gell, *A Tour in the Lakes*: 46.

7. Coleridge, S. T., Journal entry for 15 November 1799, reproduced in Hudson, R. (ed.), *Coleridge among the Lakes & Mountains* (London: The Folio Society, 1991): 69.

8. Gell, *A Tour in the Lakes*: 69.

9. Coleridge, Journal entry for 15 November 1799, reproduced in Hudson, *Coleridge among the Lakes & Mountains*: 69.

10. Southey, *Letters from England*: 165.

11. Quoted in Ousby, *The Englishman's England*: 167.

12. For the reference to the floating island in 1864 see Palmer, W. T., and Cooper, A. H., *The English Lakes* (London: A. & C. Black, 1905): 143. For the appearance in 1995 see Parker, J. W., *An Atlas of the English Lakes* (Milnthorpe: Cicerone Press, 2002): 71.

13. The British Museum was established in 1753, largely based on the collections of the physician and scientist Sir Hans Sloane, but it did not open to the public until 1759.

14. Breaks, P., 'Commercial Museums of Eighteenth Century Cumbria', *Journal of the History of Collections*, 4, no. 1 (1992): 107–26.

15. Gell, *A Tour in the Lakes*: 19.

16. Ibid.: 20.

17. Breaks, 'Commercial Museums of Eighteenth Century Cumbria': 111.

18. Ibid.: 119.

19. Ousby, I. (ed.), James Plumptre's Britain: *The Journals of a Tourist in the 1790s* (London: Hutchinson, 1992): 145.

20. Coleridge, S. T., Journal entry for 15 November 1799, reproduced in Hudson, *Coleridge among the Lakes & Mountains*: 69.

5 Wandering Lonely: Wordsworth Leaves the Lake District

1. Jean-Jacques Rousseau, *The Confessions*. Quoted in Solnit, R., *Wanderlust*: 19.

2. Wordsworth, W., Letter to William Mathews, Keswick, 7 November 1794. Included in Hill, A. G. (ed.), *Letters of William Wordsworth* (Oxford: Clarendon Press, 1984): 20–2.

3. Carnie, *At Lakeland's Heart*: 143. Calvert also left a further £300 to Dorothy Wordsworth in a codicil.

4. Wordsworth, W., Letter to William Mathews, Keswick, 7 November 1794.

5. McKusick, J., '"Wisely Forgetful": Coleridge and the politics of Pantisocracy', in Fulford, T., and Kitson, P. J., *Romanticism and Colonialism Writing and Empire, 1730–1830* (Cambridge: Cambridge University Press, 1998): 123.

6. Wordsworth, W., *The Prelude*, Book VIII, lines 92–5.

7. Bragg, M., *Land of the Lakes* (London: Secker & Warburg, 1983): 197.

8. Coleridge, S. T., From a letter to Dorothy Wordsworth written in Keswick, 10 November 1799. Included in Hudson, *Coleridge among the Lakes & Mountains*: 65–6.

9. Hudson, *Coleridge among the Lakes & Mountains*: 64.

10. Ibid.: 65–6.

11. Ibid.: 70.

12. Ibid., 71.

13. Quoted in Hebron, S., *The Romantics and the British Landscape* (London: The British Library, 2006): 33.

6 The Lake Poets: Wordsworth, Coleridge and Southey

1. Wordsworth, W., Letter to Samuel Taylor Coleridge, Grasmere, 24 and 27 December 1799. Included in Hill, *Letters of William Wordsworth*: 33–4.

2. Coleridge, S. T., Letter to William Godwin, 19 November 1801. Quoted in Sisman, A., *The Friendship* (London: HarperCollins, 2006): 187.

3. 5 April 1800. http://www.fullbooks.com/The-Works-of-Charles-and-Mary-Lamb-Vol5.html, accessed 10/04/2008.

4. Coleridge, S. T., Letter to William Godwin, Keswick, 21 May 1800.

5. Coleridge, S. T., Letter to Samuel Purkis, Keswick, 29 July 1800.

6. Coleridge, S. T., *The Major Works, including Biographia Literaria* (Oxford: Oxford University Press, 2000): 184.

7. Wordsworth, W., Letter to Sir George Beaumont, Grasmere, 11 February 1805. Included in Hill, *Letters of William Wordsworth*: 76–7.

8. Wordsworth, D., Letter to Mary Hutchinson, Grasmere, 29 April 1801. Included in Hill, A. G. (ed.), *The Letters: A Selection* (Oxford: Oxford University Press, new edition, 1985): 48–9.

9. Hudson, *Coleridge among the Lakes & Mountains*: 121

10. Johnson, P., '1828 for opportunity, 1998 for longevity', *Spectator*, 4 July 1998.

11. Pelham, E. (ed.), *Coleridge and Wordsworth* (Toronto: Morang and Co., 1902): 22.

12. Coleridge, S. T., Letter to William Godwin, Keswick, 25 March 1801, in Hudson, *Coleridge among the Lakes & Mountains*: 117

13. Coleridge, S. T., from 'A Letter to Sarah Hutchinson', in *Selected Poems*, ed. Richard Holmes (London: Penguin, 1996): 169–78.

14. Wordsworth, *The Grasmere and Alfoxden Journals*, entry for Thursday 15 April 1802: 85.

15. Woof, P., 'The Daffodils: The Journal and the Poem', in *The Wordsworths and the Daffodils* (Grasmere: The Wordsworth Trust, 2002): 7–35.

16. Sisman, *The Friendship*: 363.

17. Quoted in Byatt, A. S., *Unruly Times* (London: Vintage, 1997 [1970]): 225.

18. Davies, H., *William Wordsworth. A Biography* (London: Weidenfeld & Nicolson, 1980): 263.

19. Martineau, H., *An Independent Woman's Lake District Writings*, ed. Michael R. Hill (Amherst, NY: Humanity Books, 2004): 430.

20. Southey, R., *Letters from England*: 226–7

21. Southey, C. C. (ed.), *The Life and Correspondence of the Late Robert Southey*, vol. III (London: Longmans, 1850): 4.

22. Wordsworth, W., Letter to Sir George Beaumont, Grasmere, 11 February 1805. Included in Hill, *Letters of William Wordsworth*: 76–7.

23. Southey, R., Letter to John Rickman, mid-April 1807.

24. Wordsworth, D., Letter to Catherine Clarkson, Coleorton, 17 [actually 16] February 1807. Included in Barker, J. (ed.), *Wordsworth: A Life in Letters* (London: Penguin, 2003): 88

25. Martineau, *An Independent Woman's Lake District Writings*: 439.

26. *The Letters of William and Dorothy Wordsworth 1787–1805*, ed. Ernest de Selincourt (Oxford: Oxford University Press, 1967): 534.

27. Wordsworth, D., Letter to Catherine Clarkson, Grasmere, 12 April 1810. Included in Barker, *Wordsworth: A Life in Letters*: 101.

7 Artists among the Lakes: A New Aesthetic Frontier

1. Bragg, *Land of the Lakes*: 188.

2. Farington could have read Gray's published poems, but it is likely that his acquaintance with Gray's opinions of the Lake District came from the celebrated life of Gray by William Mason: *The Poems of Mr Gray, to which are Prefixed Memoirs of his Life and Writings* (1775). Mason made a point of including some of Gray's letters, and was one of the earliest biographers to do so.

3. A principal source for details of Turner's visit to the Lake District was David Hill's *Turner in the North* (New Haven, CT, and London: Yale University Press, 1997), published on the occasion of a major

exhibition, *Turner in the North of England 1797*, at the Tate Gallery, London, 1997.

4. Ruskin, J., *Praeterita* (London: Everyman's Library, 2005): 225.

5. *Ullswater, Cumberland* was bought by the Wordsworth Trust in 2005 for £300,000 with help from the National Heritage Memorial Fund, National Art Collections Fund, the V&A/MLA Purchase Grant Scheme, the Golden Trust and an anonymous donor.

6. Ruskin, *Praeterita*: 355.

7. About a quarter of the present-day Lake District lay in Lancashire. The county boundary extended as far north as the River Brathay at Clappersgate.

8. Quoted in Burkett and Sloss, *William Green of Ambleside: A Lake District Artist*: 31.

9. Ibid.

10. Ibid.: 15.

11. Ibid.: 66.

12. Green, W., *The Tourist's New Guide, containing a Description of the Lakes, Mountains and Scenery in Cumberland, Westmorland, and Lancashire, with some account of their Bordering Towns and Villages*, 2 vols (Kendal: R. Lough & Co., 1819): vii.

13. Ibid: vol. I: 5.

14. Wordsworth, *The Grasmere and Alfoxden Journals*: 175.

15. Extract from the diary of Joseph Farington, 12 December 1807, quoted in *William Wordsworth: The Critical Heritage*, vol. I, *1793–1820*, ed. Robert Woof (London: Routledge, 2001): 252.

16. Leslie, C. R., *Memoirs of the Life of John Constable* (London: Longmans, 1845): 19–20.

17. Estimates of the number of drawings vary. The catalogue for *The Discovery of the Lake District*, an exhibition at the Victoria & Albert Museum in 1984, mentions seventy-seven, while the catalogue accompanying the Wordsworth Trust's exhibition *The Solitude of Mountains* in 2006 puts the number closer to one hundred.

18. Rhyne, C. S., *John Constable, Towards a Complete Chronology* (Portland, OR: self-published, 1990) and at http://academic.reed.edu/art/faculty/rhyne/papers/jc_chronology.pdf. Accessed 23/06/2008.

19. Rhyne, C. S., 'The Drawing of Mountains: Constable's 1860 Lake District Tour', in *The Lake District: A Sort of National Property*: 61–70

20. Ibid.

21. The catalogue for *The Solitude of Mountains* includes an essay by Conal Shields, who says that only a solitary oil, tentatively entitled *Bowfell and Langdale Pikes*, has been convincingly linked to Constable's visit in 1806.

8 The Buttermere Beauty: Mary Robinson, Captain Budworth and the Keswick Impostor

1. Budworth, J., *A Fortnight's Ramble to the Lakes in Westmoreland, Lancashire and Cumberland*, 3rd edition (London, 1810): 251.

2. The Lake District char is *Salmo Willughbii*. According to John Watson, FLS, *The English Lake District Fisheries* (London: Lawrence & Bullen, 1899), it could be found in 'Coniston, Crummock, Ennerdale Lake, Haweswater, Buttermere, and Ullswater, as well as Gaits Water and Seathwaite Tarn'. A deep-feeding fish usually caught by trolling a line, the char was never regarded as a 'sporting fish', but it was one which nevertheless held a mysterious appeal for anglers. Char were seldom taken in Buttermere, according to Watson, but the lake produced some of the finest-flavoured pink-fleshed trout in the region.

3. Budworth, *A Fortnight's Ramble*: 251.

4. Ibid.: 252.

5. Ibid.: 385.

6. Ibid.: 389.

7. Ibid.: 394.

8. Ibid.: 400.

9. Ibid.: 408.

10. Many of the details of Hatfield's life, crimes, arrest, trial and execution are taken from *The Complete Newgate Calendar*, vol. IV.

11. Coleridge, S. T., 'Romantic Marriage II', in *Morning Post*, 22 October 1802.

12. Coleridge, S. T., 'The Keswick Impostor I', in *Morning Post*, 20 November 1802.

13. De Quincey, T., *Recollections of the Lake Poets* (London: John Lehmann, 1948 [1834–1840]): 55.

14. Quoted in Russett, M., *Fictions and Fakes* (Cambridge: Cambridge University Press, 2006): 104.

15. De Quincey, *Recollections of the Lake Poets*: 57, footnote.

16. Ibid.: 62–3.

17. Coleridge, S. T., 'The Keswick Impostor II', in *Morning Post*, 31 December 1802.

18. Ibid. 20 November 1802.

19. Coleridge, 'Romantic Marriage I', in *Morning Post*, 11 October 1802.

20. Coleridge, 'Romantic Marriage II', in *Morning Post*, 22 October 1802.

21. Quoted in Burke, P., *Recollections of the Court Room* (New York: H. Dayton, 1859): 181.

22. *The Complete Newgate Calendar*, vol. IV.

23. Hudson, *Coleridge among the Lakes & Mountains*: 179.

24. Quoted in Hebron, *The Romantics and the British Landscape*: 150.

25. Wordsworth, W., *The Prelude*, Book VII, lines 321–7.

9 'Let Nature be all in all': Wordsworth and the Origins of Landscape Conservation

1. Noyes, R., *Wordsworth and the Art of Landscape* (Bloomington, IN: Indiana University Press, 1968).

2. Buchanan, C., *Wordsworth's Gardens* (Lubbock, TX.: Texas Tech University Press, 2001). This book documents Wordsworth's principal gardens in considerable detail.

3. Wordsworth, D., Letter to Mrs Thomas Clarkson, Rydal Mount, *c.* 14 September 1813.

4. Rawnsley, H. D., *Reminiscences of Wordsworth among the Peasantry of Westmoreland* (London: Dillon's, 1968 [1882]): 17–18.

5. Wordsworth, *Wordsworth's Guide to the Lakes*: 69.

6. Ibid.: 70.

7. Mabey, R., *Flora Britannica* (London: Sinclair-Stevenson, 1996): 22–4.

8. Wordsworth, *Wordsworth's Guide to the Lakes*: 86–7.

9. Ibid.: 86.

10. De Quincey, *Recollections of the Lake Poets*: 304.

11. Wordsworth, W., Letter to Sir George Beaumont, Coleorton, 10 November 1806.

12. Wordsworth, *Wordsworth's Guide to the Lakes*: 73.

13. Green, W., *Guide Book*, vol. I (1819): 247.

14. Wordsworth, *Wordsworth's Guide to the Lakes*: 85.

15. Wordsworth, W., Letter to Jacob Fletcher, 17 January 1825.

16. Wordsworth, W., *Prose Works*, vol. III, ed. W. J. B. Owen and J. W. Smyser (Oxford: Clarendon Press, 1974).

17. Wordsworth, W., Letter to Sir George Beaumont, 17 October 1805.

18. Wordsworth, *Wordsworth's Guide to the Lakes*: 72.

19. Ibid.: 57.

20. Wordsworth, *Wordsworth's Guide to the Lakes*: 62.

21. Ibid.: 74.

22. Hudson, *Coleridge among the Lakes & Mountains*: 64.

23. Wordsworth, *The Grasmere and Alfoxden Journals*: 106–7.

24. Wordsworth, *Wordsworth's Guide to the Lakes*: 80–1.

25. A sensitivity to the use of colour in the landscape remains important in landscape architectural practice. The architect and landscape architect Michael Lancaster, who died in 2004, even made a specialist career out of it, publishing such titles as *Britain in View* (1984), *Colour in Architecture* (1996) and *Colourscape* (1996).

26. Rawnsley, *Reminiscences of Wordsworth among the Peasantry of Westmoreland*: 27.

27. Gambles, R., *The Story of the Lakeland Dales* (Chichester: Phillimore, 1997): 119.

10 'A Pleasant Sort of Fear': The Birth of Fellwalking

1. Bott, G., *Keswick: The Story of a Lake District Town* (Carlisle: Bookcase, 2005): 49.

2. Radcliffe, A., *A Journey Made in the Summer of 1794 through Holland and the Western Frontier of Germany, with a Return Down the Rhine to which are added Observations during a Tour to the Lakes of Lancashire, Westmoreland, and Cumberland*, 2nd edition (London: G. G. and J. Robinson, 1795): 332.

3. Ibid.: 340.

4. Ibid.: 340–1.

5. De Quincey, *Recollections of the Lake Poets*: 28–9.

6. Wordsworth, W., Letter to Charles Wordsworth, Rydal Mount, (probably) 17 June 1830.

7. Rawnsley, *Reminiscences of Wordsworth among the Peasantry of Westmoreland*: 24.

8. Ibid.: 31.

9. Ibid.: 36.

10. Hudson, *Coleridge among the Lakes & Mountains*: 85.

11. Ibid.: 92.

12. Hebron, *The Romantics and the British Landscape*: 41.

13. Ibid.: 144.

14. Ibid.: 249.

15. Solnit, *Wanderlust*: 84.

16. Quoted in Burkett and Sloss, *William Green of Ambleside*: 74.

17. De Quincey, *Recollections of the Lake Poets*: 288–9.

18. Wilkinson, T., *Tours of British Mountains* (London: Taylor and Hessay, 1824): 99–100.

19. Ibid.: 169.

20. Keats, J., Letter to Benjamin Robert Haydon, 8 April 1818. Full text at http://englishhistory.net/keats/letters/haydon8April1818.html. Accessed 19/05/2008.

21. Rawnsley, H. D., 'Charles Dickens in Cumberland', in *Chapters at the English Lakes* (Glasgow: James MacLehose & Sons, 1913). The original account by Collins and Dickens was entitled *The Lazy Tour of the Two Apprentices* and was published in *Household Words*, 3–31 October 1857; and *Harper's Weekly*, 31 October–28 November 1857.

11 'Speak, Passing Winds': The Protest over Railways

1. Wordsworth, W., Letter to the editor of the *Morning Post*, Rydal Mount, 9 December 1844.

2. Ibid.

3. Wordsworth, W., Second letter to the editor of the *Morning Post*, 17 December 1844.

4. Ibid.

5. Ibid.

6. Wordsworth, W., Letter to the editor of the *Morning Post*, Rydal Mount, 9 December 1844.

7. Wordsworth, *Prose Works*, vol. III: 339.

8. Wordsworth, W., Letter to Christopher Wordsworth, Jnr, August 1845.

9. In 1846 the powers formerly exercised by the Board of Trade in relation to railways were transferred to a statutory body known as the Commissioners of Railways.

10. *The Discovery of the Lake District*, exhibition catalogue, London, Victoria & Albert Museum, 1984: 107.

11. *Westmorland Gazette and Kendal Advertiser*, 24 April 1847.

12. More specifically, Wordsworth was prepared to canvass and to spy on behalf of the Lowther family to prevent a firebrand Whig, Henry Brougham, from taking a seat in Westmorland.

13. Rawnsley, *Reminiscences of Wordsworth among the Peasantry of Westmoreland*: 37.

14. Martineau, *An Independent Woman's Lake District Writings*: 446.

15. Solnit, *Wanderlust*: 115.

16. Martineau, 'Lights of the Lake District', in *An Independent Woman's Lake District Writings*: 423.

17. Martineau, 'A Year in Ambleside', in *An Independent Woman's Lake District Writings*: 174.

18. Martineau, 'The Cost of Cottages', in *An Independent Woman's Lake District Writings*: 274.

19. Hunter Davies suggests that she was suffering from cholecystitis and gallstones. Davies, *William Wordsworth*: 301.

20. Martineau, 'The English Lake District', in *An Independent Woman's Lake District Writings*: 296.

21. Burkett and Sloss, *William Green of Ambleside*: 79.

22. Nicholson, N., *Portrait of the Lakes* (London: Robert Hale, 1963).

12 The Sage of Brantwood: John Ruskin Wrestles the Capitalist Dragon

1. Quoted in Hunt, J. D., *The Wider Sea* (London: Phoenix, 1998 [1982]): 44.

2. John Dixon Hunt, one of Ruskin's biographers, suggests that this is the likely date, though the editor of *Iteriad* says that the Ruskins' first visit to the Lake District was in 1824.

3. Ruskin, *Praeterita*: 296.

4. Ibid.: 321.

5. From a letter to Charles Eliot Norton, quoted in Hunt, *The Wider Sea*: 343.

6. From a letter from Ruskin to his mother, quoted in *The Discovery of the Lake District*: 95.

7. Frost, M. A., 14 June 2006. 'John Ruskin'. *The Literary Encyclopaedia*. Accessed 23/07/2008. <http://www.litencyc.com/php/speople.php?rec=true&UID=3890>

8. Ruskin, *Praeterita*: 13.

9. From the Preface to the re-arranged edition of *Modern Painters II*, quoted the Introduction to Wheeler, M. (ed.), *Ruskin and Environment* (Manchester: Manchester University Press, 1995): 2.

10. Ruskin, J., Letter to the editor of the *Pall Mall Gazette*, Brantwood, 1 March 1887.

11. Ruskin, J., 'Railways in the Lake District. A Protest' [1876], in Cook, E. T., and Wedderburn, A. (eds), *The Works of John Ruskin*, vol. 34 (London: George Allen, 1908:140–1.

12. Darby, W. J., *Landscape and Identity* (Oxford: Berg, 2000): 155.

13. Ibid.: 142.

14. Ambleside Railway Bill. Proceedings in the House of Commons, 1887.

15. Ibid.

16. Ibid.

17. Hanley, K., 'The discourse of natural beauty', in Wheeler, *Ruskin and Environment*: 10–37.

13 'Soaped Poles in Bear Gardens': Rock-climbing Pioneers

1. Ruskin, *Praeterita*: 146.

2. Quoted in Fleming, F., *Killing Dragons. The Conquest of the Alps* (London: Granta, 2001): 142.

3. Alfred Wills (later Sir Alfred Wills) became a judge and presided over the trial of Oscar Wilde.

4. Fleming, *Killing Dragons*: 172–3.

5. Kelly, H. M., and Doughty, J. H., 'The Pioneers', in '100 Years of Rock Climbing in the Lake District', ed. A. G. Cram, *Fell and Rock Journal*, vol. XXIV (2), no. 70, 1986.

6. Quoted in Fleming, *Killing Dragons*: 295.

7. Hudson, *Coleridge among the Lakes & Mountains*: 145.

8. Haskett Smith, W. P., 'The First Ascent of Napes Needle', originally published in the *Fell and Rock Journal*, no. 8, 1914. Reprinted in Cram, '100 Years of Rock Climbing in the Lake District'.

9. Jackson, H., and Jackson, M., *Lakeland's Pioneer Rock-Climbers* (Clapham (via Lancaster): Dalesman Publishing Co., 1980).

10. Oppenheimer, L. J., *The Heart of Lakeland* (London: Sherratt and Hughes, 1908): 37.

11. Ibid.: 22–3.

12. Ibid.: 137.

13. Ibid.: 101–10.

14. Ibid.: 161.

15. Crowley, A., *The Confessions of Aleister Crowley* (London: Routledge, 1979). http://www.hermetic.com/crowley/confess/Chapter9.html. Accessed 30/03/2007.

16. Jones, O. G., *Rock-Climbing in the English Lake District*, 3rd edition (Keswick: G. P. Abraham and Sons, 1911): 250.

17. Ibid.: 195–6.

18. Abraham, G., *Motor Ways in Lakeland*, 2nd edition (London: Methuen & Co., 1913).

14 Manchester's Thirst: The Lost Battle of Thirlmere

1. Quoted in Berry, G., and Beard, G., *The Lake District: A Century of Conservation* (Edinburgh: John Bartholomew & Son, 1980): 6.

2. Manchester's population, already 350,000 by mid-century, was still rising; indeed, it would double by 1900. See http://vision.edina.ac.uk/data_cube_chart_page.jsp?data_theme=T_POP&data_cube-_TPop&u_id=10033007&c_id=10001043&add–. Accessed 22/08/2008. The number of cotton mills peaked at 108 in 1853 and the textile industry remained a thirsty consumer of water. See http://www.spinningtheweb.org.uk/m_display.php?irn=5&sub=cottonopolis&theme=places&crumb=City+Centre. Accessed 24/08/2008.

3. Berry and Beard, *The Lake District*: 6.

4. Quoted in Rollinson, *A History of Man in the Lake District*: 151.

5. Wyatt, J., *Cumbria: The Lake District and its County* (London: Robert Hale, 2004): 369.

6. West, *A Guide to the Lakes of Cumberland, Westmorland and Lancashire*: 44.

7. Some authors, including Bruce Thompson of the National Trust, call it the Thirlmere Defence Society.

8. Rawnsley, H. D., *Harvey Goodwin, Bishop of Carlisle* (London: John Murray, 1896): 193.

9. Quoted in Rollinson, *A History of Man in the Lake District*: 152.

10. Hansard, House of Commons, Deb 12 February 1878, vol. 237 cc 1504–33.

11. Ibid.

12. Hansard, House of Commons, 25 February 1879.

13. Quoted in *The Discovery of the Lake District*: 155.

14. Harwood, J. J., *The History and Description of the Thirlmere Water Scheme* (Manchester: Henry Blacklock, 1895): 179.

15. Gaze, J., *Figures in a Landscape: A History of the National Trust*: 31.

16. Collingwood, *The Lake Counties*: 155.

17. Abraham, *Motor Ways in Lakeland*: 61.

18. Quoted in Hurst, J., *Return to Eden* (Milnthorpe: Sigma Leisure, 2000): 10.

19. Berry, G., *A Tale of Two Lakes: The Fight to Save Ennerdale Water and Wastwater* (Kendal: Friends of the Lake District, 1982): 57.

20. Ibid.: 66.
21. Ibid.: 79.

15 A Sort of National Property: Hardwicke Rawnsley and the Formation of the National Trust

1. Wordsworth, *Wordsworth's Guide to the Lakes*: 92.
2. Quoted in Murphy, G., *Founders of the National Trust* (London: National Trust Enterprises Ltd., 2002): 84.
3. Ibid.: 86.
4. Quoted in Lear, L., *Beatrix Potter: A Life in Nature* (London: Allen Lane, 2007): 54.
5. Ibid.: 141.
6. Hankinson, A., 'Hardwicke Drummond Rawnsley (1851–1920)', in *Keswick Characters*, vol. 1, ed. Elizabeth Foot and Patricia Howell (Carlisle: Bookcase, 2006): 76.
7. Murphy, *Founders of the National Trust*: 90.
8. Richards, J., 'The role of the railways', in Wheeler, *Ruskin and Environment*: 123–43.
9. Murphy, *Founders of the National Trust*: 87.
10. Huxley, T. H., Letter to his son. See Leonard Huxley, *The Life and Letters of Thomas Henry Huxley*, vol. 2 (London: Macmillan, 1913). http://www.gutenberg.org/dirs/etext04/llth210.txt. Accessed 31/07/2008.
11. Murphy, *Founders of the National Trust*: 52.
12. Gaze, J., *Figures in a Landscape: A History of the National Trust* (London: Barrie & Jenkins, 1988): 18.
13. Murphy, *Founders of the National Trust*: 63–4.
14. Schoon, N., 'National Trust Marks Centenary', *Independent*, 13 January 1996.
15. Walton, J. K., 'The National Trust: preservation or provision?', in Wheeler, *Ruskin and Environment*: 156.

16. I have been unable to locate a secure first origin of this phrase, though it appears without quotation marks in Raphael Samuel's *Theatres of Memory* (London: Verso, 1994): 242.
17. http://pcwww.liv.ac.uk/~Sinclair/ALGY399_Site/national_trust.html. Accessed 14/10/2008.
18. This is the figure given by Bruce Thompson in *The Lake District and the National Trust* (Kendal: Titus Wilson & Son, 1946): 42. In *Figures in a Landscape*, John Gaze gives the area as 108 acres (p. 39).
19. Thompson, *The Lake District and the National Trust*: 43.
20. Quoted in Gaze, *Figures in a Landscape*: 39.
21. Thompson, *The Lake District and the National Trust*: 43.
22. Walton, 'The National Trust: preservation or provision?', in Wheeler, *Ruskin and Environment*: 154–5.
23. Thompson, *The Lake District and the National Trust*: 43.
24. Ibid.: 56–9.
25. Lear, *Beatrix Potter*: 395.

16 Visions of Childhood: Beatrix Potter and Arthur Ransome

1. Potter, B., *The Journal of Beatrix Potter, from 1881–1897*, transcribed and ed. Leslie Linder (London: Frederick Warne & Co., 1974 (fourth reprint with corrections)): 19.
2. Ibid.: 406.
3. Lear, *Beatrix Potter*: 301.
4. Ibid.: 320–9.
5. Ibid.: 334–6.
6. Ibid.: 10.
7. Potter, *The Journal of Beatrix Potter*: 148–9.
8. Leeson, R., 'Beatrix Potter: One of Life's Conservatives', in 'Beatrix Potter's Attitudes and Enthusiasms', *Beatrix Potter Studies VI*, papers presented at

the Beatrix Potter Society Conference, Ambleside, England, 1994: 36.

9. Potter, *The Journal of Beatrix Potter*. 390.

10. Lear, *Beatrix Potter*: 241.

11. Wakefield, E. W., Letter to *Flight* magazine, published 20 January 1912.

12. Thompson, *The Lake District and the National Trust*: 47.

13. Ransome, A., Autobiographical sketch from the *Junior Book of Authors*, 1935. http://www.mainlesson.com/displayauthor.php?author=ransome. Accessed 23/02/2009.

14. Ransome, A., *The Autobiography of Arthur Ransome* (London: Jonathan Cape, 1976): 26.

15. Ibid.: 28.

16. Hardyment, C., *Arthur Ransome & Captain Flint's Trunk* (London: Frances Lincoln, 2006 [1984]): 11.

17. Ransome, A. M., Letter to Edith Ransome (mother), Petrograd, 1 May 1917. In *Signalling from Mars: The Letters of Arthur Ransome*, ed. Hugh Brogan (London: Jonathan Cape, 1997): 43–4.

18. Hardyment, *Arthur Ransome & Captain Flint's Trunk*: 26, 71.

17 Ramblers: Rights of Way and Alfred Wainwright

1. Whyte, W., 'Sunday Tramps (*act.* 1879–1895)', *Oxford Dictionary of National Biography*, online edition (Oxford: Oxford University Press, May 2007). See also Hollett, D., *The Pioneer Ramblers 1850–1940* (Manchester: Ramblers' Association, 2002): 76–7.

2. CHA minutes, 4 and 5 January 1897. Quoted in Darby, *Landscape and Identity*: 161.

3. In response to changing aspirations, the CHA changed its name to the Countrywide Holiday Association in 1964, but the cost of maintaining its guesthouses became prohibitive and in 2004 its holiday activities were taken over

by Ramblers Holidays (the commercial arm of the Ramblers' Association).

4. Hollett, *The Pioneer Ramblers 1850–1940*: 104–5.

5. Ibid.: 183.

6. Ibid.: 103.

7. Ibid.: 166.

8. Griffin, A. H., *The Coniston Tigers* (Wilmslow: Sigma Press, 2000): 7.

9. Ibid.: 13.

10. Wainwright, A., *Memoirs of a Fellwanderer* (London: Frances Lincoln, 2003 [1993]): 23.

11. Ibid.: 24.

12. Davies, H., *Wainwright: The Biography* (London: Penguin, 2007 [1995]): 178.

13. Wainwright, A., *A Pictorial Guide to the Lakeland Fells*, Book Seven: *The Western Fells*, (London: Michael Joseph, 1993 [1964]). See 'Great Gable 3'.

14. Brady, E., and Palmer, C., 'Landscape and Value in the Work of Alfred Wainwright (1907–1991)', *Landscape Research*, vol. 32, no. 4, August 2007: 397–422.

15. Griffin, *The Coniston Tigers*: 192.

16. Ibid.: 193.

18 For All the People: The Creation of the National Park

1. Last, N., *Nella Last's Peace: The post-war diaries of Housewife, 49*, ed. Patricia and Robert Malcolmson (London: Profile Books, 2008): 105.

2. Ibid.: 106–7.

3. Richards, J., 'The Role of the Railways', in Wheeler, *Ruskin and Environment*: 128.

4. Letter from 'A Lake Visitor' to the editor of the *Manchester Guardian*, 9 March 1889.

5. Letter from A.E.B. to the editor of the *Manchester Guardian*, 8 September 1900.

6. Letter from J.W.F. to the editor of the *Manchester Guardian*, 9 March 1889.

7. Oppenheimer, *The Heart of Lakeland*: 191–2.

8. Ibid.: 196.

9. Berry and Beard, *The Lake District*: 14.

10. Wainwright, A., *A Pictorial Guide to the Lakeland Fells*, Book Six: *The North Western Fells* (London: Michael Joseph, 1992 [1964]). See 'Lord's Seat 4'.

11. Letter from Hugh Walpole to the editor of *The Times*, 19 February 1935.

12. Symonds, H. H., *Afforestation in the Lake District* (London: J. M. Dent & Sons, 1936): 20.

13. Ibid.: 56.

14. Ibid.: 63.

15. Ibid.: 29.

16. It was chaired by Christopher Addison, a minister in Ramsay MacDonald's second Labour government.

17. *Manchester Guardian*, 20 February 1939: 10.

18. Quoted in Redhead, B., *The National Parks of England and Wales* (London: Guild Publishing, 1988): 16.

19. Dower, J., *National Parks in England and Wales* (London: HMSO, 1945): 6.

20. http://www.nationalparks.gov.uk/learningabout/history.htm#1940. Accessed 05/02/2009.

21. *Manchester Guardian*, 1 April 1949: 8.

22. http://www.amblesideonline.co.uk/people.html. Accessed 24/02/2009.

23. Wyatt, *Cumbria: The Lake District and its County*: 68.

24. Redhead, *The National Parks of England and Wales*: 96.

25. http://we-english.co.uk/blog/?p=930. Accessed 16/02/2009.

26. Jaggi, M., 'Four writers revisit summer holiday spots in Britain'. This article was first published on guardian.co.uk at 00.01 BST on Monday 18 August 2008. It appeared in the *Guardian* on Monday 18 August 2008 on p. 6 of the Comment & Features section. It was last updated at 14.43 BST on Monday 18 August 2008. Accessed 2/16/2009.

27. Centre for Urban and Regional Ecology, University of Manchester. *Risk Workshop. Footpath Erosion in the Lake District*, 28 January 2005. Available at http://www.snw.org.uk/tourism/downloads/LD_workshop_report.pdf. Accessed 12/02/2009.

28. Durgan, E., 'How Whinash saw off the turbines', *Independent*, Saturday 26 January 2008.

29. http://www.coe.int/t/dg4/cultureheritage/Conventions/Landscape/ Accessed 17/07/2009.

Brothers Water and High Hartsop Dodd

Select Bibliography

Early Visitors

Brown, J., *Description of the Lake and Vale of Keswick* (Newcastle, 1767)

Budworth, J., *A Fortnight's Ramble to the Lakes in Westmoreland, Lancashire and Cumberland*, 3rd edition (London, 1810)

Camden, W., *Britannia*, transl. Philemon Holland (London, 1610)

Defoe, D., *A Tour Through the Whole Island of Great Britain*, ed. Pat Rogers (Exeter: Webb & Bower, 1989)

Fiennes, C., *The Illustrated Journeys of Celia Fiennes 1685–c. 1715*, ed. Christopher Morris (London: Macdonalds & Co., and Exeter: Webb & Bower, 1982)

Gell, W., *A Tour in the Lakes 1797*, ed. William Rollinson (Otley: Smith Settle, 2000)

Gray, T., *Journal in the Lakes*, written 1769, published by William Mason (1775)

Hutchinson, W., *An Excursion to the Lakes in Westmoreland and Cumberland; with a Tour through Part of the Northern Counties, in the Years 1773 and 1774*, printed for J. Wilkie and W. Charnley (1776)

Plumptre, J., *James Plumptre's Britain. The Journals of a Tourist in the 1790s*, ed. Ian Ousby (London: Hutchinson, 1992)

Radcliffe, A., *A Journey Made in the Summer of 1794 through Holland and the Western Frontier of Germany, with a Return Down the Rhine to which are added Observations during a Tour to the Lakes of Lancashire, Westmoreland, and Cumberland*, 2nd edition (London: G. G. and J. Robinson, 1795)

West, T., *A Guide to the Lakes of Cumberland, Westmorland and Lancashire*, 11th edition (Kendal: W. Pennington, 1821)

Wilberforce, W., *Journey to the Lake District from Cambridge 1779*, ed. C. E. Wrangham (Stocksfield: Oriel Press, 1983)

Wilkinson, T., *Tours of British Mountains* (London: Taylor and Hessay, 1824)

Young, A., *A Six Months Tour Through the North of England*, vol. II (London, 1770)

General Topography and Local History

Bott, G., *Keswick: The Story of a Lake District Town* (Carlisle: Bookcase, 2005)

Bragg, M., *Land of the Lakes* (London: Secker & Warburg, 1983)

Carnie, J. M., *At Lakeland's Heart* (Windermere: Parrock Press, 2002)

Collingwood, W. G. *The Lake Counties*, 2nd edition (London: Frederick Warne & Co., 1932)

Gambles, R. *The Story of the Lakeland Dales* (Chichester: Phillimore, 1997)

Hankinson, A., *The Regatta Men* (Milnthorpe: Cicerone Press, 1988)

Martineau, H., *An Independent Woman's Lake District Writings*, ed. Michael R. Hill (Amherst, NY: Humanity Books, 2004)

Nicholson, N., *The Lakers: Adventures of the First Tourists* (London: Robert Hale, 1955)

—, *Portrait of the Lakes* (London: Robert Hale, 1963)

—, *Greater Lakeland* (London: Robert Hale, 1969)

Rawnsley, H. D., *By Fell and Dale at the English Lakes* (Glasgow: James Maclehose & Sons, 1911)

Rollinson, W., *A History of Man in the Lake District* (London: J. M. Dent & Sons, 1967)

Singleton, F., *The English Lakes* (London: B. T. Batsford, 1954)

Whaley, D., *A Dictionary of Lake District Place-Names* (Nottingham: English Place-Name Society, 2006)

Wyatt, J., *Cumbria: The Lake District and its County* (London: Robert Hale, 2004)

The Lake Poets and Their Circle

Barker, J. (ed.), *Wordsworth: A Life in Letters* (London: Penguin, 2003)

Byatt, A. S., *Unruly Times* (London: Vintage, 1997 [1970])

Coleridge, S. T., *The Major Works, including Biographia Literaria* (Oxford: Oxford University Press, 2000)

Davies, H., *William Wordsworth: A Biography* (London: Weidenfeld & Nicolson, 1980)

De Quincey, T., *Confessions of an English Opium-Eater and Other Writings*, (London: Penguin 2003 [1821])

—, *Recollections of the Lake Poets* (London: John Lehmann, 1948 [1834–40])

Hebron, S., *The Romantics and the British Landscape* (London: British Library, 2006)

Hill, A. G. (ed.), *Letters of William Wordsworth* (Oxford: Clarendon Press, 1984)

Rawnsley, H. D., *Reminiscences of Wordsworth among the Peasantry of Westmoreland* (London: Dillon's, 1968 [1882])

Sisman, A., *The Friendship* (London, HarperCollins, 2006)

Southey, C. C. (ed.), *The Life and Correspondence of the Late Robert Southey*, vol. III (London: Longmans, 1850)

Southey, R., *Letters from England* (Gloucester: Alan Sutton, 1984 [1807])

Wordsworth, C., *Memoirs of William Wordsworth, Poet-Laureate, D.C.L.*, vol. I, (London: Edward Moxon, 1851)

Wordsworth, D., *The Grasmere and Alfoxden Journals*, ed. Pamela Woof (Oxford: Oxford University Press, 2002)

Artists

Abbot Hall Art Gallery, *Sublime Inspiration*, exhibition catalogue (1997)
Burkett, M. E., and J. D. G. Sloss, *William Green of Ambleside: A Lake District Artist (1760–1823)* (Kendal: Abbot Hall, 1984)
Darby, W. J., *Landscape and Identity* (Oxford: Berg, 2000)
Hill, D., *Turner in the North* (New Haven, CT, and London: Yale University Press, 1997)
Leslie, C. R., *Memoirs of the Life of John Constable* (London: Longmans, 1845)
Victoria & Albert Museum, *The Discovery of the Lake District*, exhibition catalogue (1984)
—, *The Lake District: A Sort of National Property*, papers presented to a symposium held at the Victoria & Albert Museum (1984)
Woof, R., *Treasures of the Wordsworth Trust* (Grasmere: Wordsworth Trust, 2005)
Wordsworth Trust, *Constable and the Lake District: The Solitude of Mountains*, exhibition catalogue (2006)

John Ruskin

Hunt, J. D., *The Wider Sea* (London: Phoenix, 1998 [1982])
Ruskin, J., *Praeterita* (London: Everyman's Library, 2005)
Wheeler, M. (ed.), *Ruskin and Environment* (Manchester: Manchester University Press, 1995)

The History of Walking and Climbing

Coleridge, S. T., *Coleridge among the Lakes & Mountains*, ed. Roger Hudson (London: The Folio Society, 1991)
Cram, A. G. (ed.), '100 Years of Rock Climbing in the Lake District', *Fell and Rock Journal*, vol. XXIV (2), no. 70 (1986)
Davies, H., *Wainwright: The Biography* (London: Penguin, 2007 [1995])
Griffin, A. H., *The Coniston Tigers* (Wilmslow: Sigma Press, 2000)
Hollett, D., *The Pioneer Ramblers 1850–1940* (Manchester: Ramblers' Association, 2002)
Hankinson, A., *Coleridge Walks the Fells: A Lakeland Journey Retraced* (London: Flamingo, 1993)
Jackson, H., and M. Jackson, *Lakeland's Pioneer Rock-Climbers* (Clapham (via Lancaster): Dalesman Publishing Co., 1980)
Jones, O. G., *Rock-Climbing in the English Lake District*, 3rd edition (Keswick: G. P. Abraham and Sons, 1911)
Oppenheimer, L. J., *The Heart of Lakeland* (London: Sherratt & Hughes, 1908)
Solnit, R., *Wanderlust* (London: Verso, 2001)
Wainwright, A., *Memoirs of a Fellwanderer* (London: Frances Lincoln, 2003 [1993])
Wainwright, M., *Wainwright: The Man Who Loved the Lakes* (London: BBC Books, 2007)

Landscape Conservation

Abraham, G., *Motor Ways in Lakeland*, 2nd edition (London: Methuen & Co., 1913)

Berry, G., and G. Beard, *The Lake District: A Century of Conservation* (Edinburgh: John Bartholomew & Son, 1980)

Berry, G., *A Tale of Two Lakes: The Fight to Save Ennerdale Water and Wastwater* (Kendal: Friends of the Lake District, 1982)

Buchanan, C., *Wordsworth's Gardens* (Lubbock, TX: Texas Tech University Press, 2001)

Harwood, J. J., *The History and Description of the Thirlmere Water Scheme* (Manchester: Henry Blacklock, 1895)

Symonds, H. H., *Afforestation in the Lake District* (London: J. M. Dent and Sons, 1936)

Wordsworth, W., *Wordsworth's Guide to the Lakes*, 5th edition (London: Henry Frowde, 1906)

Beatrix Potter and Arthur Ransome

Beatrix Potter Society, 'Beatrix Potter's Attitudes and Enthusiasms', *Beatrix Potter Studies* VI, papers presented at the Beatrix Potter Society Conference, Ambleside, England (1994)

Brogan, H., *The Life of Arthur Ransome* (London: Jonathan Cape, 1984)

Denyer, S., *Beatrix Potter at Home in the Lake District* (London: Frances Lincoln/ National Trust, 2000)

Hardyment, C., *Arthur Ransome & Captain Flint's Trunk* (London: Frances Lincoln, 2006 [1984])

Lane, M., *The Tale of Beatrix Potter: A Biography* (London: Frederick Warne & Co., 2001)

Lear, L., *Beatrix Potter: A Life in Nature* (London: Allen Lane, 2007)

Potter, B., *The Journal of Beatrix Potter, from 1881–1897*, transcribed and ed. Leslie Linder (London: Frederick Warne & Co., 1974)

Ransome, A., *The Autobiography of Arthur Ransome* (London: Jonathan Cape, 1976)

Ransome, A., *Signalling from Mars: The Letters of Arthur Ransome*, ed. Hugh Brogan (London: Jonathan Cape, 1997)

The National Trust and the National Park

Gaze, J., *Figures in a Landscape: A History of the National Trust* (London: Barrie & Jenkins, 1988)

Hankinson, A., 'Hardwicke Drummond Rawnsley (1851–1920)', in *Keswick Characters*, vol. I, ed. Elizabeth Foot and Patricia Howell (Carlisle: Bookcase, 2006)

Last, N., *Nella Last's Peace: The post-war diaries of Housewife, 49*, ed. Patricia and Robert Malcolmson (London: Profile Books, 2008)

Murphy, G., *Founders of the National Trust* (London: National Trust, 2002)

Thompson, B. L., *The Lake District and the National Trust* (Kendal: Titus Wilson & Son, 1946)

Acknowledgements

WORDSWORTH BELIEVED HE WAS fortunate in his birthplace. I think I was lucky in this respect too, and in having parents who were keen walkers and introduced me to the fells at an early age. My father was a dedicated amateur photographer and though our family excursions were punctuated by tedious halts while he waited for the sun to emerge from behind clouds, I benefited from his encouragement and his eye for a view. He once suggested that if I could combine writing with taking photographs, it would be the basis for a pleasant and rewarding career. It has taken a few decades for that idea to germinate, but I am thankful that he planted the seed. It is a pity he is not still around to see this book.

I would also like to thank all those school teachers who, in the days before Health and Safety, risk assessments and the rest, had the patience and the nerve to take their charges into mountainous terrain in all seasons and all weathers. I wonder if today's children have the unfettered access to the hills that we were given in the 1970s.

This book is the result of research using both primary and secondary sources. I am grateful to the librarians who maintain the special collections at Newcastle University's Robinson Library, where many early editions of Lake District guidebooks are kept, and to their counterparts at the Armitt Collection in Ambleside. My particular thanks go to Jeff Cowton, Curator at the Wordsworth Trust in Grasmere, where many astonishing literary treasures are preserved, and to Jamie Barnes, who was, at the time of my research visits, the custodian of the Keswick Museum and Art Gallery, and gave me access to Peter Crosthwaite's original notebooks. I am also grateful to those who have written about the Lake District before me, particularly the late Bill Rollinson, author of *A History of Man in the Lake District* (1967) and the late Alan Hankinson, whose *The Regatta Men* (1989) alerted me to the intertwined stories of Pocklington and Crosthwaite. Linda Lear's monumental biography of Beatrix Potter was indispensable, as was Hunter Davies's life of Alfred Wainwright. I've also drawn upon Adam Sisman's *Wordsworth and Coleridge: the Friendship* in my account of the Lakes Poets and their circle. Many other debts are acknowledged in the text or by way of footnote.

Very practical help was given by Frances Hinton, who was kind enough to let me stay at John Peel Farm, her cottage near Caldbeck, on several occasions. Frances also read and commented on some of the earlier chapters and lent me some useful books. Claire Lamont, Emeritus Professor of English Literature at Newcastle University, read and commented on those chapters concerned with Wordsworth and Coleridge (though, of course, any mistakes that remain are my own).

The final chapter of *The English Lakes* was the most difficult to write, since it engaged with present-day issues as well as recent history. Multiple perspectives were needed, so I am grateful to Peter Allen of Grange House Farm for giving up time on a Sunday morning to talk about nature conservation and the pressures upon hill farming; to Steve Ratcliffe of the National Park Authority and Mike Clarke, Project Director of the World Heritage Site bid, for a lively discussion of current planning issues and future scenarios for the National Park; and to Richard Pearse of the Friends of the Lake District for explaining the group's role in landscape conservation. In every case the discussion threw out many interesting tangents and I am sorry that it has not been possible to pack all of these into a short chapter.

At Bloomsbury I would like to thank Bill Swainson for his enthusiastic support, Emily Sweet, Nick Humphrey, Richard Collins, Polly Napper and Jude Drake.

My thanks, as ever, to my agent John Saddler, for his good counsel; and to my wife Mine and daughter Ella for putting up with my long absences among the fells.

Index

A NOTE ON THE AUTHOR

Ian Thompson was raised on the outskirts of Barrow-in-Furness, in a cottage said to have been built with stones plundered from the ruins of Furness Abbey. He studied philosophy at the University of Newcastle (1974–7), and later completed a BPhil and PhD in landscape architecture. After qualifying as a landscape architect he worked in practice in Glasgow, Tyneside and Gateshead. He teaches in the School of Architecture, Planning and Landscape at Newcastle University. He is the author of *The Sun King's Garden* and now lives in Newcastle with his wife and young daughter, walking in the Lake District whenever he has the opportunity.

A NOTE ON THE TYPE

The text of this book is set in Bell. Originally cut for John Bell in 1788, this type was used in Bell's newspaper, *The Oracle*. It was regarded as the first English Modern typeface. This version was design by Monotype in 1932.